D0432442

6

ON THE WATERFRONT

Budd Schulberg

ALLISON & BUSBY

For the 'saints of Xavier', the late Father Phil Carey, and Father John Corridan, 'the waterfront priest'; for their banty disciple, Arthur Browne, irrepressible 'Brownie', who led me to and guided me along the waterfront through many days and nights. And for Tony Mike, Tommy Bull, Timmy, Pete, Joey and countless others—men on the docks who gave me a hand. And for the hundreds of martyred long-shoremen who should not have died in vain.

1992

This edition published in Great Britain in 1992 by
Allison & Busby
an imprint of Virgin Publishing Ltd
338 Ladbroke Grove
London W10 5AH

First published in Great Britain in 1956 by
The Bodley Head Ltd
Reissued by Sphere Books Ltd in 1971
Reissued by Allison & Busby in 1988

Copyright © 1955 by Budd Schulberg
Copyright renewed in 1983 by Budd Schulberg
Introduction copyright © 1987 by Budd Schulberg

The moral right of the author is asserted

A catalogue record for this book is available
from the British Library

ISBN 0 74900 185 2

Printed and bound in Great Britain by
Mackays of Chatham PLC, Chatham, Kent

BH 181 956 S

INTRODUCTION
by
Budd Schulberg

Although the film *On The Waterfront* is now part of motion picture lore, the background of this novel is less familiar. This was no 'novelization', that bastard word for a bastard by-product of Hollywood success. Reviewers, actually invoking Zola and Dreiser in their praise of the work, were surprised that after all the kudos the film had received, there was still so much more to say than a ninety-minute movie—even one of the best of them—could possibly suggest.

Truth was, I had taken a rather unorthodox approach to the writing of the screenplay, applying not a month or two, but years of my life to absorbing everything I could about the New York waterfront, becoming an habituée of the westside Manhattan and Jersey bars that were unofficial headquarters, or homes away from home, for waterfront racketeers and Irish and Italian 'insoigents' alike, drinking beer and talking into the night with longshore families in the cluttered kitchens of their $26.50 per month railroad flats, interviewing longshore-union leaders and getting to know the fearless and outspoken labor priests from St. Xavier's in New York's Hell's Kitchen who gave me an insight into Catholic social action I had never had before. While I had read about the French working class priests, and the Central and South American clergy who related their devotion to Christ to the peasant (or peon) resistance movements, I had not realized that just a few blocks west of comfortable watering holes like Sardi's, there were men in cassocks and turned-around collars who were just as defiant in their stand against greed, oppression, and corruption as their brother priests in more exotic parts of the world.

I became fascinated with a particular 'waterfront priest,' Father John Corridan, a rangy, ruddy, fast-talking, chain-smoking, tough-minded, sometimes profane Kerryman, a welcome antidote to the stereotyped Barry Fitzgerald, Bing Crosby 'Fah-ther' so dear to Hollywood hearts. Days into nights, I listened intently to Father John, whose speech was a unique blend of Hell's Kitchen, baseball slang, an encyclopaedic grasp of waterfront economics, and an attack on man's inhumanity to man based on the teachings of Christ as brought up to date in the Papal Encyclicals on the reconstruction of the social order.

Long before I was ready to write either a novel or a film, Father Corridan and his rebel disciples in the mob-controlled International Longshoreman's Association had begun to obsess me. I wrote a long piece for *The Saturday Evening Post*, 'Father John Knows the Score,' and even broke into the Catholic left-liberal magazine *Commonweal*, with a short essay on this maverick priest's application of Catholic social ethics to the meat-grinder of men the New York waterfront had become.

The research took a dramatic turn. One of Father John's most devoted disciples was little Arthur Browne, proud of the fact that he was one of the stand-up 'insoigents' in the Chelsea local run by the fat cats and their 'pistoleros.' With his flattened nose, his cocky laugh, and his stringpiece vocabulary, Brownie reminded me of those tough little bantamweights who used to delight the New York boxing fans.

Brownie promised to take me in hand and 'walk me through the waterfront,' but first we had to work up a cover story. Even in the bars friendly to the 'insoigents', his pals would wonder what he was doing with an obvious outsider. They would think 'reporter' or 'cop' and in either case Brownie (and I) would be in jeopardy. Since I knew boxing and co-managed a fighter, and since longshoremen are avid fight fans, Brownie would tell the curious that we had met at Stillman's Gym, fallen into conversation about fighters and had simply drifted over to the West Side to quench our 'thoist'. 'I'll point out the various characters and shoot the breeze and you just listen 'n' drink your beer.'

It worked fine. We drank boilermakers, Brownie got a group talking, I listened and made mental notes as to how I could work the dialogue into the script. One night we worked our way from bar to bar until we were opposite Pier 18. A saturnine man in a gray suit was at the bar and somehow, on my fifth boilermaker, I forgot my usual role and asked the stranger what he did. Brownie grabbed me, and the next thing I knew we were running down the street toward our 'home block'.

'Jesus, Mary 'n' Joseph, you wanna get us both killed? Y'know who that guy was? Another Albert A. He's topped more people 'n Cockeye Dunn. I'm gonna tell Father John you're fired! We need a smarter resoicher.'

Then he gave that undefeated laugh of his. The 'cowboys' had flattened his nose, thrown him through a skylight, and even into the river, unconscious. 'Lucky it was winter and the cold water revived me.' I lived with this sawed-off Lazarus and his wife Anne in their cold-water flat. I sat at the kitchen table and wrote down lines I could never make up: 'Ya know what we gotta get rid of—the highocracy! Wait'll I see that bum again—I'll top 'im off lovely.' And for revenge: 'I'll take it out of their skulls!'

Father John (and his more prudent but equally dedicated superior, the still active Father Phil Carey) enlisted me as a journalistic ally in their efforts to prepare the men for a crucial National Labor Relations Board vote that might have thrown the 'Pistol Local', the Anastasias, and the rest of them out of office in favor of honest rank-and-file leadership. I wrote articles for *The New York Times Magazine* that helped convince St. Xavier's and the rebel movement that I was not a Hollywood opportunist looking to cash in on their 'story', but a writer devoted to their cause.

When my film script was thrown back in my face (and Elia Kazan's) by Hollywood's leading moguls, I took refuge in the thought that I had such an overabundance of material that I could develop the same material as a novel.

Even when the film had been launched successfully, I had thought so much about its potential as a novel that I simply could not resist taking a year out of my life to get it down. Having attended all the hearings of the State Crime Commission (on waterfront crime), until scrapbooks and notebooks bulged—even with that Oscar perched on the mantelpiece—I could not overcome the conviction that my job as chronicler of waterfront people and waterfront tensions was far from completed.

I found that far more was involved than extending a one hundred and twenty five-page screenplay to a four hundred-page novel. The difference between a novel and a film is more qualitative than quantitive. Film is an art of high points. It should embrace five or six sequences, each one mounting to a climax that moves the action onward to its final crescendo.

The novel is an art of high, middle and low points, and while I believe its form must never be overlooked, it's the sort of form you lock the front door against, knowing full well it will climb through one of the back-windows thoughtfully left open for it. The film does best when it concentrates on a single character. It tells the *Informer* superbly. It tends to lose itself in the ramifications of *War and Peace*. It has no time for what I call the essential digressions—the 'digression' of complicated, contradictory character; the 'digression' of social background. The film must go from significant episode to more significant episode in a constantly mounting pattern. It's an exciting form. But it pays a price for this excitement. It cannot wander as life wanders, or pause as life always pauses, to contemplate the incidental or the unexpected. The film has a relentless form. Once you set it up it becomes your master, demanding and rather terrifying. It has its own tight logic, and once you stray from that straight and narrow path the tension slackens, the air is let out of the balloon.

The film was focused on Terry Malloy, a half-vicious hoodlum caught between the waterfront mob and the groping, anxious beginnings of a conscience. His brothers are to be found on New York's troubled West Side, or along Brooklyn's Gowanus Canal, or in the corrupt political-machine towns on the Jersey shore. Elia Kazan and Marlon Brando did sensitive and brilliant things with this character, and I had written his dialogue carefully, with an ear to my wanderings along the riverfront. But the restricting form of He said-She said allowed no time to relate Terry to his background, to explore his mind with its groping efforts to shake off its sloth—to catch him off-guard, so to speak. More important, the film's concentration on a single dominating character, brought close to the camera-eye, made it aesthetically inconvenient, if not impossible, to set Terry's story in its social and historical perspective. In the novel Terry is a single strand in a rope of intertwining fibers, suggesting the knotted complexities of the world of the waterfront that loops around New York, a lawless frontier still almost unknown to the metropolitan citizenry.

In the early 50's when I was researching the waterfront, I knew that the wholesale crimes of the harbor were not to be explained merely by the prominence of certain gentlemen from Sing Sing and Dannemora in positions of authority on the docks. The shipping companies and the stevedore management had accepted—in some cases encouraged—the thugs for years, and in many cases city politicians were nothing less than partners of the longshore union racketeers. It was this unhealthy axis that made it so difficult to bring any real democratic reform to the graft-ridden docks. I even discussed with my film collaborators scenes that would dramatize this civic blight. Those scenes were not eliminated through any cowardice or fear of censorship, as some critics have suggested. No, it was another tyrant, the ninety-minute feature form, that lopped off their heads.

But the novel is both an X-ray and a wide-angle lens, the ideal medium for self-appraisal and the development of social themes. The novel isn't a straight piece of string. It's a ball of twine. In the novel, I found my opportunity to put Terry Malloy in proper focus. It only required retelling his story from another point of view, and with a different end in mind. I mean this literally and figuratively. Terry's decision, even his fate, became subordinated to the anxious balance and the fate of the waterfront as a whole. This demanded an entirely different ending, as well as fuller development of characters who were secondary figures in the film. So Father Barry, the 'waterfront priest', is brought to stage center, is allowed to share the action with Terry and to dominate the thinking of the book. As a curate in a poor parish he must take grave chances if he is to follow Christ his way. How could he reach difficult decisions except by interior monologues? The film had no time for this sort of thing. The novel has not only time but the obligation to examine this with great care. This searching becomes, in fact, the stuff of the novel, and the violent action line of Terry Malloy is now seen for what it is, one of the many moral rises in the spiritual and social development of Father Barry.

In the great novels *Moby Dick, War and Peace, The Red and the Black* we see how the action and the ideas are able to flow together with no violence from one to the other. There you have the glory of the novel, the reason why, in this age of supercommunication, we should never forsake it. I am not so vain as to claim membership in that great company for this novel, but in that tradition—from Stendahl to Steinbeck— I was able to work veins impossible to mine in dramatic art. It was not only that, having gained a great deal of knowledge and indignation from men on the docks, I was able to speak out in a way not feasible on film. I was able also to speak-*in*, to search the interior drama in the heart and mind of a church militant who dares apply the insights of his Savior to the dark and godless alleyways of the waterfront. I was able to follow him into an Irish tenement wake, to take him for a solitary, mind-troubled walk along the river, where he can measure his religious convictions against the spiritually bankrupt atmosphere of a typical waterfront neighborhood. I can listen in on his private prayers as he kneels sleepless on the cold floor of his cell-like room in the rectory, and I can end not with a dramatic close-up of Marlon Brandon, but with the deeper truth of inconclusiveness as this priest stands at night on the edge of the Hudson weighing the martyrdom of Terry Malloy and thinking bitterly of the millions on millions in the great city who do not care: 'Having eyes, they see not.'

Maybe what I am trying to say is that a film must act, a book has time to think and wonder. There is the essential difference.

The film mounted to a battle royal between conscience-troubled Terry Malloy (Brando) and his old *patron*, dock boss Johnny Friendly (Lee Cobb), ending with Father Barry (Karl Malden) urging the battered, now redeemed Terry to lead the intimidated dockers into the pier, thereby breaking the hold of the 'Pistol Local'. Even though Johnny screams from behind them, 'I'll be back—and I'll remember every last one of yuz!' his dialogue was lost in the sweeping, upbeat power of the camera.

The novel gave me a second chance to put my waterfront experience in perspective, with Terry finding his Calvary in a Jersey swamp, and Father Barry facing exile to a 'safer' parish, where his rebellious spirit may be more prudently contained.

As appropriate and effective as was our ending for the film the closing chapter of the novel afforded me the opportunity I had been waiting for, to relate the waterfront struggle to the struggle for social justice that had divided the Catholic Church for centuries, as it will continue to into the twenty-first century. 'If you say nothing and do nothing, you will escape criticism,' Father Barry remembers a wise Cardinal's warning as he prepares, in reluctant obedience, to leave his waterfront parish.

Film may be the language of the new generation—and a rich, rewarding language it is. But may this novel be a reminder of the special values of fiction: texture, introspection, complexity.

—Brookside, 1987

1

ACROSS THE HUDSON River from the grubby harbour town of Bohegan little squares of light were coming on all over the seaport metropolis. The massive verticals of the skyline were softening into a continuous range of man-made mountains. Soon the dusk would darken into night, as night had closed in over the river some 18 million times since this region was fisrt split wide by the glacial mass cutting down from the north.

In the cities clustered around the harbour were men crowded together in the subways, men going home from work. But the workday on the river had no end. Directly across from Bohegan, on the old North River, as the Dutch once called it and longshoremen still call it, Pier 80 was alive with movement, like a city of ants, and with the same kind of chaotic order, thousands of passengers and friends, shouting, whispering, embracing, waving handkerchiefs in the ritual of leavetaking. For three hundred years the weeping and the panic and the laughter and the hope and the chancing of sea journeys through the Narrows from the great landlocked harbour of the Upper Bay. Mid-river there was more ordered confusion as the old-fashioned ferries, the tugs, the coastal freighters, the coal barges, a sweeping *Queen* and a solid Dutch three-stacker called, needled, warned and miraculously avoided each other.

Along one of the Bohegan docks a Portuguese freighter bound for Lisbon was working under lights, the winches humming and growling, and the longshoremen, fifty- and sixty-year-old Irishmen and Italians proudly able to keep up with the younger men, the thirty-year-olds out of World War II with wide shoulders and muscular arms and paunches not as big from beer as they were going to

I

be after twenty years of bellying up to the bar after the shift or while waiting—the interminable waiting for work. Here in Bohegan—when they weren't short-ganged—they worked in teams of twenty-two, eight in the hold, eight on the dock, four on the deck, along with a couple of high-low drivers, and they knew each other's rhythms and ways like fellow-members of a football team. They worked at a regular, easy, knowing pace, making the most dangerous work in America—more fatalities than even the mines—look safe and casual. Steel girders seemed to be flying out of control as they swung out from the dock and over the forward hatches: an inch or two here and there and they'd slice off the top of a man's head like cheese, and if you don't get your feet out of the way in split-second time as the girders quickly lower on to the deck, it's good-bye toes. There's more than one longshoreman who can count his number of toes without using all his fingers, and more than one a little short on fingers too. It's all in a day's work. No wonder you see some of them cross themselves like miners or bullfighters as they climb down into the hatch.

Loading and unloading is an art and a fever. The dock boss is on you all the time. Unload, load and turn 'er around. The faster she puts a cargo down and picks up another, well, that's where the money is. Do a three-day job in two and there's your profit. Legitimate profit, that is. Oh, there's plenty of the other kind for the mob who's got the local and the Bohegan piers in its pocket. More ways to skin this fat cat than you ordinary citizens would ever dream. You take 16 billion dollars' worth of cargo moving in and out all over the harbour every year and if the boys siphon off maybe 60 million of it in pilferage, shakedowns, kickbacks, bribes, short-gangs, numbers, trumped-up loading fees and a dozen other smart operations, why, who cares—the shipping companies? Not so you could notice it. The longshoremen? Most of them are happy or anyway willing just to keep working. The city fathers? That's a joke on the waterfront. The people, the public, you'n'me? All we do is pay the tab, the extra 6 or 7 per cent passed on to the consumer because the greatest harbour of the greatest city of the greatest country in the world is run like a private grab-bag.

The harbour of New York makes the city of New York and the

city of New York is the capital of America, no matter what our civics teachers say. Eight billion dollars of world trade makes this the heart-in-commerce of the Western world. Oh, you simple Hendrik Hudson in your simple little ship, the original wrong-way Corrigan looking for India along the palisades of Jersey, look at your harbour now!

There goes a truckload of coffee. Coffee's scarce these days. A checker routes it off to a warehouse, only not the one it was intended for. The trucker has a receipt to turn in, and who's to find out for at least six months it's a fake receipt? Thirty thousand dollars' worth of coffee. As easy as that. Nothing small on the waterfront. Not with that 16 billion moving in and out. Now who'll miss one little truckload of coffee? Or by the time some eager beaver does, it's so long back that all he can do is pass it on to his supervisor who passes it on to the superintendent who passes it along two or three more echelons till it reaches a vice-president who passes it on to the insurance company. Just tack it on to the cost, it's part of the business, all part of the game. Nobody really feels it except the consumer, you'n'me, and we're too dumb to complain.

There goes a sightseeing boat on its tourist-spiel circumnavigation of Manhattan. Now we're passing the famous luxury lines of the West Side, some of the two hundred ocean-going piers along this tremendous 750-mile shoreline from Brooklyn to Bohegan. There's the *Liberté*, she came in last night with Bernard Baruch aboard, and the Mayor back from another vacation, and Miss America of 1955, yes, sir, folks, more celebrities arriving and departing every fifty minutes twenty-four hours a day three hundred and sixty-five days a year than ever before in the history of the world. There goes the *Andrea Doria,* the new Italian dreamboat, one of the 10,000 ships a year coming in and going out, one every fifty minutes around the clock, year in year out. And just look around you at the traffic, why, we've got three thousand tugs and barges and lighters and railroad-car floats and ferries and floating cranes and pleasure craft, even canoes and kids on rafts in the middle of all this great going and coming as if they were Tom Sawyers on the Mississippi. Only Mark Twain never saw anything like this, I tell ya Mark would've flipped his wig if he had ever turned his side-wheeler into the harbour of New York.

At the river's edge on the Bohegan side where the ancient Hudson-American piers extended 300 yards into the great harbour, the water was brackish and thinly carpeted with bits of splintered wood, half-capsized beer bottles, oil slick, dead fish and an occasional contraceptive tossed away after some random joy. Midstream the river was deep and magnificent, but here at the edge it was a watery dump. On water-worn stilts over the shallow water, in the shadow of a great ocean liner at Pier B and an Egyptian freighter at Pier C, was a two-room boathouse that had belonged to the Bohegan Yacht Club in some distant, more elegant past. For years now Bohegan had been a working town, a waterfront commerce town and—it figures—a two-bit politician's town. The sportsmen with their narrow white ducks and their nautical caps had moved on to watering places where the river had not yet gone flat and sour as spoiled wine, and where there was ample room to turn a ketch.

Now the Bohegan Yacht Club was inhabited by sportsmen of another stripe. A sign over the door read Longshoremen's Local 447. Everyone knew what 447 stood for in Bohegan. Johnny Friendly. And everyone knew what Johnny Friendly stood for. Likewise Johnny Friendly. Johnny Friendly was president of the local, and vice-president, secretary, treasurer and delegate, for that matter, though he had some of his boys filling those slots. More than that he was a vice-president of the Longshoremen's District Council. More than that he was the way you got and kept a job in this section of the waterfront, the only way, except for some special-favour guys sent down from the Mayor's office. And then even more than that, Johnny Friendly had a better than nodding acquaintance with Tom McGovern, a man whose power was so great that his name was only a whisper on the waterfront. Mr. Big they called him in the press and in the bars, some fearing libel from his battery of Wall Street lawyers, others simply fearing for their lives and limbs. Mr. Big, Big Tom to his remarkable spectrum of friends, was a dear friend of the Mayor's, not just the joker pushed into the Bohegan City Hall by the Johnny Friendly votes, the Hudson-American and Inter-State (McGovern) Stevedore Company, but the Mayor of the big town itself, alongside which Hoboken, Weehawken, Bohegan, Port Newark and the rest of them were like the rich little mines around the Mother Lode. Tom McGovern was a big, self-made, self-full man, and while Johnny Friendly had these Bohegan piers in his pocket and was frequently described as doing very lovely, Tom McGovern had a whole brace of Johnny Friendlys from Brooklyn to Bohegan, north of Hoboken on the Jersey shore.

Johnny Friendly had the build of a two-hundred-year-old oak cut off a few inches short of six feet. He was big in the shoulders and he had strong arms and legs from his longshoremen days. He was what they call a black Irishman, with eyes like black marbles ten for a nickel, thinning hair that he worried about losing, a jaw that could shove forward at you when he wanted to bull you down. He had the kind of build the tough ones have when they've made a bundle or two and like their Heiniken beers and the five-dollar steaks garnished with fat fried onions and the oversized baked potatoes fondly embracing those little lakes of butter. There was a coating of fat over Johnny's muscles that didn't conceal their existence or the potential violence they represented.

Johnny Friendly was never alone, except when he slept. He moved with his boys and they were as much a part of him as the hundred legs of a centipede. The men around him—'on the muscle for Johnny Friendly' is the way they were usually described—were picked for three qualities; that is, they had to have two of the three. 'I want 'em rough or brainy plus loyal.' Actually Johnny Friendly, whose Christian name was Matthew J. Skelly, combined these three qualities and three more in addition: ruthlessness, ambition and benevolence. This last had a streak of softness, almost of effeminacy about it. No one dared voice it, dared even notice it in fact, but Johnny Friendly had a way of squeezing and patting your shoulder while he talked to you, if he liked you. And he took very strong, sudden, and, from his point of view, perceptive likes and dislikes. He wasn't merely good to his mother, though he did try to take that bewildered lady to church every Sunday. A fed-up longshoreman's wife could come to John Friendly with the familiar story of her old man's drinking up the week's pay on his way home from the docks and there I am with the five kids and nothing in the icebox. Then Johnny would see to it that the money went right from the company pay office into the house. A king in pre-constitutional days never had more power than Johnny Friendly, McGovern's fief, had along the docks and deep into Bohegan. And many a king written up in the history books had less feeling for his subjects. Johnny Friendly would go way out for them, way out. Not just Christmas baskets, though he did that too, usually through the Cleveland Democratic Club on Dock Street that he controlled. He was always good for fifties and C-notes peeled off the fat roll, and a pat on the back, and a gravelly voiced, 'Aah, tha's all right, I understan', ferget it!' A real big man around Bohegan, Johnny Friendly. A 100 per cent when he's for you. Zero when he's not.

Right now Johnny Friendly's emotional state was pushing zero. His patience, of which he liked to think he had a great store, was all used up. That Doyle kid. That fresh-nosed little son-of-a-bitchin' Doyle kid. Troublemaker. It seemed to run in the family. The uncle, Eddie, used to go around with petitions and stuff like that way back when the local was just getting started. Johnny had been a kid himself then. They had fixed Eddie Doyle's wagon and roughed up Joey's old man a little bit. Old man Doyle's leg always stiffened up in the wintertime from where the bullet was. At least he seemed to have learned his lesson.

For years now he had gone along with the set-up, content to pick up his two-three days and his forty-fifty dollars a week. Always ready with a buck for the collection which went in (and quickly out of) 447's welfare fund. Once in a while when some crumb forced a meeting of the local, Pop Doyle had the good sense to stay away. Pop was all right. Johnny Friendly didn't mind him. But this wet-behind-the-ears pink-faced kid of his. Two years in the Navy and he comes out a regular sea lawyer: the constitution of the local calls for bi-monthly meetings. How do you like that, in the small print he finds bi-monthly. The kid has the nerve to actually go read the constitution. That's the kind we can do without around here. Very nicely. Give me the guys who can't read anything but a racing form and go get their load on after work. Peaceable citizens, that's what we want around here. Well, we gave them their meeting. We called it on twenty-four-hours' notice after posting it on the bulletin board here in the office. Sure the notice was on a scrap of paper one inch high but the constitution doesn't say what kind of notice; it just

6

says adequate notice must be given. I gave them their adequate. Only about fifty showed up. Fifty out of a possible fifteen hundred. And half of them was ours. You know, especially loyal members of 447. We all got elected for four more years. This Joey Doyle put up a squawk and Truck whose neck is as wide as some men's shoulders, Truck had to take him outside and quiet him down. He's a tough monkey, Joey Doyle. Doesn't look it, but he's there with the moxie and this trade-union bug has got him bad. Like his Uncle Eddie before him he's hard to discourage. And then comes the clincher. The Governor's got a bunch of stiffs he calls the State Crime Commission. A bunch of stuffed-shirt hypocrites who probably sponged it up good when they needed it. Now they get headlines about investigating waterfront crime. The Governor did plenty favours for Tom McGovern in his time, but it's an election year and the Governor wants to score. First that clown Kefauver and then these jokers want to get in on the act. Well, of course, it's for laughs. Who's going to go blabbing to that bunch of striped-pants bums? Only we start hearing things about Joey Doyle. He's been seen going in and out of the Court House where they sit around jacking off or whatever they do. I'm patient. On the District Council, ask anyone they'll tell you I'm one of the saner heads. I don't go off half-cocked like my old pal Cockeye Hearn, God've mercy on his soul. You don't see me going around giving it to them in broad daylight just because I don't like the part in their hair. Cockeye down there in the Village had his good points and his partner Wally (Slicker) McGhee is still as quick a trick as you ever want to meet, but you have to be pretty stupid to blow somebody off the waterfront and wind up on the wrong end of the switch. Anyway, before I move Joey out of my way with muscle I look to con him out of my way with some soft soap. For that I've got Charley Malloy. Charley ain't called the Gent for nothing. He's got a lot better education than the rest of us got. He did two years in Fordham, believe it or no. And the reason he was bounced wasn't because he wasn't smart enough. He was a little too smart. Charley's got brains to burn. He got caught selling examination answers, that's all. Charley was always smart. Would've been a helluva lawyer. He can talk up a breeze like *That matter to which you have reference to which* and stuff like that. So I sent

7

my trouble-shooter to my trouble-maker. Charley talks sense. He says he likes Joey and wants to help him, which he does. There might even be a place in the set-up for a bright kid like Joey. We don't hold grudges. I've taken in plenty guys who started in bucking me. It shows they got spirit. I can use spirit. But when Charley wastes his best arguments and comes back with no dice and the scuttlebutt has the Doyle punk blowing his nose for the Crime Commission, which no respectable longshoreman would be caught dead in their company, what am I supposed to do, hang a medal on him? I worked too hard for what I got to frig around with a cheese-eater. Know what I mean?

So Johnny and Charley, a waterfront idea of suavity and culture, worked up a little plan. Its virtue lay in its simplicity. No tell-tale firearms, not even the usual splash in the river. In the office on the creaky floating dock on the river's edge, Johnny went over the plans with Charley and Sonny and Specs, who were providing the muscle. Johnny wasn't like a lot of the Irish mob, hit 'em first and think afterwards. He had been raised with a lot of Italians and he liked to do his jobs a little more in the Sicilian manner. A certain finesse. If you didn't think there was an art to these things look at his friend Danny D. who lived in the big house on the Jersey heights. Danny D. had tradition behind him, generations of disciplined viciousness. It was in his heritage to be secretive and thorough and merciless and never to go back on his word. Johnny admired Danny D.

'Okay, Matooze,' he said to Charley, 'go get the kid brother, put 'im to work.' Matooze was Johnny's name for anybody he liked. Nobody knew where it came from or what it meant. All you had to know was you were in pretty good shape if he called you Matooze. But if he called you Shlagoom, then you better look out. Then you ship out or go to Baltimore or something. Charley had seen many a bum turn sickly white at the sound of that dark invention of a word *shlagoom*. Johnny followed Charley up the gangplank to the shore with his arm on his shoulder.

'You got enough padding in there for a football team,' he said to Charley approvingly. Charley was a very natty dresser. He had his overcoats made to order. He wore a camel's hair that was really a beaut. It looked like it must have come off a very upper-class camel. And it fitted Charley a lot better than it ever fitted the camel. Johnny Friendly, he'd buy a hundred-and-fifty-dollar tailor-made suit and after twenty minutes it'd start to hang baggy on him like it was ready made. It had something to do with the bulk of his figure. Charley was on his way to a round belly too, from too much sitting around and the big bills he ran up at Cavanagh's and Shor's, and he was softer than Johnny, having always lived off his wits while Johnny started up the hard way and smartened up as he went along. But Charley's clothes hung creased and neat on him, another reason for having picked up the affectionate billing Charley the Gent.

'Okay, Matooze,' Johnny said again. 'I'll be over at the joint.' That was the Friendly Bar, a little farther up River Street. Johnny's brother-in-law Leo ran it for him. There was as much business done there as in the union office itself. The horse play and the numbers and a lot of the kickback and of course the loan sharking, that all went on in the bar. The back room was Johnny's second home. He kept an apartment, but he only went there to sleep or jump a broad. He wasn't much for home. He saw his mother had a nice home and he helped his two sisters get places of their own, put their husbands on as dues collectors and shylocks so they could make an easy living. But Johnny was raised in the streets and in the bars, and that's where he felt at home even if he wasn't much of a drinking man. Labatt's Pale India Ale was his pleasure. He wanted to stay in this business and he had seen a lot of tough monkeys drink themselves down the drain.

Charley the Gent, in that dry, quiet way he had, said see ya Johnny, and then turned toward the row of tenements one block in from the river. It was a cool autumn evening and Charley liked the way the odds and ends of laundry fluttered on the lines. There was a maze of coloured shirts and long underwear and panties and diapers and kids' stuff. The poverty of the waterfront hung out for all to see, denims that had been washed hundreds of times, and pyjamas scarred with darning patches and the dresses of little girls that had long since washed out their colours. The poverty of the waterfront hung out for all to see. But poverty comes in bright colours too, here and there a yellow towel, a red wool shirt, a pair of green-checked socks, the life of the poor, respectable, drunken, hard-working, lazy, cocky,

9

defeated, well-connected, forsaken waterfront poor hung row on row across the steep canyons between the tenements. Charley looked up at the crowded clothesline and thought of all those wives doing all that washing, every day clothes piling up full of sweat and coffee dust and the sweepings of children with dirty streets for playgrounds and the soilings of infants, dirty clothes to soap and soak and rinse and hang out and pull in and iron and fold so they'd be ready to be dirtied again.

Suckers, Charley thought, for that was the form of his social thinking, suckers to take it day in and day out, but that's the way it had to be, or at least the way it was. At the top of the heap the real bigs like Tom McGovern, in the middle guys like mayors and D.A.'s and judges and Willie Givens, the International president who sneezed every time Tom McGovern stood in a draught. A step below them the local movers like Johnny F., then the lieutenants such as himself, then the goons and the sharks, the small operators, below them the body of regulars, the longshoremen and checkers and truckers who played ball, who helped to work the pilferage trick, and finally on the bottom below the bottom, the men who shaped up without an *in*, who took their chances, kicked back when they got too hungry to hold out any longer, lived mostly on loan-shark money they had to pay back at 10 per cent a week and got a piece of that $2.34 an hour only when a ship was calling for fifteen gangs and everybody was thumbed in to work except the worst of the bottle babies, the dead beats and the rebels.

Charley reached the entrance to the tenement he was headed for, a narrow, four-storey building that had been thrown up sixty years earlier in a hasty effort to accommodate the influx when the new (now archaic) piers were built and big-time shipping came to Bohegan. It was growing darker but a lot of kids were hollering up a stickball game in the street. On the stoop some of the older ones were idly watching. Old man Doyle was there, with a can of beer in his hand, more tired from the heavy work of the day than he'd admit, and with him, almost like a human appendage, was Runty Nolan, a jockey-sized, little gnome of a man barely five feet tall, with a face that had been hammered out of its original cast for thirty years of talking back. Not a young, up-to-date, Navy-wise, modern-trade-union-minded oppositionist like Joey Doyle but an incorrigible gadfly, a born needler, a party of one who fought Johnny Friendly in his own thick Irish way, by laughing at him, stinging him with humorous darts that were sharply defiant without quite provoking retaliation. Runty Nolan was like an old Navy man, perennially a seaman third, who knew by the book exactly how far he could push his Chief without risking court martial. A charter member of 447, in the days when Tom McGovern and Willie Givens were young dockwallopers working in the same gang, Runty in 1955 was exactly where he had been in 1915, a kind of self-appointed court jester of the docks, but too proud to serve a king, who accepted his beatings as part of a great joke he was playing on McGovern and Givens. 'Those bums I knew 'em when they was glad to steal a chop off'n a meat truck,' he'd laugh, reading in the papers that McGovern had been appointed chairman of some kind of new port committee, or that Givens had just been voted twenty-five thousand a year for life plus expenses. 'I wouldn't pay the bum twenty-five cents,' he'd make a point of telling a Johnny Friendly supernumerary, knowing how the stooge would growl back at him for abusing the exalted president of the International Longshoremen's Union.

Runty as usual had a comfortable load on, and Pop Doyle was enjoying his beer quietly, also as usual, a man whose gentle face was lined and hardened with the hard years, slightly stooped in the shoulders and back from thirty years of bending over the coffee bags and the heavy boxes, dreaming a long time ago of a better deal for the men on the docks, talking now and then on the third or fourth beer of Gompers and the stillborn hope of an honest-to-God union in the port, but tired now, his sweet wife under the ground and something of his manhood and nerve buried with her, content to sit on the stoop and let the beer make a cool river in his throat and chuckle at Runty Nolan's sly barbs and jokes.

'Well, if it ain't Brother Malloy,' Runty spoke up with the irrepressible laugh in his voice that years of heavy blows had failed to silence. Runty always made a point of calling every one of the Friendly boys 'Brother' and it never failed to raise a laugh or a smile from the men, Runty Nolan's own, ingenuous way of making clear for all to hear just what he thought of Friendly's type of union brotherhood.

'Hello, boys,' Charley said affably. He couldn't stand Runty Nolan, a soused-up wiseacre always looking for trouble and getting by with murder because he was small and somewhat comical. And Charley wasn't made any happier at the sight of Pop. There was a quiet passive resistance to Pop that could be a little unnerving if you were a sensitive man. The trouble with me, Charley was thinking, I let this stuff get me. Eight years I'm with Johnny now and I still let it get me. I should be over in City Hall where I could get the loot with a lot less of the dirty work. Just go around kissing babies, of various ages, and pocketing mine. Some day. Some day, maybe he'd make Commissioner. Maybe even Police Commissioner. Like Friendly's old chauffeur from the bootleg days, Donnelly. Donnelly was Commissioner of Public Safety now and doing very lovely. That was the way it went in Bohegan. Across the river in the big town it was a lot more complicated. A D.A. might enjoy the hospitality of Tom McGovern and go easy on the waterfront but he wasn't an out and out goniff like Donnelly. Over here in Bohegan you had a chance. Charley looked at the old man, Doyle, whose son was the job Charley had been assigned to. Pop Doyle, Charley thought, how much hard work and grief was indelibly written into that sad Irish kisser. And now more grief. And Charley the Gent, a soft sensitive type except for an ineradicable stain of larceny in his heart, had to be its messenger.

A second-storey window opened suddenly and a massive woman placed her formidable, fat arms on the window sill. Her loud, slightly nasal voice was not to be denied, even by the high-pitched babel of the street. Not even the screeching whistle of a ferry sweeping into the Bohegan slip could prevail over Mrs. McLaverty. 'Michael, Michael, next time I call you it's gonna be with a strap!'

A kid in the street turned his freckles, coated in stickball sweat, toward the offending window. 'Aw Ma, the game ain't over. Gimme ten more minutes.'

Careful not to let his resplendent camel's hair coat touch the dirty door or the walls of the tenement hallway, Charley entered the dim entrance to the railroad flats. It was one of those buildings that makes a local mockery of the city pretensions of modernity. Only some back-of-the-hand understanding between the landlord and a legman for the housing commissioner could have saved this building from condemnation fifteen years earlier. The walls along the stairway were cracked and stained and scribbled with the random observations, protests and greetings of a long succession of occupants, forming a sort of archeological strata of primitive tenement communication. The preparation of at least half a dozen different meals in this four-storey beehive created a warm, sweet and sour hallway aroma that Charley was always to associate with the life he had hustled his way out of. And the confusion of sounds, the bedlam, always a baby crying, and some bigger kid clobbering a smaller one, fighting back and bawling at the same time, and the distracted mother threatening to smack 'em both and a married couple hollering at each other in a loud, continuous debate of inconclusive affirmatives and negatives, the staccato gunfire of a radio melodrama and the Murphys who got on like lovers in their middle age of all things invariably laughing together and someone playing Frankie Laine at the top of his and the loudspeaker's voice, 'This cheating heart . . . depends on you-hoo . . .'

It was raucous and unprivate and unsanitary and un a lot of things, but one thing you had to say for it, it was living. It was no insignificant part of the mystery of from what power and to what purpose the human community endures.

Charley Malloy tried to keep his mind from wandering off into one of the dark chambers of this mystery. With somewhat the detached manner of an insurance agent checking up on an injured client, he heavily climbed the stairs, pausing on the third landing, a little annoyed with himself for being so out of breath. He ought to pick up his handball again. This was no shape for a man of thirty-five. Maybe it was time to go on a diet. The doctor said he was twenty-five pounds overweight. This whole country is overweight. They got it too good. Except for dead beats like Pop Doyle. There wasn't an extra half-pound of flesh on Pop Doyle. The best part of Pop Doyle had run off in sweat and soaked through into the floor of the hatch. Like an insurance agent, Charley Malloy plodded up the last stairway to the roof. Only in this case the accident hadn't happened yet.

2

IT WAS POSSIBLE to walk along the rooftops of the tenements all the way from Dock Street to Ferry Street, though this was no simple straightaway but a variety of different levels with a three-storey building often tucked between a couple of fours and even those of equal storeys unequal in height so that a block-long stretch of adjoining rooftops was like a great theatrical stage of multiple levels. In recent years these rooftops had sprouted television aerials in such abundance that to walk among them was to wander through a forest of steel branches. And between the aerials there were more clothes lines, and on almost every roof at least one pigeon coop, for pigeon racing was still a favourite sport in Bohegan, offering as it did a chance to extend yourself above and beyond the brick and mortar confines of the slum. Up into the unencumbered sky your flock of Belgian beauties soared, and if there was dirt and sweat and monotony in the daily life of the neighbourhood, at least here on the roof you could reach up through your birds into a freer, cleaner world.

At the top of the stairs leading from the fourth floor on to the roof Charley stood a moment, watching his younger brother at the edge of the roof with a long pole in his hand. At the end of the pole, like a makeshift flag of surrender, was an eight-inch strip from an old sheet, designed to frighten the birds into staying aloft for their training exercise. Around and around they flew in a great fluttering circle some thirty of them, not arranged behind their leader in any pattern of formation like ducks or squadrons of men, but spread out in a natural cluster.

Charley stood a moment, watching his brother Terry enjoying the sight of them, as he enjoyed this ritual two or three times a day, the birds winging out over the river and then swinging around in a quarter-mile arc to cast their fifty-mile-an-hour shadows over the tenement buildings, over the bars and the shabby seamen's hotels and the slummy streets, the pigeons unaware of the people below and the people aware of the pigeons mostly as the subject of a hoary scatalogical joke. But to Terry Malloy they were a favourite and endlessly satisfying sight. 'Look at 'em, the bums!' he'd think to himself reverently, the *th* thickening to a *d* when he actually spoke, 'my birds, the best fuggin flock o' homers in the neighbourhood.'

Pigeons, Charley was thinking, kid stuff. Why doesn't he grow up? He's twenty-eight years old already. Maybe he caught one too many in the head when he was the Pride o' Bohegan. Some pride! Look at him, the best prospect turned out of Bohegan since Truck Amon caved in to Joe Louis on Joe's Bum-of-the-Month Tour. Well, at least Truck is earning his keep on the muscle for Johnny Friendly, but what about this kid here, a grown man already who never quite grew up, with his thickened nose and his slightly puffed eyes from too much leather, a good-looking kid except for the nose and the scar tissue, always looked to Charley like a father because their real father forgot he was a father and drifted off into some skidrow heaven and was neither dead nor alive so far as Charley and Terry were concerned. All they ever got from him was the name, Malloy. Charley had to hustle and use his head. And he looked out for the kid, Terry, when he could. Only how much could you do for a kid like this, flapping his silly pole at a bunch of silly birds? And a couple of neighbourhood kids in bluejeans and basketball jackets with block letters spelling out 'Golden Warriors' on their backs, a brace of reform-school candidates called Billy Conley and Jo-Jo Delaney, helping Terry with the birds and looking up to him as if he were something big and not just Terry Malloy, an ex-pug who had had it for a little while and now was only accepted by the big men in the neighbourhood because he had the good fortune to be the brother of Charley the Gent.

Charley came up behind Terry and spoke softly, but the unexpected presence startled the kid—as most people still called him—and he pivoted quickly.

'Oh, Charley, I didn' hear ya come up.'

He lowered his pole and the leader of his flock, a firm-looking blue-checker full of its importance, circled in for a landing on the roof of the coop, all the others following him smoothly.

'I'm gettin' 'em ready for the Washington race,' Terry said. 'I come in twelfth last time. Number one in the neighbourhood. I made myself a coupla hundred bucks from the pool.'

'He'd a-come in eleventh or maybe tenth if Swifty had gone right inta the coop so we could punch the band in the clock,' Billy put in.

'That's his one bad habit,' Terry said, as if reluctant to admit any fault in his prize.

Charley looked at the birds, bored. 'Kids, vamoose,' he told the two Warriors. 'I want to talk private with Terry.'

The boys withdrew with the sullen obedience of soldiers. The prestige of Charley the Gent in this neighbourhood was something like that of a general's aide. The day would come when these kids would want commissions in the only organization with a future on the banks of Bohegan.

'Good kids,' Terry said as they scampered off. They made him feel good. Asking him about them Garden fights. The night he took DeLucca out with a big left hook. The Brooklyn wallios thought they had something in Vinnie DeLucca until that night Terry tagged him with a left hand. Terry liked it for the kids to ask him about DeLucca. Or when they came to him for pointers on how to handle the Blue Devils. Good kids.

'Punks,' Charley said. 'The kids around here get dumber every year. It's a disgrace.'

Then seeing Terry look at him uncomprehendingly—with a certain patient lack of expression he always assumed when Charley got too far ahead of him in the think department—the older brother came to the point of his visit:

'They'—which could be anybody from Johnny Friendly down— wanted to talk to Joey Doyle. But Joey had been playing it cute. Ever since his trips to the Crime Commission, when he spotted Sonny tailing him, he had never gone out at night except with two or three young, tough longshoremen for protection. Johnny wanted to get Joey alone. It was highly important they should talk to him. Before Joey went and did something very foolish. Now Charley had an idea, That's what he was expected to have, ideas. He glanced over at the pigeons. A number of them had flown into the coop and were fussing and cooing in their elaborate ritual of settling down for the night.

Joey Doyle raised pigeons too. For years there had been a friendly rivalry between him and Terry. A friendly piracy. There was the old trick of tying a piece of ribbon to your homer's leg. A pigeon is incorrigibly curious. Sometimes a bird from a strange or rival loft would follow that ribbon right into your own coop. Terry had picked up some nice birds that way. Army birds and prize stuff off their course. In every long-distance race hundreds of birds were lost. Sometimes they followed others home. Terry had mentioned this to Charley once and Charley hadn't paid much attention as he always thought this pigeon business of Terry's was a kid's waste of time. One of the things helping to keep him small. Twenty-eight years old and no regular job and nothing going for him on the docks where the livin' was easy if you just worked one or two little angles. There was no excuse, simply no excuse for not making four or five bills a week. A little initiative, that's all. Charley wasn't a driver, a congenital go-after-it like Johnny Friendly. But thank God he wasn't a drifter, a fringer like his poor slob of a kid brother, too slow to come in out of the rain, or even to know if it was raining half the time. Had it been the punching that did it? It was hard to tell. Terry had racked up before those little blood trickles washed away his reason and his reflexes. Maybe it had something to do with the old lady dying. Charley was sixteen then, Terry only nine. He had taken it pretty hard. For a couple of years he hadn't talked very much. The doctors had some fancy word for that. Something inside of you feels so cheated and mean you just don't respond to nothin'.

It was the boxing that had brought Terry out a little. Right away he was better at it than the other kids and it gave him a position. Everybody needs a position. There goes Terry Malloy, he's the boxer—that's position. Some little thing you do, or are, in particular. Up at the dump they stuck him in, it was called Saint Joe's Home, he could lick the big boys of fifteen when he was only eleven. It gave him something to hang on to. It still did, a little bit, the way he shifted his shoulders when he walked and the way he carried his hands and the way he felt inside and the little wake of admiration he still left behind him as he heel-and-toed along River Street—'There goes Terry Malloy. Useta be a pretty good fighter.'

'—I figured maybe if you call up to him you got one of his pigeons, you could get him to come up on the roof so a couple of

17

the boys could have a little talk with him,' Charley was saying.

Terry frowned. He had a little more work to do banding some squabs and cleaning up around the coop and then he had figured to drop in and shoot a little pool with Chick and Jackie, then wander over to Friendly's, have a few beers and watch the fight on TV. One trouble with Charley and Johnny's business was they were always working. Day and night there was something to take care of. That's the trouble when you get too big. Always something or someone to look out for.

'—now you sure you got it straight?' Charley was saying.

'Yeah, yeah, okay, okay,' Terry said. 'It sounds kinda corny, but . . .'

'Yours not to reason why,' Charley recited.

'Huh? What's that?'

'Poetry. Kipling I think it is.'

'You and your double talk,' Terry said, proud of Charley's brains and knowledge. 'No kiddin', Charley, when they put you together they stuck in an extra tongue.'

'And a good thing,' Charley said. 'Since I always had to talk for the two of us.' He tapped Terry twice, fondly, on the shoulder in semi-conscious imitation of John Friendly. 'Now get on it. And don't goof it up. It's important to Johnny, highly important. Tell 'im you'll meet him on the roof and then cut over to the joint. I'll be waiting for you.'

'Okay, okay,' Terry said heavily. He was like a boy whose father tells him to go help his mother with the dishes in the kitchen. He felt lazy and the chore was dull, but how do you stand off a thing like that?

Charley took a last look around as he headed for the steep stair-way leading down from the roof. 'Jesus it's filthy up here,' he said.

'Whatta you want the Waldorf Astoria Roof Garden?' Terry said.

'I guess a pig-sty looks clean—to a pig,' Charley said gently. 'I'll see you, slugger. Don't goof. And by the way, there's a sawbuck in it for you.'

The immaculate camel's hair coat, incongruous on this roof-top dusted with soot from the nearby factories and spotted with pigeon droppings, disappeared into the stairwell. A loud, rasping blast from the *United States* swinging out into midstream and pointing for the Narrows, made Terry forget for a moment what it was he had to do. Those pilots, he wished he could've learned something like that. There was only a hundred of 'em in the entire harbour and they could average fifty bucks an hour. Twenty-five thousand a year just for steering a boat. Only trouble was most of 'em cracked up from all that pressure after a while. But they always had the pension waiting and meanwhile it was something to come aboard the *United States* or the *Liberté* and take over from the captain himself. Now the *Liberté* is yours, to run like a outboard and you work her down through the main channel and then into Ambrose Channel until you're out beyond the Light. 'Okay,' you say, 'from hereon it's easy, no problem, just the open sea. Here, bub,' you say to the four-striper with his rows of ribbons, 'I guess you c'n handle it from here.'

Now the ship's whistle sent its raucous, moody song echoing down the watery canyon between the eastern and the western shores, its harsh and mournful song. Terry ran his fingers rapidly backward across his upper lip and against his nose, a vestigial gesture from his boxing days when the blood used to gush into his nostrils and his glove had to serve for a handkerchief. Behind him his pigeons, conventional creatures with orderly manners, had squatted down on the perches to which habit and some brief but violent give-and-take had assigned them. Their cooing was lower in their throats now and modulated to the night.

Terry reached into his coop, expertly, and grabbed the nearest of his birds, careful to come down on it from above, spreading his hand across its back from wing to wing so it would lie quietly in his hand and not upset the others. He placed the bird inside his black-and-red checked windbreaker. That goddamn 447, he thought. Sooner or later they got into everything, even into this flock of pigeons which were his alone.

As he reached the third-floor landing, Billy and Jo-Jo were underfoot, flipping nickels in an impromptu tossing game.

'Hey, Terry, where you goin'?'

'Yankee Stadium, me 'n Marciano,' Terry said.

'No kiddin', Terry, c'n we go with ya?' And Jo-Jo: 'Yeah Terry, we're goin' with ya.'

Terry liked these kids. Good tough kids. They'd do anything for him. Always running little errands for him. He was to them something like Johnny Friendly was to him. Or McGovern was to Johnny Friendly. That's the way it was down here. You had to look up to someone. You had to have someone looking out for you.

'Get lost,' Terry said, humorously, and went on down the stairs, stroking the head of the pigeon to keep it quiet inside his jacket.

The two kids grinned at each other, pleased at the warmth of familiarity in Terry's remark, and went on with their game.

Terry walked around the corner and down a narrow alley into an open courtyard used by a dozen tenements as a handy place for their empty cans and old papers. Foresight and care, or just plain common sense, might have turned this yard into an organized playground for the kids, but instead this littered plot of wasted ground was a squalid rectangular monument to civic neglect—despair—call it what you will. A couple of half-wild cats hungered and prowled among the cans. The Hudson was as black as a river of oil now, and seemed to be flowing as slowly and thickly. But the boats were ever on the move in their restless coming and going. Turn 'er around and get her out. Cargo plus movement equals money. And the harbour was a greedy bitch. The harbour was Hetty Green with muscle.

As Terry came under Joey's window he could hear someone singing in the distance in a toneless and terrible voice. Some drunk, some sauce hound lifting his whisky rotten voice in an unrequested number:

> '*Tippi tippi tin tippi tin*
> *Tippi tippi tan tippi tan* . . .'

Oh, my good God Christ. The bums they got around this neighbourhood. As somebody said, maybe Charley, the asshole of the universe is Bohegan and midtown Bohegan is Paris compared to the Bohegan docks. The piers themselves are thirty years behind the times. The pilings are rotten. The human scum wandering from bar to bar looking for something they'll never find because they haven't the slightest idea of what they're looking for. *Tippi tippi tin*, what the hell kind of song is that? At least if the juice-head got to sing let him sing Galway Bay or something. Galway Bay was a beauteeful song. That scuffed up little clown, Runty Nolan, when he had enough balls in him, he could really give out with Galway Bay.

Terry looked up at Doyle's window, his vision obstructed by all that wash on the line and the lattice of fire escapes. He felt inside his jacket for the pigeon. The pigeon felt nice and warm and peaceful. He wished he didn't have to call Joey out. He got along pretty good with Joey. Always kiddin' him about how his birds were nothin' but a bunch of lousy park culls, and stuff like that. Joey would laugh. Joey had a pretty good sense of humour. It was hard to figure a kid like that getting in all this trouble. Getting himself marked lousy in Johnny and Charley's book. An agitator. Talking in the bars about all the things he found wrong with the union. Fifty years behind every other union in America, he'd say, spouting the stuff his Uncle Eddie had learned him. Where's our seniority? Where's a decent pension plan? Where's a hiring system that ain't based on some Sing Sing hiring boss doing you a favour? Where's an up-and-up election? Where's a public accounting for the five G's in dues we pay in every month? And on and on with that kind of talk. Some of the men would argue back. Those that worked regular and had Johnny and Charley to thank for it. And some of the men just hung their heads and drank their beers and tried to change the subject to the respective merits of Mays and Snider.

One time, listening to Joey shoot his mouth off about the old men and how the railroads or the mines would be looking out for them at sixty because those outfits gave out in services what they took in dues, Terry listened to all he could stand and finally asked:

'What's in it for you, Joey? That's what I can't figure. You're only twenny-three-four years old. You're a good worker. Your old man stands in pretty good. You could get all the work you want if you'd only keep your mouth shut. Why worry about a lot of washed-up stumblebums? Why don'cha look out for you?'

And Joey had answered, 'There's a right and a wrong, Terry. Takin' over our union and runnin' it with a pistol like Johnny's doin', that's wrong. And if more fellas had some guts down here they'd stand up and holler it's wrong.'

This Joey Doyle must be crazy. Terry had had to walk away. Talk like that wasn't healthy, and right in Friendly's Bar. A nice, clean-looking kid, but with a noggin full of the kind of ideas that can get you hit in the head.

Under Joey's window Terry cupped his hands to his mouth and hollered, 'Hey Joey, Joey Doyle!'

Three stories up a window opened and Joey peered over the sill, cautiously.

'Terry?' He tried to see the figure standing in the empty court-yard. He knew what it was to buck the Johnny Friendlys. The cops were looking the other way. City Hall, the whole town was looking the other way. When it came to protection, the waterfront was an orphan. You were on your own. His old man had begged him to take it easy. His friends had warned him not to go out.

'Whaddya want, Terry?'

Terry reached into his windbreaker and held up the pigeon. The bird was frightened and when it sensed the open air it tried to thrust itself forward out of Terry's hands. It managed to work one of its wings free and beat wildly to wrench itself from Terry's grasp. Terry held it firmly by its legs and with his other hand pinned its wings down with authority.

'Ya see this,' he shouted up through the limp and gaudy laundry. 'He's one o' yours. I recognized the band.'

Joey leaned out a little farther. He had the young, pink-cheeked, slightly fleshy good-looking Irish face associated with choir boys.

'Lemme see. Maybe it's Danny Boy. I lost 'im in the last race.'

Terry wasn't thinking what he was doing. Just doing it like he was told. 'He followed my birds into their coop. Here—you want 'im?'

It was nice of Terry to bring his bird back. Joey had felt bad about losing Danny Boy. He had figured to mate him with a fast hen, Peggy G. He started to say he'd be right down. But the animal watchfulness of the Bohegan docks was in him and the words wouldn't come out. The rat-quickness of the docks was in Terry too. Without having to think about it, Terry added, 'I'll bring him to the roof. Meet ya at yer loft.'

The pigeons were the peaceful and satisfactory part of Joey Doyle's life, as they were of Terry's, and the sight of the sleek, firm bird in Terry's hand, and the mention of the loft, Joey's only escape from the bruising immediacy of the waterfront, were reassuring.

'Okay, okay,' Joey said, 'I'll see ya on the roof.'

As Joey Doyle turned away from the window, Terry took a couple of backward steps and released his hold on the pigeon. It flew aimlessly upward, brushing the aerial laundry in awkward, night-blinded flight. On the roof Terry could see the silhouette of a couple of hulking business suits waiting for their quarry in the dark. They were a couple of pistols, Sonny and Specs, and he hoped they wouldn't give Joey too much of a hard time. If Joey would only get smart and come around. This is the way it was and this is the way it would always be and you had to be an awful meatball to go against the set-up or think any different. It was no skin off Terry if Joey wanted to louse himself up. Terry backed away into the alley, crab-wise and with a crab's instinct for pulling his head in.

The cracked record behind him was croaking its miserable tin-pan-alley dirge.

> *'Tippi tippi tin tippi tin*
> *Tippi tippi tan tippi tan . . .'*

Jesus, these rummies down here, they could sure get on your nerves. The unkempt, staggering form lurched into Terry and a wave of disgust broke over him as he recognized Mutt Murphy, a one-armed dock-worker rotted out with cheap whisky, who started his day in the afternoon like a gentleman, made the rounds of the bars (usually on the end of a quick heave-ho) until the early hours and then flopped in a hallway or a tenement basement.

Mutt had left his arm between a couple of packing cases some ten years back. He had been wandering around griping about his compensation and cadging drinks ever since. Terry had heard the sob story and had had the sour whisky breath blown in his face too many times. As Mutt made contact with anyone who happened to wander across his stumbling path, his left arm shot out automatically, his palm uplifted in the classic gesture of supplicants, at once ashamed and aggressive.

'A dime. Got a dime you don't need? For a crippled-up member of 447?'

'Go on, get outa here,' Terry said, pushing the wreck away from him and farther along the alley.

23

Being pushed was an all-day every-day experience for Mutt and he wasn't even slightly discouraged. He had learned to accept being pushed and cuffed around as his principal contact with these river-front people among whom and off whom he lived. His life would have been unbearable without these signs of attention, if not affection, from passers-by.

'A dime—a dime for a cupa coffee?'

'Don't give me that coffee, you juice-head.'

Angered by Mutt's refusal to go, and nervous about what was going to happen to Joey up there on the roof, Terry leaned over and spat savagely into Mutt's upraised hand. Mutt drew his hand back indignantly and wiped the spittle on the sleeve of his stump. The violence of the gesture seemed to bring the sturdy, swaggering figure of the young man into focus for Mutt.

'Terry. I shoulda known.' He straightened up a little and wiped his hand against his filthy slept-in denim pants. 'Thanks fer nuthin', ya bum.'

'Get lost,' Terry mumbled as he watched the one-armed bottle-baby drift off into the evening mist.

'Tippi tippi tin . . .' the wanderer went back to his hoarse and mirthless chant, some ritual of his own, as if in a stroke of revelation, he had found an anthem for his emptiness.

Terry took a last, wondering look at the roof-top where Joey must be already involved in critical conversation with Sonny and Specs. Then he brushed his fingers against his nose, boxer style again, and started walking in his rolling, light-footed, shoulder-shifting way towards the Friendly Bar and Grill over on the corner of River and Pulaski.

3

BY THE TIME Terry Malloy reached the end of the alley, giving on River Street, he had pretty well succeeded in putting Joey Doyle and the pigeon out of his mind; maybe, without his being aware of it, it was merely pushed back and buried in the dense undergrowth of forgotten or half-understood impressions that lay entangled in Terry's mind. The luxury of anticipation and the pain of contrition and afterthought were unknown to Terry. Sometimes the corner cowboys tapped their heads and laughed, meaning Terry was punchy. But Terry's inability to look into himself or to experience anything other than immediate pleasure or pain was nothing but sloth.

You ate, you slept, you drank, you copulated, you took in a movie or shot a little pool and you worked when you had to, at the softest job you could find, to keep a few dollars in your pocket. That was the day-to-day existence of Terry Malloy. Johnny Friendly called you by your first name. You usually had enough cabbage or credit to get your load on Saturday nights. There was always a tramp somewhere to come up to your room and help you get the hot water off your stomach. What more could you want? What more could you want? What more could you possibly want?

Feeling like that, full of life in a deadened sort of way, on his own, on the prowl, ready to run or bite or snatch off something good, ready for the minute but with no sense of time or urgency, Terry walked tough along the bars of River Street. There were at least half a dozen to every block, and each one doing business in fifteen-cent beers and thirty-five cent shots; here and there a juke box blared, the Honeydreamers and the Four Aces, 'I feel so lonely when I'm . . . here without you . . .' And bars where the old aimless conversations were displaced by television sets, drawing the row of customers' faces in one direction and fixing them so rigidly as they nursed their beers that they seemed a depersonalized line of wax dummies.

Except for this singular invention, the saloons were unchanged for generations, many of them a century old, with time-polished mahogany bars, elegant brass spittoons and brass rails that had supported the heavy feet of the great-grandfathers of the present company. The men among whom Terry walked along River Street had not changed their style either. There was something about this waterfront that stubbornly avoided progress, or even change. As in the days of the sailing ships, the street along the river was peopled with barrel-shaped men with faces weathered by sea air and drink,

25

burly in their wind-breakers, with heavy-toed shoes and caps tilted at a rakish angle. They were hard workers who carried their liquor and got their pay safely home to the wife, and staggering among them the casuals who picked up just enough work to keep themselves in whatever it was they drank in search of reassurance or forgetfulness.

Terry said Hi to this one and threw a friendly jab at that one and pretty soon he had come to the Friendly Bar on the corner across from Pier B. There was nothing special about the Friendly Bar; it looked like most of the other gin mills along the street: a plate-glass window with a green blind running half way up so the wives couldn't spot their truant husbands, a beautiful old bar, exquisitely carved in the old rococo manner, surrounded incongruously by unscrubbed walls of corrugated brown sheet metal decorated with pictures of fighters, ball players and calendar nudes. A few humorous signs—'In God We Trust—No Exceptions'—'Ladies, Watch Your Language. There May Be Gentlemen Present'—and a Back Room for the big and little wheels, that was Friendly's, a deceptively unimposing command post for the Bohegan sector of the harbour.

Johnny Friendly (through his stooge brother-in-law Leo) didn't pay any rent for the street corner outside the Bar and Grill, but it was considered an integral part of the establishment. There were always half a dozen or a dozen or more of the Friendly boys standing around, leaning against the plate-glass window or the lamppost, talking shop or sports or doing a little business. 'J.P.' Morgan, bat-eared and weasel-faced, was a familiar figure on the corner as longshoremen sullenly accepted his loans of fifty or a hundred, to be paid back at the generous rate of 10 per cent a week, which didn't sound too bad until you remembered the 10 per cent was accumulative, and that if you failed to come up with the hundred the first week, the interest was 10 per cent of $110 and so on and on until you were paying 30 or 40 per cent. If you fell too far behind 'J.P.' would signal a hiring boss, Big Mac McGown or Socks Thomas, to put you to work. The debtor would turn over his work tab to 'J.P.' and 'J.P.' would collect straight from the pay office, so there was no chance of the guy drinking it up or turning it over to the wife before 'J.P.' (really Johnny Friendly) got his. So one way to be sure to work (eventually) was to co-operate with 'J.P.' Morgan's street-corner banking system.

The financial see-saw of the labour set-up on the waterfront balanced on a nondescript but vital little fulcrum like 'J.P.' Most longshoremen lived all their lives in debt, spending the last dollar in their pockets on a Saturday night and starting from scratch, or rather, behind scratch every Monday morning. Loan-sharking plus two or three men for every job, keeping a floating population of insecure and hungry men—these were the two prongs of Johnny Friendly's power in Bohegan. And it was the power of dock bosses in Port Newark and Staten Island and Red Hook and every section of the harbour split up into a dozen self-sufficient multi-million-dollar operations according to the tacit understanding of the underworld executives who referred to themselves as union leaders. These waterfront lordlings were smiled upon by President Willie Givens, who could pound his chest and weep at union conventions and communion breakfasts about his love for his dock-working brothers who expressed their gratitude by voting him twenty-five thousand dollars for life and an unlimited expense account. The vote was 100 per cent legal, as well as phony, for the convention delegates were hand-picked, opposed only here and there by an obstreperous, irrepressible Runty Nolan, or a serious, young parliamentarian like Joey Doyle. The rank and file spent their resentment in undercurrent humour, calling their President 'Weeping Willie' and 'Nickel and Dime Willie' because his contracts with the shipping association always resulted in notoriously paltry wage increases, and 'Willing Willie' because he was so pitifully eager to please the shippers and the stevedores (and his high-and-mighty benefactor Tom McGovern) who remembered him gratefully with Christmas envelopes containing crisp thousand-dollar bills. Yes, it was always Merry Christmas for Weeping Willie, yet somehow no one questioned the fact that this bit of formalized corruption was meant to celebrate the birthday of Weeping Willie and Tom McGovern's Father and Saviour.

It seemed a long way from Bethlehem to the corner of River and Pulaski Streets. There 'J.P.'s' pockets bulged with Johnny Friendly's ready cash and there 'Jockey' Brynes, an ancient gnome ruled off the tracks as an apprentice in some dust-covered scandal, ran a book that longshoremen were expected to patronize. At least it was no secret that Jockey worked for the set-up along with 'J.P.', Big Mac, and Socks Thomas, familiarly known as 'A 'n B' in honour of the number of times he had been charged with assault and battery.

These were some of the people standing outside the Friendly Bar and Grill when Terry appeared. Leaning against the bar window, waiting calmly, was Charley, flanked by Truck Amon, a fat fortress of a man who was said to consume three gallons of beer every day, and Gilly Connors, another fat boy, who was once told by Charley to use his head in handling a certain situation, whereupon he butted the fellow so effectively the victim went to the hospital with fractures of the nose and jaw.

When Terry was close enough, Charley said in his habitually soft voice, as if the vocal cords had been designed for conspiracy, 'How goes?'

Terry nodded impatiently. 'He's on the roof.'

'The pigeon?' Charley's voice was barely audible.

'Like you said,' Terry grumbled, still resenting the conversation, as if merely avoiding the subject could disassociate him from whatever they were doing with Joey Doyle. 'It worked.'

'You're sure? You saw 'im go up?' Charley pressed him.

'Yeah, yeah, it worked, it worked.'

Truck Amon tapped his temple, pressed his thick lips together and nodded sagely at Terry. 'That brother of yours is thinkin' alla time. Alla time.'

'*All* a time,' Gilly Connors agreed, his lower lip protruding and his head bobbing in a characteristic series of abbreviated nods.

Terry looked at his brother questioningly, not knowing what more to say. Usually he waited for Charley to peg the conversation, but this time Charley was silent and pensive. There was a sad, sweet, distracted look on his face, an expression of concentrated preoccupation. As Terry looked at him, wishing he could figure what was on his older brother's mind, that brainy mind, a sound came to his ears, and to the ears of everybody in the neighbourhood, for it could be heard for blocks around, that was the most terrifying he had ever heard. It was a scream, such as might have been torn from

28

the bloody throat of a savage animal being ripped apart by fiercer beasts. It was a scream, a cry, a shout, a prayer, a protest, a farewell. Unmistakably it gave voice to death, sudden and violent, a tongue ripped from its living mouth at the very moment of its outcry against the act, a shrill, hoarse, descending wail choked with agony.

'I'm afraid somebody fell offa roof,' Truck Amon said looking from Gilly to Charley for appreciation of his wit.

The barflies were pouring out of Friendly's in the direction of the scream and the sickening, thudding punctuation that had ended it. Only Charley didn't move. Truck and Gilly and 'J.P.' and a few others sat there with blank and withdrawn faces, curtained against the act of mercy or a show of compassion. Terry looked into their faces, into the purposely bland face of his brother. Suddenly he saw what they had done to him. He had been a decoy, like the pigeon, as ignorant and almost as innocent.

Around the corner there was an increasing babel of voices. A police car sirened in. Charley and Truck and Gilly watched, with tired, mind-our-own-business eyes. Terry watched Charley and Gilly and Truck. Truck said, in his dry, thick-toned monotone:

'He thought he was gonna sing for the Crime Commission. He won't.'

Terry said to Charley quietly, more befuddled than accusing, 'You said they was only gonna talk to him?'

Charley wouldn't look at Terry. He kept staring straight ahead, at the passers-by, as if it were any other night. He tried to be as cold and business-like as Johnny Friendly. 'That was the idea.'

'I thought they'd talk to 'im. Try to straighten 'im out. Get him to dummy up. I thought they was only gonna talk to him?'

Terry's was less a question than an awkward searching of himself.

'Maybe he gave 'em an argument,' Charley suggested.

'I figured the worst they'd do is work 'im over a little bit,' Terry said.

'He probably gave 'em an argument,' Charley persisted. He said it in a way intended to cut off further discussion. Terry was a funny kid, a roughneck, a natural cop-hater, but not quite a working hoodlum in the Specs or Sonny or Truck or Gilly sense. A little too much of a loner. People didn't realize you had to have an organization sense to rate as one of the boys. Terry was like a masterless half-vicious mongrel dog that never ran with the pack. He was satisfied to gnaw on any stray bone he picked up in the street when he could be stealing meat off a butcher truck. A hard guy to figure, hard to trust, in a funny way. That's why Charley had never bothered trying to get Terry into the organization. People wondered why Charley with his connexions didn't do a little more for the kid brother. The reason was in Terry himself. He couldn't do a simple favour without asking dumb questions about it.

'Just work 'im over a little, that's what I figgered,' Terry was muttering.

'That Doyle's been givin' our boss a lot of trouble lately,' Truck said in a righteous, almost prim tone of voice. To Truck Amon, born and raised in Bohegan to respect muscle and power, any flaunting of the authority of Johnny Friendly was an affront to his sense of order. Johnny had made him and Johnny could break him. He was on the payroll for a bill and a half a week and what he could look to steal. That's all he knew and all he needed to know.

Terry was still talking to himself. Charley had an eye on him. What was the kid eating himself for? Maybe he should have given him the whole picture. But it was bad security. Don't tell nobody no more than he has to know to do what ya tell him to, Johnny Friendly always said. Like many a successful racket guy, Johnny would have made a pretty good division commander. So how could Charley give Terry the whole story? He hadn't figured Terry would give him any trouble. Terry knew certain things had to be taken care of in this business. He had to know that much.

'He wasn't a bad little fella, that Joey,' Terry said under his breath.

'No, he wasn't,' Charley said.

'Except for his mouth,' Truck said.

'Talkative,' Charley said.

'Yeah, talkative,' Gilly seconded, liking the sound of the word.

'Wasn't a bad little fella,' Terry couldn't seem to stop saying. Maybe if he had known it was to be his pitch to call Joey out for the knock-off, if he had had a little time to get used to it, it might have been okay. Joey had been asking for it, that's for sure. So he had only himself to blame. Terry could see that. But what was getting under his skin was this not telling him. As if he was too dumb to be trusted with the job if he had known they were going all the way. That's what was crawling inside him. That's what he figured it was. All he knew was he felt bad. Until the time Charley had come up to get him on the roof, he had felt okay, his usual okay self, and now he felt something like a bellyache in his head, the way his head had buzzed and felt heavy and big when an opponent had scored with a combination to the jaw and the ear, and he knew he was hurt and needed to cover up until he could shake his head clear.

Everyone on the corner was looking in the direction of the tenement roof-top from which Joey had fallen unwillingly into the littered courtyard.

'Maybe he could sing,' Truck said with his guttural wit, 'but he couldn't fly.'

'Definitely,' Gilly rumbled, with his abbreviated St. Vitus nods, and a bull-frog chuckle in his throat.

Terry looked at them and he felt he was catching blows to the head again. It was like being caught in a flurry and trapped in the other guy's rhythm. Charley saw the look on Terry's face and figured he better get the kid away from Truck and Gilly before they said anything else to rub it in worse. Especially that Truck, who wasn't satisfied just being a thickneck and had to double as a comedian.

'Come on, kid, I'll buy you a drink,' Charley offered, sliding his arm over Terry's shoulder.

'You go in. I'll be in in a minute,' Terry said.

'It happens, kid,' Charley said philosophically.

'I know. I know. I just wanna get some air,' Terry said, ashamed to be caught soft in front of Charley.

Charley hesitated for a moment and then turned toward the entrance, giving Truck and Gilly the eye to follow him in.

With his mind full of confusion, Terry watched the stream of people, longshoremen, truckers, wives and kids and drifters, moving in the direction of the accident.

4

IN THE CLEARING behind the row of tenements at least fifty people had gathered around the heap of inert bone and flesh and crumpled clothing that had been Joey Doyle. Their heads were bent in the age-old attitude of grief, in this case genuine grief, for Joey had been a popular kid before developing into a respected neighbourhood figure. But there was also in this atmosphere a deep sense of shame, as if the entire neighbourhood was implicated in this sudden and yet not unexpected violence.

Group resentment, smouldering, was silent and invisible, and yet a force, like a field of electric current coursing around the body, which someone had had the grace to cover with pages of a daily tabloid. In fact, if one looked carefully he could see the dark headlines crying out the day's rapines, holdups and murders, so that the rags of violence covered the remains of violence in the back alley of this river town.

Pop Doyle stood with his friends, Runty Nolan and big, bull-voiced Moose McGonigle, a Mutt-and-Jeff combo who did a lot of drinking and clowning together and liked to abuse each other. They knew the whole story of Joey Doyle and they also knew—while often straying from—the narrow, twisting paths of waterfront survival. So they weren't saying anything. The three of them stood mute and guarded near the body. And although the motionless grief of Pop Doyle was deeper, for Joey had been a beloved only son (an infant brother losing to pneumonia years before), Pop's face, like the faces around him, made an effort to hide its feelings and its knowledge. To know nothing, or to act know-nothing, was the one sure way of survival on the waterfront.

As always, the city had put smoothly into motion its machinery for handling personal tragedy. Joe Regan, the cop on the beat, had called for the ambulance while Mrs. Geraghty, a neighbour, had sent her boy running for Father Barry over at St. Timothy's, a block and a half away. The intern and the neighbourhood priest had arrived only minutes apart, the rangy, fast-talking and usually chain-smoking young parish priest pushing people aside with a rough 'Outa my way, outa my way,' and having time to administer the

32

last rites while the body was still warm and the intern was listening in vain for a faltering heart beat. As Father Barry was praying for God's mercy and the gift for Joey Doyle of a life everlasting, the intern was telling Regan, the cop, to pencil his report D.O.A. Another Dead on Arrival from River Street.

Regan had asked a few routine questions of the onlookers—had anyone seen the fall and did anyone know whether young Doyle had been alone on the roof?—questions that had to be asked to cover Regan in case he was checked. Then, for the same reason, because it looked like an accident but probably wasn't, he sent for the homicide squad. They drove up a little later, a pair of first-grade detectives who took over, especially the old man Foley, a fatgut who had started out doing a job on these waterfront cases until his captain had straightened him out. Most of the action in town was on the piers: the horse play and the dice and a cut of the pilferage, not to mention the pay-off on the ship jumpers and the nose candy from the Italian mob who maintained an uneasy truce with the Irish and Johnny Friendly in Bohegan. Foley had been ready to play it straight at the beginning but with a take-artist like Donnelly as Commissioner you would just louse yourself up and push yourself back into a uniform if you didn't play along.

So Foley knew what kind of a report he was expected to bring in, but he also knew enough to make his questions hard and official. There would be days of this, all the motions of a thorough investigation, for there was nothing the Bohegan police force was better schooled in than covering up its tracks. The neighbours were watching warily as Lieutenant Foley turned to Pop Doyle.

'You're Doyle, aren't you? The boy's father?'

Pop stared at him, angry behind his mask. 'That's right.'

'Would your son usually've been up on the roof at this time of night?'

Pop shrugged. 'Once in a while. He'd be up there with his boids.'

'Any idea whether he was alone or not?'

'How should I know? I wasn't up there.'

Mrs. Collins was pushing forward to have her say. She was a thin, once-pretty, nervous and overworked woman in her early thirties whose husband had been a hatch boss fished out of the river in the

33

late 40's. 'Billy Conley and Jo-Jo Delaney are up on the roof all the time. Maybe they could tell you something about it.'

Pop glared at her. Helping cops was a waterfront taboo, no matter how you felt about the bums who muscled your union. 'Buttinsky,' you keep outa this,' he told her harshly.

The Conley and Delaney kids were standing near the front of the crowd. Foley knew them. They were marked tough juves who bore watching. The familiar blank look of caution-with-cops slipped over their faces.

'We ain't been up on the roof for a nour. We didn' see nothin'.'

Foley turned away from them. Punks. He'd have trouble with them one of these days. Everybody was staring at Foley and his partner with the same cold, disdainful look. The lips of old man Doyle were pressed together in a melancholy sneer. He was waiting for the next question.

'You're sure you got no idea what he was doing up on the roof after dark? And whether he was expecting to meet anyone?'

A low growl of resentment came out of Pop. Cops! Who wants cops? Any ideas, he wants to know. A helluva lot he'd do if I filled him up to the eyebrows with ideas. Just get in more trouble, like poor Joey here.

'Any ideas, Pop?' Foley said again. 'Any suspicions? Anything like that?'

'None,' Pop said.

Mrs. Collins pushed forward again.

'It's the same thing they did to my Andy five years ago.'

Pop wheeled on her. Busybody. All of them. Why couldn't they leave him alone with his heartache and his kid? All these questions and people poking their noses in. For what? Another whitewash. 'You shut up,' he told Andy Collins' widow. 'You keep your big yap outa this.'

Mrs. Collins glared at everybody. She was always talking about her Andy and the thing they did to him five years ago. He had been a hatch boss on Pier C who hadn't forgotten his years with a hook in his hand for one-thirty-seven an hour. He liked to give the men a break. Johnny Friendly had warned him, but he wouldn't play. Beaten him up, but he kept on. There was talk he was ready to buck the outfit and try to take over the local and run it like a union. Mrs. Collins was a little out of her head on the subject. 'Every time I hear a key in the door I think it's him comin' home,' she'd keep saying. Pop Doyle could shout at her all he wanted. She was going to have her say.

'Joey Doyle was the only one with the guts to talk up for his rights around here. He was for holdin' regular meetin's. An' he was the only one with the moxie to talk up to them Crime Investigators. So this whole stinkin' mess could . . .'

'Shet up!' Pop was trembling, the pain of his loss meshed in with his rage and frustration.

'Everybody knows that.'

'Who asked ya? Shut ya trap. If Joey had taken that advice he wouldn't be . . .'

Pop looked at what was left of Joey Doyle and turned away with his face growing damp as tears and sweat mingled in a slow, salt flow. The whistle of another ocean liner went WHOOM WHOOM WHOOOOOOM on the river. In his mind the river and Johnny Friendly were one, endlessly dangerous and never sleeping.

'Everybody knows that,' Mrs. Collins was whimpering to herself.

Mutt Murphy had come along and was shouldering his way in and trying to talk to people who turned aside to avoid his stale breath and the sight of his livid, swollen-from-drinking lips.

''s a good boy,' he muttered, accustomed to talking to himself. 'Oney one ever tired t' get me me compensation, God bless 'im . . .'

Lieutenant Foley had had enough of Pop. He turned to Moose McGonigle and Runty Nolan.

'How about you fellas, any of you ever hear any threats to . . .'

Moose had a bull-necked voice, made emotional by a hard life, and his ordinary conversational tone was louder than most men shouting.

'One thing I loined—all my life on the docks—don't ask no questions—don't answer no questions, unless you . . .'

He stopped, and looked at the lump of flesh lying under the alley-newspapers, waiting for its senseless ride to the city morgue.

'He was all heart, that boy,' Runty said reverently, lowering his face full of broken bones, unable to see the body at his feet because he had been beaten for back-talking until his sight was only a shifting screen of shadows.

'Guts,' Pop said it as if it was a curse. 'I'm sick o' guts. He gets a book in the pistol local and right away he's gonna be a hero. Gonna push the mob off the dock single-handed.'

'In other words, you're pretty sure it wasn't no accident,' Detective Foley said, not so much probing as covering himself either way.

'Listen, Foley,' Pop said. 'I ain't sure o' nuthin'. And if I was I wouldn't tell ya. You'd bury it in the files and they'd bury me in the river.'

Foley made a few routine notes. The whole thing was routine. Everybody knows and nobody says and you fatten the waterfront file, just as the old man says, push another report in the file and wait for a next time.

'Okay, you c'n take it in,' he said to the intern. 'Another D.O.A.'

Father Barry, a tall, lean, fast-talking product of Bohegan, praying for Joey while anointing him, told God he thought Joey deserved mercy in heaven since it had been so rudely denied him in his short visit on this earth. He was born and raised in Bohegan, Father Barry, and he was no pious-tower religious. His old man had been a cop, honest, therefore in trouble, getting the Siberian treatment, pounding a beat on the outskirts, believing in his religion as an ethical guide as well as a sacramental experience and not afraid to tirade against the birettas and the high cloth when he thought them too worldly and overimpressed with wealth and position. A natural-born rebel, an independent man had been Patrolman John Francis Barry. His son, the priest, thinking what a poor end this was for young Doyle, remembered the funeral of his father nineteen years earlier, when he was only eleven. Look at a priest and you may think, what does he know of the world, his collar cutting him off from knowledge of the world, secure for life in the bosom of the Church. But a priest is a man, small-minded or truly catholic, easily frightened or lion-brave, buttering up the parish richlings, or as concerned for the poor and the wretched as was Christ Himself.

Mrs. McLaverty, a plump woman whose slip was always showing, said to a neighbour woman, 'Poor Katie. They was as close as twins.'

The other woman moaned. 'The poor sweet thing. It'll kill her, it will. Her only brother and she too good for this world.'

Mrs. Collins nearby could not be quieted. A little off her head since Andy was taken from her, everybody said, and good reason, with four kids half-orphaned, half-dressed, half-fed.

'You wait and see, God'll be the judge.' She was talking sort of crazy. 'The rats, they'll burn in hell until kingdom come.'

Mutt Murphy staggered closer to the widow Collins and crossed himself elaborately. 'Amen,' he said. 'Lord've mercy on him. He was a saint, that Joey. Oney one tried to get me me compensation. He filled out me report fer me 'n . . .'

He was talking to himself again.

'Come on, outa the way, comin' through . . .' The morgue wagon attendants were pushing through the crowd of curious and bereaved. A cop shoved the bleary Matt Murphy roughly out of the way, so the basket could pass.

Mutt tried to slobber his condolences to Pop, but Runty also pushed him away. There was something about Mutt that was irresistibly pushable. And pushed or cuffed away he always swung back in your direction like a heavy punching bag. 'Beat it, ya rummy,' Runty told him, throwing out his small tough chest in a characteristic bantam-cock gesture. 'Leave the old man alone.'

Mutt shrugged and walked away, shaking his head at the world. Runty and Moose helped Pop along by their closeness as they all followed the body to the morgue wagon. Most of the people in the neighbourhood were gathered solemnly on the sidewalk to watch the wagon drive away.

'C'mon,' Runty said to Pop. 'Le's go get a coupla balls in us.'

5

LONGSHOREMEN WHO HAD hurried to the tenement court-yard were streaming back to the Friendly Bar, in need of a drink.

There wasn't much talk about Joey Doyle. There were wiser things to do, with so many goons on the Earie, than to express any sympathy for him, safer just to dummy up and go about your business, have a drink, watch the fights, keep your nose clean. If there was any law in this jungle, that was it. There was a fight on TV, selling the beer, and the men who had stayed in the bar, for reasons of their own, and those whose curiosity had led them outside into the cluster around the priest and the intern and the cops were now drawn together into their common escape, the 21-inch screen where the violence was vicarious and relatively harmless.

Terry Malloy usually watched the fights, Monday, Wednesday, Friday nights, looking on in a careless, hands-in-pocket, face-in-the-beer sort of way, shrugging off the guys who kept telling him what he could have done to those harmolas in the ring, but privately thinking a lot of young bums were getting away with murder to pull down the $4,000 television money with nothing to go on except willingness and sometimes not even that. Not that Terry had been a ring master. He had been easy to hit; there was scar-tissue swelling over both eyes to prove it, but he had been strong and he had had the spirit for it and he knew a little about pacing himself and closing in on an opponent when he was ready to be taken. Only lost seven fights in forty-three, a pretty fair average for a kid brought along too fast, thrown in over his head a couple of times, and under wraps for the long odds in a couple of others. So Terry watched the fights, and once in a while dreamed the ex-pug dream of a comeback: maybe he'd get his gear out and fool around in the gym just to get the feel of it. Hell, he was still in pretty good shape, only three-four pounds over his best weight, and at twenty-eight—look at Rocky Marciano, Jimmy Carter. They were all around thirty now and seeing more money than they ever knew at twenty.

'Hey, Terry, watch doin' out there? Riley's makin' a bum outa that Solari.'

It was Specs, who had been up there on the roof with Joey, Specs and Sonny. Now they were both inside belting whisky with beer chasers and watching the fight as if nothing had happened. Specs didn't look like a pistol, slight and pasty-faced, but he had the guts or the craziness to take men's lives without flinching, which means without thinking too much about it. He was a nervous man with poor eyesight and he gave Terry the creeps, but he would do anything Johnny Friendly told him, that was for sure. Sonny was just a big meathead who went along, mostly because he had so much respect for Specs. People didn't realize that it took something extra to go all the way with another guy's life. The average bruiser like Truck or Gilly couldn't do it. They could beat you so you died of it, leave you to spit out your life in an alley somewhere. But this other, premeditated thing, the average guy in the mob wasn't up to that. You had to have something special, something big or sick in your character. Terry knew that He knew Specs and even Sonny were tougher or more desperate than he was. He himself was just a hanger-on, a crumb-catcher, usually trusted only with the smallest errands, which was perfectly all right with him. Small potatoes were all right with him. The rest of it was too much trouble, like being President. Who the hell wanted to be President? Look at this Ike and all the headaches he was into. Five stars on his shoulder and he's a hero, George Washington, with the whole world calling him Champ. A year in the White House and he's a bum and Pegler is calling him all the lousy names he used to save for the Democrats. President, or even delegate of Local 447 like Specs Flavin, who wants it? A couple of clams in his pocket and a good-looking oyster lined up for the night-o, that was for Terry. Only now he was in a little more than he had figured. The hell with the fight and Specs and Sonny. He'd tie on a good one tonight and wash it out of his system. It wasn't his fault, not as long as he figured they was only gonna be talking to Joey. Of course he knew Specs and the jobs he would do for Johnny Friendly. But it wasn't his fault if something happened without his knowing it was going to happen.

In the bar, the same old arguments, the same old bull, the same old aimless talk, the ball games and the fights and which stevedore official was the biggest S.O.B. and whether or not Flat-top Karger would get his old hiring-boss spot back when he got out of the can.

'Come on over, have a shot,' Sonny beckoned.

Terry waved them aside and went on into the backroom. The backroom was just an old, stale rectangle with the boxers and the ballplayers and the horses and a few broads on the wall—art studies

—and some pictures of the big shots (from Johnny Friendly up) arm-in-arming one another. There was a touching picture of Johnny right in there with International president Willie Givens, Tom Mc-Govern and the Mayor of Bohegan, snapped on the joyous occasion of the last testimonial dinner for Willie, an annual affair given by the Willie Givens Association, with a list of sponsors featuring everybody of importance from the Mayor and the political bosses to Murder Inc.'s Jerry Benasio, who brought business efficiency to murder. Politicians, shipowners and racketeers, that was the axis on the waterfront. They gave beautiful testimonial dinners. Each year Weeping Willie thanked them with a voice full of tears and whisky and heart-felt clichés.

The principal piece of furniture in the room was a pool table, which served Johnny Friendly as both a desk and a playground. Pool was his game and though he lost money easily ('It's only money', a favourite phrase) he lost this game of skill with great reluctance and would badger the victor until he had evened the score, then play again and again until his superiority was there for all to see. Competitive. Wanting to beat everybody at everything. That's what had made him so big on the docks.

The television was on in the background too and everybody was watching with one eye because the other eye was on Johnny. This was Friday, payday on the pier and the paynight in Friendly's Bar where the take was cut up among the henchmen who called themselves the union officers. All over the harbour the locals were paying off tonight, on Staten Island, along the East River and out in the Benasio country of Brooklyn, a stack of blue chips for the loyal favourites, a piece of the pilferage and the horse money and the short-gang gimmick (hire sixteen men for the work of twenty-two and pad the payroll with ghosts). All over the harbour it was pay-night and the boys had their hands and their tongues out. Johnny Friendly was a big man all week, and could tell Willie Givens what to do and carry out the unwritten, unspoken orders of Tom Mc-Govern, but bigger tonight because now the loot was in the hand and he dealt with realities, was moving around the backroom with the authority and dignity and bad manners of an old-fashioned king.

Jimmy Powers was narrating on the television, building up a guy who shouldn't have been up there. 'He's being beaten to the punch but he's always dangerous, he's got a lethal right hand,' the comment interrupted the fight.

Johnny Friendly laughed. 'Lethal shit,' he said. 'The kid's nothing.'

Terry was in the room, just inside the door, in a mood, looking at all of them, Jocko, the big-faced bartender, poked his head in the door.

'Hey, boss, Packy wants another one on the cuff-o.'

Packy was an old longshoreman and ex-con, helpful in a minor way until the sauce got him.

'Give it to 'im,' Johnny waved Jocko out. He was always generous in public and he was nearly so in private. If you were able to accept his way of life without question, he was rather an exemplary character.

Big Mac came up to the pool table with a wad of bills. He didn't say anything because it was just a routine pay-in, the cut from the shape-up, five days, 850 men paying Big Mac two to five bucks a day for the privilege of being thumbed in over some other guys. Better than ten thousand dollars. Two piers. And Johnny had a third opening up any minute. Big Mac lingered and Johnny knew there was something on his mind. Johnny took him into the cubicle washroom, the inner sanctum for the business that even the Johnny Friendly boys didn't have to hear. Johnny had a general's sense of security.

Big Mac, a material witness in a couple of local murders, including the Andy Collins job, a man with a hard jaw encased in the fat of easy living, put his mouth close to Johnny's ear.

'We got a banana boat comin' in at B tomorra, the *Maria Cristal* from Panama. I was just wonderin'. Them bananas go bad in a hurry.'

Big Mac looked at Johnny, waiting for the word go. What he meant was a work stoppage. You dream up some labour grievance—the company is using its own men to speed the unloading—any handy gimmick, and then you pull the men off and leave the bananas to rot. In twenty-four hours the banana people—the ones who contracted to buy 'em are the ones who get stuck—are singing

41

yes we have no bananas. Then Big Mac whispers to them he can get the men to call off the strike for a consideration—some bills slipped into an envelope like it was Christmas. They had worked it with tulip bulbs from Holland last spring and shook the Dutch uncles down for 25G in cold cash. There's a fortune in tulip bulbs and 25G is a small price to get them into America before they rot in the hold.

'Okay, ask ten G,' Johnny said. 'But be sure you don't pull the men out without a good reason. Be sure it looks legit. So I c'n bull the press how we're fighting for the rights of our men.'

'I got ya, boss,' Big Mac said. 'I don't think we'll have no trouble. That banana outfit ain't got no guts.'

They came back into the big room and the television fight was still on. 'Solari's hanging on,' Jimmy Peters was saying. 'Riley had him hurt, but he can't seem to finish him off. Only thirty seconds now. Solari had him tied up, the referee can hardly get them apart. They're both pretty tired boys.'

'Aah, turn it off,' Johnny said. 'Them clowns can't fight. There's nobody tough any more.'

He said it in a roar, looking around to challenge everybody, and the goons and the runners and the pier bosses and the shylocks and the gambling concessionaires and the stooges with big titles all nodded. Terry was standing there by the door, not coming in or throwing a few friendly hooks at his chums as he usually did. Johnny saw him and grinned.

'There he is! You could of licked 'em both with one hand tied behind ya.' He put his thick arms around Terry's chest and lifted him off the ground with affection. Then he fell into a favourite gag, cowering as if afraid he was about to be felled by a terrible punch. 'Don't hit me. Don't hit me now!' Usually Terry was glad to go along with the gag, pleased at all this attention from the big man of the neighbourhood. But this time he hung limp in Johnny's arms and he didn't feint at him and fall into the by-play as he had been in the habit of doing.

Johnny lost interest in the kid. After all, he was around mostly for laughs and as a little pay-off on the old-time boxing skills, and he looked around for one of his shylocks, keeping in his mind all the

42

transactions and aware that one of the loan sharks had yet to turn in his yield for the week.

'Where's Morgan? Where's that big banker of mine?'

Morgan, a waterfront Uriah Heep, who looked like something dredged up out of the foul waters of the slip, came forward. He was on his feet but he seemed to be crawling.

'Right here, Mr. Friendly.'

'Well, "J.P.", how's business?' Johnny said.

'I'm havin' trouble with Kelly again, boss,' 'J.P.' recited his complaint with reproachful side glances at Big Mac. 'He won't take no loans and Big Mac keeps putting him to work anyway.'

'I got to put him to work. He's my wife's nephew,' Big Mac insisted.

'But he won't take no loans.' 'J.P.' was bold when Johnny was here to keep Big Mac off him.

'I got to give him work. You know my wife. She'd murder me.'

Johnny Friendly laughed. 'That's why I stay single.'

Big Mac glared at 'J.P.' He liked to run the pier a little bit the way he, Big Mac, felt like running it and he was sick and tired of this little wormy 'J.P.' always running home to Johnny with his tattle-tales. 'J.P.' reached into his crumpled gray suit for a worn wallet and took out a wad of bills. 'Here's the interest on the week, boss. Six-thirty-two.' 'J.P.'s' take would be 20 per cent, around $125, nice pay for just nosing around into other people's troubles.

Johnny handed the roll to Charley Malloy. 'Here, count it. Countin' makes me sleepy.'

Johnny liked to have his people checking up on one another. It was one of his ways.

Skins DeLacey, a checker on Pier B, a sharp-looking, dressy kid with a knack for not working, and a reputation for stealing from himself just to keep in practice, came in and presented himself to Johnny.

'Howja make out with the sheet tin?' Johnny asked softly.

'Lovely,' Skins said. 'I wrote a lovely receipt if I do say so myself.'

'Stow the receipt. I'll take the cash,' Johnny said.

Skins had the wad. 'Forty-five bills.'

Johnny looked around for Terry. Terry was standing there glum, trying to think. He wanted to say something, but he didn't know what to say, much less how to say it. He felt funny, like being down on the canvas without feeling any pain and yet unable to get up. That had happened to him the time McBride had knocked him out in Newark. His head was clear and he could hear the count and he felt he could get up and fight, but there was something cut off between his head and his legs and he was still down on his hands and knees at the count of ten.

'Here, Terry, you count this,' Johnny handed him Skins' fistful of cash.

'Aw, Johnny . . .' Terry started to say.

'Go ahead,' Johnny ordered. 'It's good for you. Develops your mind.'

'What mind?' Big Mac dead-panned it.

Terry turned on him, relieved to find a target. 'You're not so funny tonight, fat man.'

Big Mac bellied up to Terry, ready with his hands. The kid was nothing, as far as he was concerned. Charley was smart and useful but he could see no point to Terry.

Johnny moved between them, and put his arm around Terry. 'Back up, Mac, I like the kid. Remember the night he took Faralla at St. Nick's? We won a bundle.' He dug a grateful fist into Terry's still boxer-toughened side. 'Real tough. A big try.'

The blow and the talk and the headache Terry came in with threw him off his count. 'I gotta start over,' he said.

Johnny laughed and slapped him on the back. 'Skip it, Einstein. How come you never got no education, like your brother Charley?'

Charley looked particularly scholarly with his glasses on. He read a lot. He was proud of having finished *From Here to Eternity*. He liked books he thought were true to life.

Big Mac nodded toward Terry, out to get his goat. 'The oney arithmetic he ever loined was hearin' the referee count up to ten.'

It got some laughs and Terry was ready to bury a fisted right hand in Big Mac's paunch. Johnny didn't like roughhouse in the back room. This was a business room and Johnny never looked for unnecessary trouble. He had smoothed out a good deal with prosperity and Charley had helped to dress up the operation. Legitimatize it,

44

Charley called it. He represented the local on the District Council and could sound more like an upright trade unionist than Reuther himself. Now Johnny pulled Terry away, blocking him off with his squat, authoritative body and asking his brain-man:

'What gives with our boy, Charley? He ain't himself tonight.'

'It's the Joey Doyle thing,' Charley spoke softly. 'You know how he is. Things like that. He exaggerates them. Too much Marquis of Queensbury.'

Johnny pulled the kid toward him with hard-jaw affection.

'Listen, Terry boy, I'm a soft touch too. Ask any rummy on the dock if I'm not good for a fin any time they put the arm on me. But my old lady raised us kids on a stinkin' city pension. When I was sixteen I had to beg for work in the hold. I didn't work my way up out of there for nuthin'.'

Terry knew the story. Johnny liked to recite it when he was feeling mellow and sometimes he struck back with it as an argument for doing whatever it was he wanted to do.

'I know, Johnny, I know,' Terry said, wishing he hadn't opened this can of peas.

'Takin' over this local you know it took a little doin',' Johnny went on with the self-righteous dramatics that always coloured the old story. 'Some pretty tough fellas were in the way.' Violently, he raised his head, stretching his bull neck taut to show the long, ragged, celebrated scar. 'They left me *this* to remember them by.'

Charley nodded. 'He was holding his throat to keep the blood in and still he chased them out into the street. Fisheye thought it was a dead man coming after him.'

Terry had been a kid when it happened. Fisheye Hennessy and Turkey Smity had the Bohegan piers in those days and Johnny had worked up to hatch boss. He was taking plenty and building up a following. Then one day he just walked into the office of the local, the little joint on the wharf. and when Fisheye came in he threw him out, into the scummy water of the slip, for all to see. 'I'm the new president of Local 447,' he explained. That's how union officers won elections on the waterfront. A few days later Hennessy came into the Friendly Bar (the Shamrock it was called in those days), and offered to shake hands with Johnny, but the hand had a knife palmed

45

in it and in a flash Johnny's neck was wide open like a jack-o'-lantern mouth. Ten days later the water-logged, fish-mutilated remains of Hennessy were brought to the surface with grappling hooks. Johnny was brought in as a material witness, along with Specs Flavin. But no one could be found to testify as an eye-witness, so they were released in a few days. Turkey Smith was found in the Jersey marsh about a year later. He had been eaten away by lime and looked more like an anthropological discovery than a recently departed member of the human race.

Terry knew the old story, chapter and verse. The rapid and thorough way Johnny Friendly had come to power on the docks of Bohegan had a mythical hold on the local imagination. As did the promptness with which President Willie Givens and the bunch of lushes he called his District Council recognized and embraced the new slate of officers for 447. Of course Willie Givens, the Communion breakfast star, old Weeping Willie, professed to blissful ignorance when anyone so much as suggested that his Bohegan local was manned by the wrongest bunch of trade unionists this side of Dannemora. It wasn't his job to inquire too closely into the doings of the locals. He was a champion of local autonomy. As long as the locals paid their per capita to Willie and the International, Willie was all for their independence. With his twenty-five thousand annual and his unlimited expense account and his special fund for fighting subversives and his welfare fund and his gratuities from the shipping companies (Merry Christmas, Willie!) he could drink to his heart's content and his liver's distress at the Fleetwood Country Club with his good friend Tom McGovern while the Johnny Friendlys did the dirty work. *Takin' over the local took a little doin'.* Terry knew the whole story, chapter and verse.

'I know what's eatin' you, kid.' Johnny kept his arm around Terry and Terry wished Charley hadn't brought this up. He didn't need all this crap. What he needed was to get gassed somewhere and knock off a little piece. He'd be all right in the morning. But Johnny was hanging on to him. Maybe they should've spelled out the whole thing for the kid, Johnny was ready to admit. So it wouldn't come as such a shock. But Rule One was: only tell each fella what he needs to know. One of these days maybe they could tie Terry in a little closer. But he always seemed like a kid, a natural fringer, a bum in his heart, and in this business as in any business you needed a little ambition. Just the same, Johnny remembered the Faralla fight and some favours in the ring that had paid off in thousand dollar bills. So he took the trouble to explain to Terry. Hell, he liked the kid. And he was feeling good tonight. It was a relief to have Joey Doyle out of the way. Longshoremen were unpredictable. Johnny had been one of them, and he knew. They could lie smouldering for years, and all the time you think you've got them. Then all of a sudden something sets them off and whammo! it's like snoozing on top of a volcano. Joey Doyle might have thrown the switch on him if he had had a chance. And there were rumblings of revolt in other parts of the harbour. And a new contract with the Shippers was coming up in a few months and that was always a touchy time.

'Look, kid, you know I got fifteen hundred dues payin' members, that's fifty-four thousand a year *legitimate*. And when each one of 'em is willin' to put in a couple of bucks to make sure of gettin' a day, and they're good for a dollar every time we pass the cigar box for the welfare fund, and we got the numbers and the horses going, and some other stuff—well, you figure it out. We got a couple of the fattest piers in the fattest harbour in the world. Everything that moves in and out, we take our cut.'

'We had to work hard for it,' Charley said. 'And there's plenty of headaches and responsibilities. Believe me, whatever we make, we're entitled to it.'

Terry was between them now and wishing he was on his roof, waving his long exercise pole at his pigeons. But Johnny was on top of him, talking close into his face.

'So now look, kid, you don't think we could afford to be boxed out of a deal like this—a deal I sweated and bled for—on account of one lousy little cheese-eater, that Doyle bum, who goes around agitatin' and squealin' to that friggin' Crime Commission. Do you?'

Terry was on the floor. He was crawling on his hands and knees and the referee was counting and what the hell was wrong with him so he couldn't get up. Like the breath was knocked out of him .

'. . . Well?'

Terry frowned and said, 'Sure, Johnny, sure. I know he had his nerve givin' you all that trouble. I just figured if I was gonna be in it I shoulda been told what was goin' t' . . .' He faltered, feeling Johnny's eyes on him, and Charley trying to signal him off. 'I . . . just . . .' His voice trailed off. Why bother? They knew what he meant.

Charley was watching Johnny anxiously, but the boss was still in a soft mood where Terry was concerned. The kid had done his piece of it well and Specs and Sonny had taken care of the rest and everything was okay. Right now it was a hundred to one the coroner was handling it as a routine accident. The police would close it out ditto in a couple of days. There wouldn't even be the bother of a few minor arrests. Sam Millinder, who was now riding a seventy-five-thousand-a-year retainer, wouldn't even have a chance to show off his legal figure-skating. It was the kind of smooth operation that's only possible when you've got everybody with you. Johnny reached into his pocket, drew out a fifty and tucked it into the neck of the sweater Terry was wearing for a shirt.

'Here, kid, here's half a bill. Go get your load on.'

Dully, darkly, as in an overclouded dream, a bleary snapshot torn out of the frayed album of beer-sodden sleep, Terry remembered the fresh young face of the Doyle kid leaning out over the sill. The money would only remind him. 'Naw, thanks, Johnny.' He tried to hold it off. 'I don' need it, I . . .'

Johnny didn't like to be refused in anything, even handouts. He pushed the bill deeper into the neck of Terry's sweater, with a laugh that was hard and generous. 'Go on. A little present from your Uncle Johnny.'

He turned around to Big Mac, who was waiting docilely for his split so he could spread money on the bar in a dozen traps and be a big man among cronies and freeloaders.

'Hey, Mac,' Johnny commanded, 'tomorra morning when you shape the men put Terry in the loft. Number one. Every day.'

Big Mac nodded, sucking in his puffy cheeks, a sign of reluctant obedience.

'Okay, Matooze?' Johnny told Terry. 'An easy ride. Check in and goof off on the coffee bags.'

48

That was ninety bucks a week for reading *See, She, Pic, Quick, Tempo, Stare, Dare* and the *Police Gazette*.

'Thanks, Johnny,' Terry said. He couldn't shake the mood of he-didn't-know-what. He stuffed his hands into the pocket of his jeans and went walking out with the fifty hot on his chest like a mustard plaster.

Charley had been watching his brother with shrewd, seasoned sympathy. 'You got a real friend here, and don't you forget it,' he felt the need to call after the kid.

Terry didn't turn around. He walked slowly toward the door, just as a beaten fighter, his head down, makes his way up the aisle through the crowd to his dressing room.

'Why should he forget it?' Johnny said grandly. And proceeded to pay off his boys, dealing out the week's take like cards across the pool table, and saving sheafs of bills for the Mayor and the Police Commissioner, whom he'd be seeing over at the Cleveland Democratic Club a little later.

Specs and Sonny and Gilly were at the bar rolling dice as Terry shouldered his way through. They called to him again, but he kept on going. He walked along River Street until he came to a little hole-in-the-wall bar called Hildegarde's which always struck him funny because Hildegarde was a good two hundred pounds, a great slab of warm-hearted, incongruous femininity who carried on a tearful running battle with her skinny, allergic-to-work husband Max. It was usually quiet in Hildegarde's, especially after she had thrown out Max. Terry sat there at the bar absently listening to Helen Forrest singing 'My Secret Love', over and over and over again because Hildegarde's fat, damp hands kept feeding nickels into the box.

'Whatsa matter you so quiet tonight?' Hildegarde said.

Terry shrugged and gulped his fake-bottom jigger of Four Roses like something too hot to hold in his mouth. Hildegarde moved away from him, an experienced bartender respectful of her customer's mood. There was nobody else in the place, so she leaned the fat folds of her body in the juke box and crooned in a thick guttural accent:

> '*Vunce I hoff a secret luff*
> *Dot liffed vit-in da heart off me . . .*'

49

Ordinarily Terry would have kidded her, as they had a kind of running gag about her boy friends—'Who's da new poy fran?' Terry would elbow her. 'How's about you 'n me sneakin' off for the week-end? The No-tell Motel, huh, you may not be the best piece of ass in town but nobody c'n say you ain't the biggest.'

Hildegarde would pretend to be angry and call him a dirty-mouth fresh guy, but she liked Terry and she'd wind up buying him drinks, and letting him run up a bill until he had enough chips. But tonight it was different and big Hildegarde embraced the juke box in her loneliness and left Terry to whatever it was that had hold of his mind.

6

IT WAS AFTER ten o'clock, but the kids on Market Street were still playing a noisy game of stoop-ball in the misty light of the sidewalk lamps. The ball bounded back into the street and a sweaty-faced twelve-year-old pursued it almost under the wheels of a taxi that had suddenly turned the corner. The people of this neighbour-hood travelled by subway and grumbled about the hiked fifteen-cent fares. A cab pulling up to a tenement doorway was an occasion. As it parked in front of the Doyle house, all the kids came running to surround it, some of them climbing on the fenders to the profane resentment of the driver. Before Katie Doyle could step out of the cab her name went whispering through the crowd. The kids bunched themselves around the door, pressing for a look at her, like the teenage fans of movie stars. Aside from her connexion with her brother Joey, she was something of a celebrity in the neighbour-hood, because as a freshman at Marygrove College, up in Tarry-town, she had made an unusual break with the bluejean, shirt-out, fresh-talking younger set of Bohegan. She was a quiet, perhaps over-serious girl, sent off to school at the delicate age of twelve because Pop Doyle had been determined, to the point of obsession, to keep her off the streets and out of the trouble the best of pretty girls can stumble into on the Bohegan river front.

In her first year at Marygrove as an eighth-grader she had stood out from the class as the only one to recite the catechism as if the words had meaning, while the others were satisfied to repeat by rote what they were hardly thinking and certainly not feeling. It had made Katherine-Anne a difficult pupil. Within the frame of obedience she tried to think for herself. If the teaching sisters of Marygrove had given Katherine-Anne the key to Heaven, it could be said that she immediately tried to fit the key to the lock, and that she was prepared to examine the Room inside with an inquisitive persistence that was often a little more than the good sisters had bargained for. Sister Margaret who taught English poetry and disapproved of Gerrard Manley Hopkins complained with fond irritation, 'I wish she didn't ask so many questions.'

The frankly staring, dirty-faced children of the neighbourhood pressed toward her as Katherine-Anne paid off the driver. She had adored Joey, almost to the point of distraction if not sin, and now she seemed totally enclosed within her loss, still faint from the shock of the phone call that had pierced the seclusive barriers of Marygrove and pulled her back to Market Street and the terrible events that darkened the river. She was still wearing her blue middy blouse and skirt and in a number of less material ways she had not yet made the transition from the college campus on the outskirts of Tarrytown to this insistent row of crowded tenement dwellings around the corner from the piers. From the cab she walked straight up the outside steps and into the worn, familiar hallway.

Billy Conley, looking up at her from his strategic position at the bottom of the stoop, was moved to comment: 'Boy, that Doyle kid really growed up since she was home last Easter.'

Jo-Jo Delaney laughingly agreed: 'And in the right places. He moved his hands in a grown-up way to show them what he meant.

A fat, twelve-year-old girl scolded: 'Ain't ya got no respeck for the dead?'

At the mention of this final word, the smirking, sex-bothered boys fell silent. Billy could be a beautiful Irish boy when his face was in respose and now he looked like an angel-faced choir-singer at High Mass as he raised his eyes not to heaven but just to the third-storey window where the lights of the Doyle flat were burning.

It was a railroad flat, one of sixteen in the sixty-year-old aged-brick building, with an entrance into the narrow kitchen, with its small stove and its bathtub, covered by a lid on which Pop always sat to make room for visitors at the kitchen table. Beyond the kitchen was a dark cubicle, hardly twelve feet long, from which the doors had been removed to leave space for a bed. Another small bedroom and the front room which had once been a parlour but had been converted to a master bedroom (with a television set still being paid for) completed the living quarters. A railroad flat. Well-named, for the width is little wider than a pullman, with each room opening directly into the next, and with no outer hallway to allow more privacy. In the hall was a small toilet for the families of that floor, and if this was clearly not the way a majority of Americans lived, it was still the way the waterfront cargo carriers of Bohegan existed. Some of the tenement houses in this blighted stretch of coastline offered nothing better than outhouses, ramshackle monuments to social lag, erected in the paper-and-refuse-littered open squares between the Market Street apartments and the bars on River Street.

A half dozen people could give the Doyle flat a sense of being overcrowded and now there were at least twice that many present: Pop in his underwear shirt, and Runty and Moose passing the bottle, and a roomer from across the hall, Mr. Mathewson, who was North Irish Protestant but still welcome, and Jimmy Sharkey, a young friend of Joey's. There was also Mrs. Gallagher, a motherly neighbour who had eleven kids and was engaged in a lifelong tug-of-war with her husband as to who would get hold of his Friday-night check and yet somehow found time to mother the entire tenement. She was now in the cramped kitchen filling in for long-absent Mrs. Doyle, making sandwiches of ham and cornbeef and cheese that other neighbours had brought in. And there was Uncle Frank, a sergeant on the Force, a plump, red-faced, kindly man, who for some mysterious reason had never married and was always good for a nickel or a dime to the kids on the street. It was a cross-section of the neighbourhood crowded into these small rooms, drinking and talking loud and telling stories and sometimes weeping with the neighbours who kept dropping in and passing through with a hug for Pop and a nip of the bottle and the ancient fumbling words for the poor lad's passing.

As Katherine-Anne came along the creaky upper hallway to the open kitchen door, Runty Nolan was holding the floor with a whisky story told in an effort to lift Pop's sorrow.

'So I comes out of the swingin' door of McCarty's'—Runty was acting it out with the mimic gifts of the old country—'an' do a header into a snowbank . . .'

Moose was refilling Pop's glass and Pop was trying to laugh. 'Go ahead, go ahead, Pop,' Moose shouted. 'Drink up.'

'Well, just a little one,' Pop said, dazed by all the people and the suddenness.

'. . . an' when Pathrick here (indicating Pop) tries to rouse me, I sez, "Ya got ya noive disturbin' a man in his own bed an' pullin' off his sheets." "Sheets, that's *snow*, ya rummy," this old coot sez.'

Runty had a hearty ho-ho-ho laugh and everybody joined in, those who didn't feel like laughing saying hah-hah-hah even louder than the others, until the crowded, stale-smelling, shabby wall-papered rooms were truly waked with the unnatural, mournful laughter. So it sounded when Katie came in, a tall, straight, pink-skinned, remote figure in the sardine-crowded, whisky-smelling kitchen.

The sight of his daughter entering so quietly that she was among them before they even noticed her coming was just what Pop needed to break down completely. Now his true feelings flowed at last as he held his Katie close to him and she felt his creased, un-shaven face against her smooth cheek. Then he was sobbing into the harbouring curve of her neck and shoulder. She held him quietly while he sobbed, 'Katie girl . . .'

Softly, still dry-eyed from the shock of it, she said, 'Pop . . . Pop . . .' and the friends around them turned to each other both from embarrassment and to make an invisible wall of themselves behind which father and daughter could bare their sorrow.

On the other side of this invisible wall, Runty Nolan was offering the bottle to Mathewson. 'Come on, Matty, ye're fallin' behind.'

'Behind! One more 'n I'll be fallin' down,' the North Irish Protestant said.

Katherine-Anne, watchful and remote, praying in her mind to her dear Mother Mary, was groping toward her own awareness of what had happened. In the seclusion of the Tarrytown convent school, guided by the sisters of St. Anne, she had lived with an almost feverish sense of sin and corruption and human misery. The Holy Family, in her eyes, was engaged in an hour-by-hour struggle against ignorance and error. The Trinity was as real to Katie Doyle as the cash register in Friendly's Bar and Grill was to Johnny's brother-in-law Leo. But slowly, Katie was beginning to sense, pushing blindly underground like a half-grown mole, what a world of pious dreams her moral being had been drifting through. Now, for the first time in her life, Katie had a real human misery, a live sin, a raw and vicious corruption thrusting through her faith. In her mind, cut off from the forced festivity of the wake, she was calling on her Blessed Mary as she would have turned to her own mother if only she had still been here. And when she cried to herself, *Our Mother full of grace, help me, help me to understand,* she was searching without yet knowing it for a real answer to a question of life or death, not far away on Calvary, with the angels sweeping down to their silent triumph over coarse soldiers, but here, on River Street and shabby Market Street, where the ships went WHOOOO-WHOOOOOM in the night and the oil-slick tongues of the monster river licked greedily for victims—not far away on Calvary in the pocket-sized Missal, but here, on the hillock of misery and violence between Market and River streets on the Bohegan Banks.

'Yes, sir,' Jimmy Sharkey was saying, for the fifth time at least, to keep the talk going, to keep this kind of party alive, 'it'll be a long time before anybody stands up to them gorillas like Joey Doyle.'

'Enough guts for a regiment,' Moose shouted.

'A real bravadeero,' Runty Nolan put in.

And Runty knew what it was to be a bravadeero on the docks. He went back to '14 when Local 447 got its charter. Willie Givens and Tom McGovern were charter members who worked right alongside him. Willie was a young blowhard always cadging drinks. One day he had a few too many and didn't see a piece of steel plating swinging past him toward the hold. Willie was laid up for three months, and Runty, out of the goodness of his heart, suggested to the membership, still in its unencrusted, democratic stage, that a job be made for Willie as assistant financial secretary of the local to see him through his convalescence. Willie took to bureaucracy like a waterfront kid takes to beer. He never did a day's work with a hook again. He went up and up. President of the Local. Vice-Chairman of the District Council. Finally President of the International. Twenty-five G and unlimited expenses. And presents from the shippers for being so understanding of management's problems. And a secret fund for 'fighting Communism' that every firm in the harbour felt its patriotic duty to support, an ostrich-sized nest-egg accountable only to Willie himself. The last Convention, a fine group of amiable rubber-stamps, had made Willie President for life, all in favour say Aye and God help the poor slob who dares raise his voice in the negative. Thus had Willie Givens developed into a parliamentary front for Johnny Friendly below him and Big Tom McGovern on top.

Big Tom was on the Board of Directors of the Knickerbocker Athletic Club and the Gotham Club and the Mayor jumped when he whistled and he had stevedore companies and tug companies and oil companies and sand-and-gravel companies and trucking companies and companies that owned other companies. In other words, he had the city by the head and the tail and while he was pouring twenty-five-year-old for the judges and the politicos, his strong-arms in the stevedore outfits were muscling the men who refused to knuckle under. From the penthouse on Fifth Avenue to the gutter on River Street where the blood ran, Big Tom had it all. But Runty could remember when young McGovern, a two-hundred-pound bully who had been told once too often that he resembled Jim Jeffries, was loading meat for the A.E.F., with his own meat-like hands, off a horse truck at Pier B, and steering into the black market more beef that he was loading for our boys over there.

And Runty could remember how in three years Tom McG. rose from a loader at forty cents an hour to the owner of ten meat trucks of his own. Thus was born the Enterprise Trucking Co., and enterprise of a most direct kind it was, for Big Tom acquired his two trucks by the efficient method of threatening their owner with extreme bodily harm if he did not sign them over.

Runty saw him use his own, brine-hardened fist to fight his way up to power on the docks. And he knew of the teamster-union official taken care of in one of the first waterfront murders so that Big Tom could push one of his own stooges into the teamster leadership, as soon after he was to set easy-dollar Willie Givens in the top spot with the longshoremen. And all the time that Big Tom was punching his way into the city's inner circle, and Weeping Willie was spreading his whisky-tipped wings as a silver-throated labour leader, Runty Nolan remained the lowliest of longshoremen, the wielder of a hook in the hold, and that in the old days before all the equipment, when the main piece of equipment was your own back. A strong back and a weak mind was a hold-man's formula for doing the job.

But Runty, for all the whisky and the long nights around bars, had a strong or at least a consistent mind when it came to Willie and Big Tom. When he saw what they were up to, back there in the first War, when Tom was on his way to his first million and Willie was oiling his union machinery, Runty swore against them his undying hatred, or more accurately his dying hatred, swore on his sainted mother and his Cobh pierman father who died in a set-to with the Black and Tans in the days of the Trouble. And when a Nolan swears on these, he swears for eterntiy. So he talked up and he spoke back and he got himself flattened and kicked for good measure. But a life of beatings had failed to deaden the twinkle in his eyes.

Runty Nolan was always for seeing the funny side, even when he was looking down the business end of a triggerboy's .38. While other longshoremen turned away in fear, Runty seemed to take a perverse delight in baiting the pistoleros, as he called them. Sometimes they laughed him off and sometimes, if he went on provoking them—and longshoremen were watching to see if Runty could get away with it—they would oblige him with a blackjack or a piece of pipe. The stories of these beatings had become a riverfront legend.

In the bars they told of the time he was left face-down in an alley, after enough blows on the noggin to crack the skull of a horse. An hour later, when everybody figured he had a one-way ticket to the morgue, damned if he didn't stagger back into Friendly's and pound the bar for whisky. 'I should worry what they do t' me. I'm on borried time,' Runty liked to say. And tossed into the black river for dead, he swam out, and got up. A gift for gettin' up, his cronies called it. His was a lone, lost, almost comic cause, for he wasn't a unit in an organized rebellion but a gadfly, a thorn in the heel of progress, if you can call progress the elaborate harbour-wide set-up of Tom McGovern, with the connivance of too many of the shiping companies, the boss stevedores and the pot-bellies who masqueraded as labour leaders. Runty Nolan had been a bravadeero—as he called it—for forty years, with more lives than a pair of cats and more spunk than was healthy for one little man.

So here at the wake, when he called Joey Doyle a bravadeero, in Joey's case a modernized, better-organized one, he knew whereof he spoke. He did not use the word lightly.

Pop, who loved Runty but had had the spirit beaten out of him long ago ('I just wanna woik and mind me own business and get me money home,' he used to tell Runty in their friendly arguments), this old man with the bitter life of the docks cutting unmistakable lines in his face now moved to the centre of the room, waving his thin, steel-muscled arms as the .86 proof brought him to a trembling line between rage and sorrow.

'Don't talk t' me of bravadeeros,' Pop yelled. 'There's oney one place a bravadeero winds up on this waterfront. On a slab. Jus' like our Joey.'

'Lord've mercy on 'im,' everybody mumbled, and grabbed for their drinks. Moose went around refilling the glasses and Runty, sorry for the bravadeero line that had aroused such bitter sadness in Pop, raised his glass in an obvious but none the less effective reach for a better, brighter mood.

'Well, here's to God, Ireland and present company,' he said with that irrepressible coating of humour in his voice. And then, like the Elder Cato insisting upon the destruction of Carthage, he added: 'And mud in the eye of Willie Givens.'

There was a general assent of 'Right', and 'Here's health' and 'God bless', and Runty was thinking to himself now we've got this wake on the right track at last, when Katie, still on the outer edges of the gathering and as quiet and remote as when she had entered, asked her little question:

'Who did it?'

The question dropped explosively into the middle of the room. Moore, Runty, Pop, young Jimmy Sharkey and three or four other longshoremen passing through looked at one another and hung their heads in a gesture that had become a fixed reaction on the waterfront whenever such a question was asked.

'Who did it?' Katie asked again, her question as simply put as the disconcerting ones she had a habit of asking her patiently impatient teacher in Christian Apologetics at Marygrove.

The room was silent. A hush had fallen over the wake. And just when Runty had hoped to rouse a little life in it. You had to go on. It was rough, but life had to go on. That's what a wake was supposed to say. Belt Irish whisky all night and wind up in the kitchen when dawn began to seep in at the windows, singing 'Galway Bay', that's how a wake was supposed to brace the bereaved and shake the living from the dead.

But here was the girl, asking the question that even Runty, for all his bravadeering, felt bound—tradition bound—not to answer.

Katie turned around to everybody, perplexed, and not yet realizing what she was doing.

'Don't you hear me? Who'd want to harm Joey? The best kid in the neighbourhood. Not because I'm his sister. Everybody loved him.'

Silence can be so intense that it becomes a force in the room as great as sound. Katie felt she had to raise her voice to overcome it.

'Are you all deaf? Has that horrible stuff you're drinking eaten through your ear-drums? *Who'd want to harm Joey?*'

Pop came over and put his hand on Katie's arm, gently. He had sent her out to Tarrytown not just to keep her from the boys who loitered around the cigar-magazine store that was really a horse room, but because he was determined to keep her innocent of the vices that crawled along the waterfront. An anthropologist could have studied this waterfront as if it were an island culture of the South Pacific with its special mores and taboos. In this harbour community there was no stronger taboo than the silence of dock-men not only with law enforcers and outsiders, but even with their womenfolk. A longshoreman didn't even like to tell his wife the number of the pier he was working, so she wouldn't know what danger he might be in and would be unable to name his assailants if she ever were asked.

Pop led Katie into the narrow cubicle behind the kitchen. He was a little drunk—half-gassed, he would have called it—and the creases of his face were moist, his eyes were misty and his voice was low and deliberate. His long underwear top, serving as a shirt, was stained where his unsteady hand had spilled whisky from his chin.

'Pray for 'im, Katie goil. Ask our Maker t' grant 'im etoinal peace. But don' ask no questions. Please, Katie, fer yer own good. Becuz you won't get no answers. You won't get nuthin' but a snootful o' trouble.'

Katie glared at him.

'Trouble? Can there be any more trouble? Joey is dead. Joey is dead . . .' It came out as a moan.

Pop put both hands on Katie's arms and tried to reason her back to quietness. 'Don' be sayin' 'hat, darlin', don' make it worse. If it's God's will . . .'

'God's will!' She pulled away angrily. 'Don't blame it on God. Since when was God an excuse for acting like *pigs*?'

Pop let her go, helplessly. If only Joey had done as Pop had told him: mind yer own business. 'But, Pop . . .' The boy would look at him with his clear blue, believing eyes (almost a twin of Katie's in the fierceness of their faith). 'But, Pop, that bunch of stiffs running our local like they owned us, letting the shippers chip our contract away because they're on the take. What could be more our business?' Trouble with Joey, and now Katie who knew nothing about it and already putting her two cents into it. Jesus, Mary and Joseph, he thought to himself, I sure hope I find a little peace in the next world.

In the kitchen Runty was keeping the party going with a crack-voiced rendering of 'The Rose of Tralee'. It was only a matter of time—another half-hour perhaps—until he'd be offering again to take Kathleen home again. Poor sentimentalized Kathleen, Katie thought. The good-for-nothing drunken Irish bums who were forever raising their voices in song to offer themselves as escorts for that perennial homeward journey with Kathleen. Irishmen, at least

59

the ones she knew, were romantic fools, Katie had decided. Actually it was the Kathleens who did all the work and held things together. They didn't have time to sing.

Uncle Frank was finishing his beer, ready to button his uniform coat and fasten his gun-belt around, or rather under, his comfortable belly. The sight of his uniform suggested something to Katie and she scurried between people to get to him.

'Uncle Frank, you're the one. Why don't you do something? You know Joey. You know he'd never—kill himself like that. He believed in God.'

Uncle Frank was a hulking, temperate man who was ready to slack off on his retirement pay in a couple of years and was looking forward to the vacation after having had to observe the worst side of man's nature for twenty-eight years. He drew Katie out the kitchen door into the hallway. People were passing to and from the wake, and to avoid them they went all the way back to the corner of the hall where there was, if not actual privacy, at least tenement privacy.

'Katie,' Uncle Frank began, 'you know the facts of life. I think Pop's makin' a mistake to keep you ignorant of them here on this waterfront. It c'n get you into trouble. A different kind o' trouble from runnin' around with the drugstore cowboys, but trouble all the same. It's time you knew the score.'

'Pop'll never talk about it,' Katie said. 'And even Joey—he'd say, some day, when I was older. As if I was still nothing but a kid to be babied. But the way they acted—almost like, like criminals themselves, looking at each other, and changing the subject, I knew something was wrong.'

In the kitchen Kathleen had been taken home again. There was a pause, and then Moose's booming voice cried out, 'He had a heart o' gold, that kid, a heart o' gold,' to which the ample Mrs. Flanagan responded as in a catechism, 'Aye, the good die young, they do, I never seen it fail . . .'

Katie was searching the plump, ruddy face of Uncle Frank for answers.

'Katie, down to the station house, we've got a file this thick of waterfront cases—deaths and disappearances and the like—at least four or five every year since I was a rookie back in Prohibition days.

A hundred murders if there's a one. And you know how many arrests? I'm not talkin' about convictions, mind you. Just arrests?'

Katie shook her head.

'Five. And convictions? Two. Just two in all the twenty-eight years I've been on the force.'

'But Uncle Frank, in civics we learn . . . In America . . .'

'Katie, walk around the corner, over to River Street, and you're out of America. It's a jungle down there, a no-man's land. The file tells the story.'

'A hundred murders . . .'

'It could be more. A fella falls in the river. They say he's drunk and slipped off the stringpiece. Or a high-low backs into him or a sling slips. There's a dozen different ways. There's more industrial accidents in ship-loading than anything else in the country. I guess you know that. One in every five hundred longshoremen's gonna wind up dead before his time. So these fellers help the accidents along a little bit. It's hard to prove.'

'But you're supposed to protect them. Isn't that what you're there for, Uncle Frank?'

'In the books you study, positively. But Katie, there's a lot you don't know, a lot of things about the way a city runs that never gets into them civics books. Things I'd lose my pension for telling you if it ever got back to my superiors. Donnelly, the Police Commissioner, appointed by the Mayor, used to drive a beer truck for Johnny Friendly. See what I mean?'

'The Police Commissioner . . .'

'Everybody knows that.' Uncle Frank nodded sadly. 'I could tell you stories. Like what happened to me when I was on the water-front squad and tried to arrest a loan shark.' Uncle Frank gave a short, bitter laugh. 'I could of qualified for lieutenant six years ago except through Pop I was seeing too much of Runty and Moose who got themselves marked in Johnny Friendly's book. Oh, I could tell you stories.'

Katie shook her head. 'I knew Bohegan was full of politics. I've heard Pop say that much. But the Sisters say we live in a Christian world.'

Uncle Frank tightened his gun belt around his waist. 'It's a world with Christians, you c'n go that far. It's pretty tough sleddin' for 'em here in Bohegan—and I don't know if we're any worse 'n the West Side or Staten Island or Brooklyn. It all stinks to high heaven.'

He turned to go, back to the night desk and the unprotected crimes that could be brought safely to justice.

'Thanks, Uncle Frank, thanks for being so truthful,' Katie said.

Uncle Frank, a small worn cog in the wheel of Bohegan justice, turned to warn her. 'Katie, I didn't tell you all this to steam you up. It was to make you see how hopeless it is, so you'll take this as you've got to take it. In pain and resignation, Katie, pain and resignation. Some day, maybe, it'll be different. I mean better. Maybe you, or your children, will be seein' this social justice our Holy Fathers have been talkin' about. Maybe it'll take Christ Himself to come back like He promised. But God knows, and I mean *God knows* there ain't no brotherhood now, nor love 'n justice in Bohegan. That's why nobody talks. That's why I can't arrest a two-bit chiseller on River Street. Donnelly'—years of humiliation and frustration were boiling up in Sergeant Frank Doyle—'I hope he burns in hell.'

He pulled his belt a notch tighter, taking a deep breath, a deep inhaling sigh. 'Remember what I told you now, Katie. This is just between us, so you'll know to do what your old man says and not push into it any further. If you mention I told you, whiff (he made a whistling sound) goes my pension.'

Then he trudged on down the stairs.

On the second landing Katie could hear Uncle Frank say, 'Evenin', Father,' with the note of boyish respect that Irish males always put on when addressing a priest. A moment later Father Barry came into view as he mounted the stairs at his usual rapid pace. A cigarette dangled from his mouth. Katie saw him remove it, snuff the lighted end and drop it into his pocket to save for later. He was a chain smoker (two packs a day minimum) who felt guilty at spending fifty cents daily on this luxurious vice. He had convinced himself that it helped him in his work. High-keyed, furiously energetic, he needed something in his hands or in his mouth to keep him occupied while he went full-speed about his parish duties. Caught between two vices, he had to choose between spending and begging, so he had become an accomplished cadger of cigarettes.

Father Barry, a pretty good ball player and something of an

62

amateur boxer in his college days, took the stairs two at a time until he reached the fourth-floor landing.

'Well, Katie,' he said when he saw the girl standing alone in the rear of the hallway. 'I'd hardly recognize you since the summer. You've grown up.'

'Yes, Father,' she said, in no mood for small talk.

'It's rough about Joey,' Father Barry said. 'He was the best. We're all gonna miss him. But . . .'

He groped for something consoling, some assuaging promise of the hereafter, but he was a product of the Bohegan banks, raised tough and poor and he couldn't help being a realist. No use filling them with a lot of high-sounding pap, he had often told the pastor, Father Donoghue, when he assisted at St. Timothy's. These were plain-talking people. They deserved plain answers.

The priest and the girl looked at each other and he hung his head, seeing impatience in her eyes and sensing it was a time for saying nothing.

'Pop is inside,' she said. 'He'll be glad to see you.'

'How's he takin' it?' Father Barry asked.

Katie shrugged. 'He's all right. He's taking it.'

'I'll be sayin' the Rosary in a couple of minutes,' Father Barry said as he went in.

'I'll be there, Father,' Katie said. But she lingered in the hall, with tears stinging the corners of her eyes. She waited until she was sure she had herself under control before walking back through the kitchen to the front bedroom. There Pop and his friends and the well-wishing neighbours were grouped around Father Barry. The priest would have looked and sounded like a tall, rangy, ruddy-faced longshoreman except for his shiny-worn black suit and the turned-around collar damp from body-sweat and soiled because he had been too rushed all afternoon to go back to his room for a change.

The beads in the hands of the priest were not beads but progressive stations in their Lord's tortured last miles to Golgotha. Katie, as she responded in muffled, chanting tones with the others, lived again the five sorrowful mysteries, the sweating of blood and the scourging at the pillar, the piercing pain of the crown of thorns, the weight of the cross and the final agony of flesh and bone hanging from the crude, cruel nails. In real pain, with her heart crying tears for *Joey Joey*, she chanted the Our Fathers and Hail Marys and those mysteriously soothing words *as it was in the beginning is now and ever shall be world without end Amen* . . .

The saying of the Rosary came to an end, with Father Barry talking rapidly and slightly out of the corner of his mouth, in the nervous rhythm of the Irish lower class, sounding much as he did when he discussed the chances of his beloved Giants, but yet with the feeling there for all to sense. He didn't know how to pretend with these Bohegan riverfronters, how to sound pious or deliberate or even priestly.

When it was over Mrs. Gallagher brought the Father a ham sandwich and Runty said, 'Here, Father, here's something to wash it down with,' and stuck a can of beer into his face. Father Barry took it gladly, and even eyed the bottle of Paddy's Irish, a beverage he was overfond of and had to struggle against. He unbuttoned his collar at the back and sat down to relax a little, a roughneck at heart but a shrewd, strong-minded, dedicated one.

The saying of the Rosary and the physical presence of a priest had eased Pop's mind. Father Barry felt he had accomplished what he could. They would meet again in Paradise, he had assured them. What more could he say?

Father Barry allowed himself a second and final beer and a cheese sandwich. He was a ready eater even if his body, going softly only slightly at the waist, belied this. The fat was burned off in nervous energy. Then he set the time for Joey's Requiem Mass, gave Pop his blessing, slapped him forcefully on the shoulder and hurried toward the door. Mrs. Glennon, around the corner, was on her way out with cancer. Her husband, Beanie Glennon, a longshore casual, wasn't much of a provider and five kids, from two to thirteen, were going to need plenty of help.

As Father Barry took his leave with a snappy 'So long', and 'See ya, now,' and 'Be good, Jimmy,' and a last buck-up-God-bless for Pop, Katie followed him into the hallway.

'Father . . .'

Father Barry wheeled as he was starting quickly down the stairs.

He wasn't prepared for this unexpected delay. He had strong, personal feelings about the violent passing of young Doyle, but he was a professional man too, and he had been here almost an hour. It had been a particularly demanding day, and there was this Glennon call, sure to be a trial, before he finally got a chance to flop down on his bed and read the bull-dog edition sport pages until it fell out of his hands and he was deep in his six-hour sleep.

'Yes, Katie?'

'Father, Joey was *pushed,* you know that, don't you?' She was trembling, with a helpless, dry-sobbing anger. 'Don't you know that? Don't you?'

Her rage found him and lashed him. He put his hand out to soothe her.

'Take it easy, Katie. I know it's rough. I can't give you the easy answers. But time and faith . . . time and faith are great healers.'

'Time and faith!' Katie flung his own words back at him so hard that they had the impact of a sudden blow that knocked him off balance. No ordinary Marygrove freshman would defy a priest. 'Time and faith. My brother's dead, pushed off this roof by beasts who hate the face of God. And you stand here talking drivel about time and faith.'

'It may not be enough, Katie, but I do what I can.'

Her eyes blazed. 'Are you sure, Father? Are you *sure?*'

The way she breathed fire into the words made him unsure.

'Katie, be reasonable. All I can do is help the family. Pray with you and—try to ease the loss.'

But she would not be held off. 'Only God has the power to give and take a life. Isn't that true, Father?'

'Of course, Katie, you know that.'

'So if—if those filthy animals take Joey's life, and the police— Uncle Frank told me—just turn their backs and forget about it, isn't it up to you to do something about it? To try and do something about it? If somebody takes a life, if there's all this evil on the waterfront, how can you pretend you've got a Christian parish— and, and all those fine things we're supposed to be learning?'

Father Barry took a step backwards down the stairs, as if increasing the distance between them would diminish the sting.

'Katie, the Glennons are waiting for me. I'll be glad to discuss this with you any time. As I was saying, I want to do what I can. I'll be in the church whenever you need me.'

Katie glared at him and then laughed angrily. The blow of Joey's death and the sickening resignation of her father and the painful flash of insight into Bohegan justice her uncle had just given her had all combined to depress her to the point where she no longer knew what she was saying.

'*In the church when you need me*,' she repeated, in a way that made Father Barry wince. 'Was there ever a saint who hid in the church?'

The question spun the priest around as if he'd been struck by one of Specs Flavin's .38 slugs. He went rapidly down the stairs and did not look back.

'O Mother, Mother of God, help me,' Katie said aloud.

Inside they were singing an old song that Runty's father had passed on to him, 'The Green Above the Red'. Runty Nolan was fond of saying, 'My entire inheritance consisted of *The History of Ireland*, a bottle of Irish whisky and the ability to absorb punishment like a sponge sucks up water.'

Katie listened, resentfully, to the bleary voices trying to lift the spirits of the house:

> '. . . *and freely as we lift our heads*
> *We vow our blood to shed*
> *Once 'n forever more t' raise*
> *The green above the red . . .*'

It was an old song of Irish independence and it said something about the universal yearning of man to be free, but it sounded to Katie like a hymn of lost causes, a whistling in the dark, as Pop and Runty and Moose and the rest of them made the long hard journey through the black tunnel in which they had trapped themselves.

'Mother, our Mother, help me find a way,' Katie prayed.

A block away the wide black river bowled its deafening answer along the giant alley of water between the Jersey and Manhattan shores as another transatlantic liner (one every fifty minutes, day in, day out) swept down river to the open sea.

MRS. GLENNON WAS dying in front of Father Barry's eyes, a little each day, and her kids were dirty and poorly dressed. Beanie Glennon had been down in the corner bar when Father Pete—as the Glennons called him—arrived, and the oldest boy had been sent down as usual to fetch the old man. The priest dreaded what would happen to the kids when Mrs. Glennon checked out. And he wondered why it should have to be so hard for Mrs. Glennon, suffering illness and poverty and, worst of all, uncertainty for the five kids. He had tried to comfort her, assure her, and his words had helped a little. But again, as with Katie Doyle, were these only words? Was there more he could be doing? Sure it was a hard day, a long day, from 5 a.m., when he began with his own prayers and his preparations for six o'clock Mass to this last family call at eleven. And an almost endless chain of chores and services performed along the way, a fairly average day in the life of a parish priest in a working-class neighbourhood. But doubt nagged him in his end-of-day weariness. Was there more he could be doing? Weren't these more than a continuous series of needy individual cases? Wasn't there a pattern here of insecurity, lawlessness, of Cain-and-Abel destruction?

He could have reached the rectory by walking the several blocks along Market Street, but he felt himself drawn down to River Street. The events of the day cut into his mind with sharp edges. He looked into the bleary faces of the men who wandered past him and he wondered: why are they drinking their lives away? Why are there six bars, at least, in every block? Bars, and no playgrounds, no tennis courts, no reading centres? No place to go on the Bohegan waterfront except into a bar or a church? Father Barry's mind was tired, but the persistent questions would not let him rest. Everything is wrong as hell, and it is more than physical poverty closing in over the port, apathy, amorality. These were fancy words and he didn't go in for them. Hell, he was a Bohegan kid himself. Who was he trying to fool? It plain and simple stank. A good boy like Joey Doyle could be knocked off and nobody lifts a finger. The men themselves accepted murder as if it was nothing worse than a black eye. Catholics, a good 95 per cent of them had accustomed themselves to the idea that a member of the Mystical Body of Christ could be violently removed from its other living parts without their feeling called upon to cry out against this violation of His previous gift. He had felt defensive when Katie had slugged her question at him, *Was there ever a saint who hid in the church?* His immediate reaction had been, Get off my back, sister. You call this hiding? After a tough day I'm here at the wake and then off to the Glennons'. I've sat in the kitchens of hundreds of families, and not only the God-seeking ones but the backsliders and forsakers. You don't have to take my word for it. The Pastor can tell you I'm tryin' to do a job down here.

Was there ever a saint who hid in the church? The simple question nagged him and ragged him. It was almost too simple. And yet that Doyle kid had a point. Name five saints and at least three of them make you think of trouble. They knew danger. They were independent souls skirting the abyss of heresy and excommunication. They were desperate men and women, defiers and innovators, reaching out, plunging deeper, taking terrible chances, as Paul chanced, and Stephen and the first Ignatius. And now, on Bohegan's ginmill row, around this harbour, through the great city and in the sink holes of the world, that kid's question was actually a charge that we are defaulting the spiritual vitality that had spread the idea of love through the whole world. Father Barry had reached the park in front of his old red-brick church, but he kept on walking.

Outside the Crow's Nest, a popular bar next to the Sailor's Home, two burly drunks were pummelling each other's faces. The smaller of the two was knocked down and as he rose from the pavement he snarled at his assailant through his bloody teeth. 'I'll kill ya, ya son of a bitch.' In a moment he was knocked down again. The bigger man laughed. 'I'll fix that sonofabitchin strike-breakin' sailor. Went through our lines in Fifty-one, huh? Git up ya bum, I ain't finished with ya.'

Father Barry could not bear to see the smaller punished any further, so, somewhat against his better judgement, he moved in like a referee, 'Okay, you fellers, break it up. What d'ya say?'

To his surprise it was the smaller, far more battered one who most resented the intrusion. 'What're you doin' here, Father? Why doncha get back to ya choich where ya belong? Comin' down here 'n buttin' in.'

The bigger man, with whom the priest had expected to have the trouble, was apologetic.

'Don't mind him, Father. He's been at it all day. He don' know what he's sayin'. He'll sober up in time for Mass, you watch 'n see, Father.'

'Okay, boys, the fight's over. Go back to your corners.' Father Barry pulled out of it and walked on, with the same long, rapid stride he always used, as if he still had a half dozen calls to make. He was tired in his head and his muscles from the long physically and emotionally draining day. But he wasn't ready for bed. The questions nagging him were a bottle full of Benzedrine.

Take those two rummies beating each other's heads in. Probably perfectly good Catholics, in a formal way. Go to Mass every Sunday, well, nearly every, and receive the Eucharist to fulfil their Easter duty. *This is my body which is being given for you* . . . Good God, we go looking for pagans in Africa and China and our own neighbourhood parish is overflowing with them. *If you do it to the least of mine you do it to me.* How deeply Father Barry had felt that once! But how easy it had become to say it, recite it, without feeling it, without living it. Just as the stolid, sleepy faces at the six o'clock received Christ in an obedient way, merely because they had been baptized and had made their First Communion. But ours is the religion that preaches and teaches the dignity of man, the preciousness of man. What was it St. Bernard had called him, a noble creature with a majestic destiny? Get a load of these noble creatures! Here is our flock. This is what they've come to, defeated, drowning their miseries, bashing each other's faces generation on generation. How, this priest was asking himself, can we figure our batting average: by the number of worshippers tradition pulls in on a Sunday morning? Or do we score our cards according to the quality of the lives they are living in this dark corner of the harbour? '*If somebody takes a life,*' the girl had lowered the boom on him, '*if there's all this evil on the waterfront, how can you pretend you've got a Christian parish?*'

He was close to the water now and could hear its rippling against the shore. At the next pier down a freighter was working under powerful lights. What were the dangers of working the bottom of the hatch at night? What was their overtime for keeping the cargo moving while the city slept? Was it true that every one of them had to buy his job each day from this fellow Johnny Friendly? But Father Barry had heard Monsignor O'Hare speak very well of Johnny Friendly as a generous contributor to Catholic causes. Was the opposition to Johnny Friendly 'a bunch of Communists', as the Monsignor had suggested? If Joey Doyle was a leader of the local opposition, he was indeed a strange breed of Communist, never missing Confession and dying in a state of grace.

Pete, stay with this, he was thinking. You're catching hold of something. Hang on to it, Pete. He had been feeling a vague dissatisfaction with the routine of the Masses for the past year and had even talked to Father Donoghue about introducing the dialogue Mass, so as to intensify its meaning for the parishoners. But now the angry eyes of Katie Doyle were looking into his mind. They were accusing him of failure. Never mind the mere improvement of the Mass. Had he brought Christ and what He stood (and died) for into the lives of these people? Had he, Father Pete Barry, made them aware of Him and each other here on the waterfront. Hell, every family he touched was affected by this problem, the question of whether or not they worked, and how they worked. Under what conditions of degradation, and to what extent they were in danger for daring to improve those conditions. This was no political problem to be piously avoided by smoke-pot swingers. Hell, no, this was a moral-religious problem! And you, Pete, you've been ducking it. You've been afraid to plunge in. The river was dark and treacherous and unknowable, like the river of humanity into which Paul plunged when he went out from Jerusalem into the unfriendly gentile currents in search of brothers.

Brother, we've got another first century on our hands, and converts to reconvert. Man redeemed must be redeemed again. My God, what a different place Bohegan would be if these harps really knew in the innermost depths of their beings what it means to take Christ's Flesh and Blood as food and drink. Let the Commies talk about their revolution, economic salvation by purge trial and forced labour camps. What a revolution we could make if Christians in name should ever develop into Christians in deed! We've been missing the boat. Every few days a ship comes in, turns around and goes out, and we're not on it, not with it, waiting for the faithful to come to us instead of throwing a line out to them.

A filthy, slightly bent-over, one-armed river rat staggered backward out of a bar as if he had been pushed. When he saw the priest his hand extended automatically. 'A dime. One thin dime for a cuppa cawfee.'

Father Barry reached in his pocket for a coin, part of his carefully hoarded cigarette fund. Every day he bought a pack and scrounged a pack. Here was his brother with no right arm and no money and probably no place to flop, one of a thousand drifters in the harbour. Here was the least of mine, pushed from bar to bar, from gutter to gutter. Father Barry remembered seeing him at Mass occasionally. He had had to walk him out of the church one morning because he was disorderly drunk in the confession queue. Mutt Murphy, that was his name, a little off his rocker from drink and the kicking around he had taken. Yes, but again, where was the Church? Where was Father Pete Barry himself? What was he doing to protect the least of mine?

'Here,' Father Barry said. 'Go have a beer on me.'

'God bless ya, Father. God bless ya,' Mutt mumbled through his swollen lips. Then he looked into the face of the priest. 'Oh, Father, you was the one give Joey Doyle his last rites.'

When Father Barry nodded, Mutt brought his face so close to the priest's that the sour breath offended him. But Father Barry did not pull his head back.

'That Joey Doyle was a saint, Father, ya know that? Went right in the union office t' try 'n get me me compensation. Them bums threw him out. They woik hand in hand with the shippers. Ya know that, Father? They ain't inter-rested in *this*'—he slapped his stump roughly—'even if I got it on board ship. All them bums is inter-rested in is *this* . . .' He put out his good arm and rubbed his fingers together to make the ancient sign of greed for money. 'Jesus Mary 'n Joseph, if we had a honest t' God union down here instead of a bunch of safecrackers, I'd be drawin' a hundred bucks a month easy. I ain't no bum, no beggar in me heart, Father, that's the God's truth. But I can't get no job and I never stood in good enough with Johnny Friendly. What's a fella gonna do, Father?'

'This kid Doyle,' Father Barry asked, 'you're sure he was pushed?'

Mutt Murphy took an unsteady backward step. 'Are you kiddin', Father? What you lookin' t' do, dump me in the river?'

Mutt withdrew rather haughtily. On his way toward the corner bar he turned and cried out in an ugly croaking voice, 'Jesus'll save me! Jesus'll save me!' Then he disappeared into the brief shelter of the bar.

Father Barry walked on. He walked out to the end of a railroad pier and stared at the broken pattern of little square lights twinkling in the massive buildings across the river. There was the mightiest city in the world half sleeping, half revelling. Millions and millions and millions of people and not one of them aware of Mutt Murphy and his lost arm. Or of Joey Doyle and his lost life. And if they were to know—if the morning papers were to headline at breakfast the terrible deed done to Joey Doyle (*for these sheep I lay down my life*), who would really care? A tabloid banner and a few sensational pictures and then—who cares? Who really cares? If even here in Bohegan, where they knew him, nobody cared enough? Increase our church attendance and you improve our moral climate, the glib ones were always saying. But here were the churchgoers following Christ in such a slipshod way that it was a cruel joke on Him to call them Christians. And the priests, even some priests, intoning but not feeling the least of mine—even some priests.

By God, Father Barry now realized, he had come from the poor and had gone into the priesthood to serve the poor. But the years had made him prudent. Hiding in the church, Katie had said. Father Barry had only walked a few miles but he had come a long way from Katie Doyle's angry question. Now he was asking himself the questions. Man, St. Bernard had insisted, was a noble creature with a majestic destiny. Was it Joey Doyle's majestic destiny to go hurtling down through the tenement clotheslines, tossed into the filthy courtyard like an empty beer can?

So that Katie's blunt question 'What are you going to do about it?' linked the priest to God on one side and man on the other. You could call it politics or a police problem and hide from it in the church, but you were in it, brother, you were in it, in it deep, just as sure as there was the Mystical Body of Christ and everyone a member, one of another. Joey's death and the search for the meaning of it, the motive of it, the cure of it, would lead his parish church back into the streets of Bohegan where the people were Christian for one hour on Sunday and enemies one of another all week long.

Father Barry felt exhilarated. More than the breeze rising from the river was bracing him now. He didn't know exactly what he was going to do, but at least he was ready to take the first step. By God, he wasn't going to be just another swinging smokepot. *Duc in altum.* Launch out into the deep. Those words always had fascinated him. Be ready to venture out into unknown depths. Was he up to it? Did he have the gospel guts to launch out into the depths?

He turned and started walking rapidly back to the rectory a mile away. Crossing River Street a few blocks farther down, a tough compact figure came lurching toward him, a young fellow in dark corduroy pants and a black-and-red checked wool windbreaker, with hands pushed deep into the pockets, and his head down.

'Hey, kid, you don't happen to have a cigarette on you?' Father Barry asked.

Here he was again using his ecclesiastical position to pressure small favours. Like showing up at shops when the doors opened Monday mornings on the chance that superstitious shop owners would give him free the things he was after. Bad luck to turn away the first customer, and to double it, a wearer of the cloth. Father Barry had learned to scrounge early. There was a touch of larceny in him that remained a vestige of the street kid's scramble to survive.

'What's this—a gag?' the moody young man—Terry Malloy—asked angrily. 'Ten to one you ain't a priest at all. I seen that racket plenny o' times.' Terry walked away, muttering profanity.

Father Barry shrugged and strode back to the rectory. That kid, that punk had probably been baptized, gone to parochial school and received Communion. But look at him, a foul-mouthed Bohegan hoodlum, hostile, suspicious, dangerous and alone.

8

AWAKENING ON THE metal frame bed that almost filled the small, stuffy bedroom, Katie felt confused. Her window at school faced east into the morning sunlight, and she always liked to linger a few moment between the clean white sheets, stretching and letting the sunlight bathe her. It was a precious moment to her, a brief interval between sleeping and waking, between the ease of sleep and the active schedule of the day. But this morning there was no sun, and no sheets. She was still in her clothes, on top of the bed where she had fallen at last into exhausted sleep. The single window in the north wall of the narrow room opened on the side of the adjoining building a scant foot away, so that even on the brightest day the light had to filter down from the roof above. It was airless and gloomy. Heavily, with a sense of discomfort, of a slovenliness that she loathed, she remembered where she was and why she was here. A neat girl, proud of the clean, scrubbed look that was natural to her and that she cultivated, she rose guiltily, straightened out the worn spread and tried to smooth out the wrinkles in her navy-blue skirt.

In the front room there was an unmusical counterpoint of masculine snoring, as the loyal members of the wake lay where they had fallen. Runty Nolan was sprawled on the floor with his arms outflung as if he had been impaled in mid-gesture as he was telling one of his stories. Jimmy Sharkey lay asleep in the big easy chair with the stuffing working out of it. Moose was boisterous even in sleep; his big body rose and fell with his heavy breathing. Pop's stringy, small-muscled arms hung over the edge of the day-bed. His twenty-four hour growth of beard and the soiled long underwear top added to the gloom. The room was littered with the leavings of the wake, a couple of bottles of Four Roses toppled on the floor like the men into whom they had been emptied; a cigarette stand on its side, its accumulation of blackened tobacco, used cigars and crushed cigarettes making a small dumping ground on the carpet; a shirt draped over a lamp; shoes spread about like ducks after a shoot; and glasses —dirty glasses, half-filled glasses, broken glasses, overturned glasses, glasses that would remind Katie of whisky and death and the stale horror of the morning after.

Katie went into the kitchen, saw the disheartening clutter of plates in the small sink, the left-over sandwiches, the spill of whiskies souring the atmosphere. Again her mind went wishfully back to Marygrove where the Sisters moved immaculately and the faces of her classmates were scrubbed clean. Dutifully, Katie turned her mind away from Tarrytown to the reality of dirty dishes and a need for coffee to stir Pop and his friends to the efforts of the day. This cold, drizzling sunless day, this Joey-less day.

The sound of coffee perking and Katie rattling the dishes as she stacked them in the sink had begun to penetrate the fuzzy sleep of Patrick Doyle. He swung slowly to a sitting position on the couch and rubbed his face in his hands with his eyes still shut against the day. He stretched and groaned and Runty shifted position on the floor and opened his eyes to a slit.

'A grand wake, Patrick,' he muttered with a cheerfulness that was almost automatic. 'As handsome a send off as I've seen since I buried me own father.'

'Me achin' head,' Pop groaned.

Runty struggled to his feet and stretched himself to his full height of five feet two inches. Then he looked around for the fallen Moose and kicked his rear end with a well-concealed affection.

'Git up, ya bum, you. Whatta ya think ya are, a goddamn millionaire?'

Moose woke up in a hurry and cocked his fist. 'If it wasn't we was out visitin', as God is me judge I'd beat the hell outa ya.'

'You ain't big enough,' Runty challenged his two hundred-pound companion.

Jimmy Sharkey rose stiff-legged from the easy chair. His eyes were bloodshot and his head felt as if it had been clubbed by a Gaelic hurling stick.

'Awright, awright, knock it off, you two juiceheads. Have a little respect.'

'Don' mind 'em,' Pop said soothingly. 'They always stood by me. They just like to string each other along. They don't mean no harm.'

Katie came in with a pot of coffee and some clean cups. Her lips were pressed together in anger. What made them behave like this, lost and beaten down, accepting Joey's death as a dead-end?

'Morning, Pop,' she said. 'Here's some coffee for you. And for your friends.'

She set the coffee down, with the cups and spoons, and went back to the kitchen.

'She's a grand goil,' Runty said. 'Lucky for you she favours her mother.' He gave his ho-ho-ho laugh.

They drank their coffee down in silence. From the river came the hoarse vibration of a boat whistle. Pop could tell the time from the sounds of the river traffic. 'Seven o'clock ferry gettin' ready to pull out for Christopher Street,' he said. 'Time we was gettin' down to the corner.'

There was a coffee-pot across from the pier, on the opposite corner from Friendly's, an informal information centre where —in lieu of some more orderly system—the men picked up their info on the ships coming in. One of the things Joey had plugged for was a hiring centre, where the men could get regular advance information on what ships were docking where and when, and how many jobs would be available. 'The shipping companies ought to be able to tell us two days ahead,' he had insisted, 'exactly how many gangs they'll be needing. A decent union 'd systematize it. Instead of every morning the same old rat race.' That was Joey talking. But around the entire harbour there was only a handful like him, stand-up guys, with their necks out a mile.

The men were rubbing the sleep out of their eyes and pulling on their windbreakers. Pop took his worn wool workcoat off a hook with the dirty canvas gloves that were a mark of his trade, along with the stubby cargo hook that was almost a physiological extension of a longshoreman's right arm.

'Put ya hook down,' Runty said. 'This ain't no day for you t' be woikin'. The lads who get woik t'day 'll be chippin' in gladly.'

'Sure, Pop, stay home. We'll pass the box for ya,' Jimmy Sharkey said.

'Ya bet we will!' Moose shouted.

'Thanks, boys, but I'm gonna shape,' Pop said, sticking his hook through his belt over his rear pocket. 'Who d'ya think's gonna pay for the funeral? Tom McGovern an' his stinkin' stevedore company? Or Willie Givens, the bum? Nobody's passin' no box for me, thank you just the same. I'm gonna shape.'

76

He led them through the bedroom to the kitchen door. From a hook on the door hung Joey's windbreaker, a fur-lined Navy issue that Pop had filched in the hold. Impulsively Pop reached for it and handed it to Runty.

'Here. Ya might as well get some use of it. Yours is more full o' holes 'n the Pittsboig infield.'

Runty nodded, slipped out of his old woollen windbreaker and tried on Joey's. It hung loosely on his small, bony frame.

'Plenny o' room for stuffin' steaks or Johnny Walker,' he said approvingly.

'It'll start to fit 'im after a while,' Moose laughed. 'After all he's still a growin' boy.'

'Le's go down get some more joe,' Jimmy said. 'My eyeballs are draggin' on the floor.'

'Whatsa matter with these young fellers?' Runty winked to Pop. 'Looks like they're gettin' soft, the lot of 'em. Show me one of 'em c'n stand up to the amber like us old timers.' Half-way through he was sorry for the saying of it, for the look on Pop's face changed, the lines seeming to cut deeper, the light of false banter fading out of the eyes. Runty knew he was thinking of Joey again. It was just a show they were putting on and they all knew it. Nobody was fooling anybody else, but they had to keep trying, keep it bubbling. That was the tradition.

Pop turned to embrace Katie, who had been standing behind them, watching them with troubled eyes.

'Have a good day, Pop,' she said tightly.

Pop took it as a reproach and his voice edged up to her carefully, wanting to soothe her and afraid that any recognition of the subject would rouse her again.

'Katie, I know it ain't easy. Maybe when ya get back to Tarrytown the Sisters c'n help ya accept it.'

'Why must we accept it?' Katie said.

Pop shrugged. 'God must know what He's doin'.'

'It's not as simple as that,' Katie said.

Pop put his hands out, as if to appeal to the others, in a rather comic gesture. 'Jesus, Mary 'n Joseph. I been coised with stubborn children.'

77

'It would have to be drizzlin',' Jimmy said, thinking of accidents. 'It'll be just our luck t' get sheet copper in the rain.'

'Or bananas,' Pop said. 'When you start slippin' on them rotten bananas . . .'

Runty chuckled. 'Wouldn't it be a sight now t' see a ship come in from Ireland herself, Gawd love her, the *Maple* or the *Elm*, loaded t' the gunnels with Jameson's Irish.' Runty stuck his small, broken-knuckle hands into the pockets of his new windbreaker. 'That'll be the day this loot jacket comes into its own.'

Katie watched them disappear into the lower stories of the tenement, laughing and talking out loud. Had they no feelings? Yes, of course, she knew how Pop cried to himself, and Runty was soft as cheese under his bantam swagger. And Moose was rough and loud, but she knew inside he was almost too gentle for the bruising give-and-take of the life on the docks. But there had been too many 'accidents' like Joey's on the waterfront. Too many ribs caved in. Too many faces hacked with steel pikes and gun handles. Until finally even the best of them, like Pop, were as accustomed to homicide and assault as they were to the sound of foghorns and ship whistles. It was, she thought, as if their hearts had developed a coating as thickened and difficult to penetrate as the callouses that years of rough work had grafted on to their hands. Though Pop had been careful not to speak of it to her, this violence they had learned to live with was in the air the neighbourhood breathed. She had heard it whispered in the grocery store when she was home for week-ends, accepted it herself as just another harsh Bohegan reality, and never dreamed it would break down the door into their own life.

From the roof the cold morning sun could be seen across the river, rising behind the jagged range of steel, concrete and glass. In the summer these rooftops made a tenement riviera where the poor could bare their torsos to the sun, watch the sparkle and movement of the river and sometimes sneak a night's sleep away from the stifling heat of the airless bedrooms. But in the early morning November chill the rooftops were deserted, except for the pigeon fanciers who were up at dawn to feed and exercise their flocks before going off to work.

This morning there was only one figure on the roof. He was

78

Terry Malloy, who had rolled in from the bars only an hour or so before, his fifty clams spread around a score of ginmills from Bohegan to Manhattan. The Bohegan bars closed their doors at two and re-opened at five, not so much as a moral curfew as a respite providing time for a badly needed clean-up. The Manhattan joints were in business until four, so an enterprising boozer could shuttle over on the ferry at two, nurse his drinks in a West Side pub until he was pushed out into the sick-blue light just in time to hit River Street spots on the Bohegan side again. A small but convincing demonstration of the American talent for jimmying through any law that tries to violate the pleasure principle.

The brain of Terry Malloy was smoky with thirty-five cent whiskies and beer chasers. His tongue felt—he thought with heavy humour—like the bottom of his pigeon coop. But there was relief in leaning back against the tar-papered side of a skylight and watching the birds circle out across the river. He inhaled deeply the cold air of the river that filtered out the soot and the factory smog. He liked the way the pigeons flashed the light undersides of their brown and blue and silver-grey wings as they swept overhead.

Hot damn, they were beauteeful, and they were his, the one thing in his life over which he had complete say-so, his to keep flying with his long be-flagged pole, his to send off into the unknown of distant cities to be released for the race home to Bohegan. He'd run for his coop as soon as he saw his bird dart through the movable bars, pull the racing band off its leg with quick, sure motion and push it into the racing clock without a lost moment to register the split-second time of arrival. Some feeling it was to have that first band in the clock.

How in hell as they flew high over the cities of East Jersey they could pick out his—Terry's—one little roof-top loft—that he would never understand. They must have plenty of brains packed into those perky, smooth-feathered little noggins. Brains and guts, that's what it took to be a racing pigeon, something like being champion of the world. Don't let anybody ever tell you they're born that way, Terry was thinking. Hell, he'd like to have a buck for every one he had lost on the practice flights. They had something special, the ones that came through. Like you take this here Swifty, he thought, his lead bird, the master of the flock, who had fought his way up to the top perch and had come through two tough five hundred-mile races, once with some of his head feathers gone and blood showing where a pigeon hawk had tried to make a meal of him. Another time he had flopped through the entrance bars with a broken leg. Terry never knew how it happened. But a bird with the true homing gift won't stop for food or water or injury. As long as he's able to move his wings he'll keep homing. Swifty was crippled now but still formidable, a powerful, hustling, proud cock of a bird. Something like Johnny Friendly, the way he cock-of-the-walked it over all the others. You had to admire him as you admired Johnny Friendly, the way he fought his way up, the way he had hustled to the front of the pack, the way he had pecked off anybody threatening that top perch, It took guts and know-how and . . .

Terry shifted his position, finding the thought uncomfortable. Why couldn't he just squat here and enjoy the big circle his flock was making over the river and the roof tops instead of thinking . . . Jeez, with a head on him like a five-day-old watermelon, this was no day for thinking. Just lean back into the tar paper and look up into the cold sky, think of the races he'd win and the easy-come goof-job he'd have in the loft. Think of Melva, the neighbourhood's favourite teen-age cooze, a jazzed-up kitten still fleshy with baby fat yet to be rubbed off, blue-jeaned Melva with 'Danger—T.N.T.' proudly crayoned on her sweatshirt over her fat young teats, a funned-up member of the young ladies auxiliary of the Golden Warriors, with her gold-and-purple Golden Warriorette blazer.

Yea, man, that's better, forget last night and think of all the good, loose stuff around, and of those beauteeful homing bastards, and eight hours of two thirty-four per for goofing on the coffee bags. Think of the things you can look to steal, Spanish brandy and French perfume and high-grade steaks from ships' stores, Fundador and Chanel and tender filets, and tender Melva and twenty bucks a day for studying the endlessly fascinating female form in the art magazines like *Girlie* and *Scanties*, that was the life, the old sporting life. 'Sha-boom, sha-boom, tatata-tatata-tatata-tatata-tatata . . .' Terry hummed a not bad imitation of the Crew Cuts.

'Get him. Eddie Fisher without talent,' came a fresh voice from around a corner of the coop. It was young Billy Conley, the ace man of the Golden Warriors and, in the informal but intricate feudalism of the Bohegan dock country, Terry's vassal.

'Whasamatter, you don' like the Crew Cuts?' Terry demanded.

'Sure I like the Crew Cuts'—it came back like a ball off the stoop —'but I ain't heard 'em lately.'

'Ha ha,' Terry said derisively.

''Samatter, you roll outa the wrong side of the bed this mornin'?'

'I didn' roll outa no bed this mornin', tha's the matter,' Terry explained.

'Man, ya look like an unmade bed yaself,' Billy said. 'What ya doin' up so early anyway?' He used the *oi* sound that was known as River Street brogue.

Terry regarded the question sourly. 'None o' ya goddamn business.'

Billy was offended. 'Well, gee whizz, ya don' hafta blow ya stack about it!'

'I come up here early becuz I wanted t' come up here early and nothin' else,' Terry insisted.

'Jeez, whatta ya wanna do, make a Federal case?' Billy was indignant. His lord and master turning on him. 'Fa nuttin',' he'd be telling his Golden Warrior buddies in a little while, 'he toined on me fa nuttin'.'

Billy reached under the raised coop to pull out the tin of scratch feed. It was his job to pour the scratch grain into the feeder every morning. Terry paid him a quarter for this chore, which kept this fourteen-year-old retainer in cigarettes.

''S all done,' Terry called. 'I took care of 'em myself already.'

'Jeez, you was really on the ball this mornin'. A reg'lar early bird.' In Boheganese it was 'oily boid'.

'Yeah, yeah.' Terry wanted to cut the kid off. 'I figgured I was up anyway, so what the hell.'

Billy looked at him wonderingly. Terry Malloy, whose proud picture in fighting togs had a place of honour in the Golden Warrior's rooftop headquarters, was acting kind of funny. The boy nodded toward the edge of the next roof. 'Jeez, I wouldna wanted t' be that Doyle bum last night makin' the high dive inta no water.' He shook his head with a nasty little laugh. 'Would you, Terry?'

'Christ, what a gum-beater,' Terry said irritably. 'Yatata-yatata.'

'Jo-Jo's lucky,' Billy went on. 'He saw it land. It busted Mrs. McLaverty's clothes line. He swears it bounced once, this high, like a ball. How about that? I think he's a goddamn liar.'

'Will ya fer chrizzake knock it off?' Terry raised his voice.

'Jeez, what is this, Russia? I can't say nuttin' around here no more,' Billy protested.

The flock followed Swifty in a sharply banked turn that carried them within twenty feet of the roof, then up again in a graceful, sweeping circle. Terry's preoccupied frown changed to a grin of admiration as his head panned with them.

'Those bastards really got it made,' he said wistfully, mostly to himself. 'Eat all they want, fly around like crazy, sleep together every night 'n raise gobs of squabs.'

'You ain't got it so bad yourself,' Billy said. 'A big in with Johnny Friendly and a free ticket when you take in the fights down in Newark. An' all the broads in the neighbourhood puttin' out for ya becuz ya name was up in lights in the Garden . . .'

'Once,' Terry reminded him.

'What's the diff?' Billy continued. 'The broads all a time wantin' t' feel ya muscle.' He made a suggestive, grabbing gesture for Terry's crotch and laughed evilly. 'You ain't got it so bad.'

'Jesus, get the talking machine,' Terry said, vaguely troubled. He hitched up his dark corduroys and cuffed Billy playfully, but hard enough to make the kid's eyes tear a little. On the river an early-morning ferry hooted at a slow-moving train of coal barges. Terry turned his thoughts to the river and the morning shape. 'I'm gonna go down t'the coffee-pot n' grab me some sinkers 'n coffee. You c'n clean out the water pans.'

Terry winked and jabbed the air twice, sharply, in a breezy gesture of farewell. He half-turned as he entered the sheltered stairway leading down into the building.

'An' don' be spillin' no water on the floor now. I don' wan' them birds t' catch cold.'

For a moment Terry's glance was drawn to the adjoining roof

where Joey's birds were hopping around and making anxious sounds for their breakfast. 'Hey, ya might as well toss some scratch over there in that other coop too,' Terry called casually.

'Hey, that's an idea,' Billy responded. 'You c'n prob'bly add 'em to yours.'

'Just do like I told ya,' Terry commanded. Then he squared his shoulders and started down the steps in a rapid, rope-skipping rhythm.

On the second flight down Terry was moving so fast that he almost collided with Father Barry who was hurrying up the stairs.

'Look where ya goin',' Terry grumbled and hurried on.

The priest hardly noticed him. His eyes were red-rimmed from his sleepless night. It had been a night of pacing and reading, of meditation and prayer. He had thumbed the works of the Church scholars from the dark-skinned Augustine through Aquinas to the social thinking of Pius XI and Maritain. He had thought hard about the martyrs, Paul, the first Ignatius, Stephen, St. John of the Cross and Thomas More, fierce, unbending men. And the saints of mercy and service, Francis Xavier, an old favourite, and the other self-denying Francis, barefoot from Assisi, walking the hard road. St. Jude crossed his mind, and Vincent de Paul.

He had heard the chimes in the town hall strike three and as the final tone burrowed back into the silence of the night he had thrown himself into bed in his shorts because he had a six o'clock Mass to say. But in the darkness he heard again the Doyle girl's clean, angry, slightly childish voice: *Was there ever a saint who hid in the church?* Was there, indeed? He thought again of his slight, shabby-looking, large-minded Francis plunged into Goa in the pagan East, who had first to brave his way through the graft and intrigue and moral chaos not of the Asiatics, but of the European Christians greedy for temporal riches, mocking Christ in every covetous breath. No saint hiding in the church was that boy. Pete Barry, at Fordham, had written his master's thesis on the good-looking selfless little Basque aristocrat who had no patience with the Portuguese Catholic profiteers and their worldly priests, but who had the patience of Job and Jesus when it came to the beggars and slaves, whores and landless farmers, the city poor and foul-mouthed sailors with whom occasionally he sat down to a game of cards on the docks.

Father Barry sat up and groped for the light and lit a cigarette to help himself think more clearly. Then he got out of bed and reached into his few shelves of books for his worn copies of the letters of Francis Xavier, with bits of yellowing paper calling attention to pages he had underlined and mulled over as a seminarian. The parishioners of St. Timothy's hardly knew this side of him. They saw a young, gruff, ruddy-faced Irishman who sometimes ran through his mass too quickly and who didn't seem to have in him any of the spirituality that made the Pastor, Father Donoghue, an impressively religious figure in the parish. 'That Father Barry is about as holy as a sack of flour,' had been Runty Nolan's first impression, and when it got back to Pete he chuckled to his fellow curate, Father Harry Vincent, 'I'm glad he said flour. It could've been worse.'

But what Father Barry had in him, held in check since he came to St. Tim's, was a live memory for what it meant to be poor, the humiliations his mother had endured when the social-service workers came poking around, the way the crushing poverty of the less fortunate, less well-connected on the waterfront could depersonalize and degrade. He had vowed in his last year of theology never to let himself forget this, and to work as He had laboured among the lowest of the low.

Well, had he welshed on himself? Not exactly. He was here at St. Timothy's on Pulaski Street because the Bishop had granted him his preference for a slum section of Bohegan. But in his second year a certain complacency, some of Father Vincent's prudence, had rubbed off on him. Damned if Bohegan wasn't in the same hypocritical, inhuman, therefore un-Catholic, slough as Goa when the young Xavier disembarked there four centuries ago. Only the difference is you haven't got the guts, the Xavierian guts, to speak up about it. Okay, Pete, you hear that, *Father* Barry, and if so what're you gonna do about it?

In the book he was holding he paused over one of the letters he had marked a few years earlier. He got back into bed to read it, for the Pastor was stingy (or, as he and Father Vincent jokingly said, pious) with the coal. The rectory was always ten degrees colder than comfort. But the bed was warm and the pillow, which his mother had made specially for him, softly cradled his head. The words floated before his eyes. Too much reading of that small print in the breviary. What was he doing all this for anyway? This wasn't the seminary; there was no longer any need to grind away like a school-boy. His alarm was set for five-thirty, allowing just enough time for a wash, a quick shave and a morning prayer before the six o'clock Mass. One of these days he'd be a pastor and make his curates say that pesky six o'clock! Then guilt grabbed hold of him and pulled him out of bed. He had chosen the toughest and easiest job in the world. Not so different from the Army, really, with its infantry platoon leaders, its front-trench fighters, its high-level strategists and its headquarters politicians.

Pete Barry had thrown off the comforting blankets and lowered himself to his knees on the cold floor beside his bed. Using the bed for a desk, he studied the words of the penetrating Xavier, woven into a letter addressed to a young priest about to take up his apostolic life in India four hundred years ago. The words had not only been underlined but annotated: even so they came back to Pete Barry now as something fresh and new:

When in the sacred tribunal of penance you have heard all that your penitents have prepared to confess as their sins, do not at once think that all is done, and that you have no further duty to discharge. You must go on further to inquire, and by means of questions to rake out the faults which ought to be known and to be rendered, but which escape the penitents themselves on account of their ignorance.

Ask them what profits they make. How and whence? What is the system that they follow in barter and loans, and in the whole matter of security for contracts?

You will generally find that everything is defiled with usurious contracts; those very persons have got together the greater part of their money by sheer rapine, who nevertheless assert themselves so confidently to be pure from all contagion of unjust gain; having, as they said, the true testimony of a conscience that reprehends them in nothing. Indeed, some persons' consciences have become so hardened that they have either no sense

at all or very little sense of the presence of vast heaps of robberies which
they have gathered into their bosoms.

'Vast heaps of robberies . . .' Father Barry read on with a mounting sense of awe and excitement. Here was a priest who had gone
from Spain to Paris, from Paris to Portugal, from Portugal to India,
from India to Japan and the coast of China, a priest whose church
was the wide, wide world, a priest who didn't take every kneeling
Catholic for a Christian and who set out to reconvert by word and
deed the paganized, oppressive, lip-serving Christians-in-name, a
priest who lived and suffered the knowledge that Jesus had many
lovers of the kingdom of heaven but precious few bearers of his
cross. Father Barry read on:

. . . Interrogate all these people by what means they grow rich on the
discharge and income of their office. If they are shy of telling you, search
and scent out in every way and the most mildly that you can. You will not
have been long on the hunt before you come on sure tracks which will lead
you to the very dens and lairs of their frauds and monopolies, through
which an unconsiderable number of men divert to their own private hoard
emoluments belonging to the public . . .

'Search and scent out in every way . . .' What a hep kid that
little Xavier was! Get the way he knows all the tricks of the trade,
the whole stinkin' set-up, never letting himself get boxed into the
argument that talk of profiteering or racketeering has no place in the
pulpit or the confession booth. This is no accident, no sportive
growth, Father Barry was thinking: it's one of the pillars of our
Faith, as our Holy Father was saying just the other day, and not the
least of them either. If Man is the only creature on earth created in
God's image, then by God you're thumbing your nose at Him
every time you stomp on the dignity of that creation.

Still in his shorts, with his knees and arms reddening from the
cold, but with excitement as always able to anaesthetize discomfort,
Father Barry wondered if the girl was saying more than she knew.
Hiding in the Church. It had hit him like a sling-load of steel ingots.
In a couple of head-spinning hours he had ranged nearly two

thousand years, from the Saviour to the social genius of Pius XII and back to his catholic Catholic Francis X:

When you have squeezed out of them the confessions of these monopolies and the like, drawing them out by many and cautious questions, you will be more easily able to settle how much of other persons' property they are in possession of, and how much they ought to make restitution of to those they have defrauded in order to be reconciled to God, than if you should ask them in general whether they have defrauded anyone. For to this question they will immediately answer that their memory upbraids them with nothing. For custom is to them in the place of law, and what they see done before them every day they persuade themselves may be practised without sin. For customs bad in themselves seem to these men to acquire authority and prescription from the fact that they are commonly practised.

Father Barry put the book down and picked up his rosary. Give me, O Father, the wisdom and the know-how and the moxie, he prayed.

There were the chimes again, now striking five. He pulled on his shiny, shapeless black suit and his battered, black hat and hustled around the corner to the twenty-four hour diner where an old woman kept an all-night news-stand. 'Hullo, Fadder, you hopp oily dis mornin'!' From one of the obliterated countries of the Baltic, she spoke with a thick accent that thirty years of Boheganese had not displaced, but only embellished.

Father Barry bought the local Bohegan tabloid, the *Graphic,* and the Manhattan scream sheets that had just been trucked through the tunnel under the river. He sat on one of the diner stools and tipped his hat back, then spread the papers before him on the counter. He felt hungry from the night's exertion, but his lips were meant this morning to touch the blood and body of his Lord. Coffee and doughnuts would have to wait. He had half-expected the Doyle killing to be front-page, but the big headline was for the capture of a young, good-looking sex maniac who had bludgeoned a waitress. Lighting a cigarette, he turned the pages full of sin and violence— teen-age beatings, angry divorces, paternity suits, public-housing scandals involving party girls, breaches of promise, malfeasance in office, a small-town week-end orgy, wife-swapping, a sailor's beating of a sex deviant, a mouth-smacking exposé of midtown Manhattan after midnight—the tabloid's daily confession of the city's inability to keep the commandments. The towns around the harbour wallow in sin and filth, Pete Barry read between the lines, like big and little hogs in a mudhole.

Still looking for the headline on Joey Doyle, he came at last to a filler lost among the ads for relief of backaches, headaches, piles and pimples:

LONGSHOREMAN FALLS TO DEATH

Joseph F. Doyle, a longshoreman, 225 Market Street, Bohegan, died last night when he fell from the roof of the apartment house in which he resided. He lived only a few minutes after being discovered by neighbours in the courtyard behind the tenement building a block from the waterfront. Whether the fall was accidental or due to foul play police were unable to determine in an on-the-scene investigation. According to a spokesman for Chief of Police William Donnelly, 'All possible efforts will be made to ascertain the facts.' Surviving are . . .

Father Barry drew hard on the cigarette. Joey Doyle had been reduced to a few lines of filler in the Bohegan *Graphic*. The cynicism of Katie's Uncle Frank swung back at him like an Australian throwing stick: 'If the police just turn their backs and forget about it— like Uncle Frank says—isn't it up to you to do something about it?' Father Barry looked at the big clock on the diner wall. 5.20. He would have to get a move on to get ready to celebrate the Mass. He hurried back to St. Timothy's with such a rapid stride that a milkman called out, 'What's yer hurry, Father?'

In the sacristy when he tied the cincture around his waist he thought of its meaning in a way that had not occurred to him since he was first ordained; he was actually girding his loins for battle. And at the low Mass at six, which he had to admit to himself he often had run through mechanically and even sleepily, he felt to an almost unbearable degree the passion of the sacrifice. The chalice into which he poured the wine would hold the blood of Christ, the pledge of martyrs, of Joey's too.

He liked to think he was as rugged as the fellows who swung the

88

hooks, but his hand trembled this morning when he realized that once more, at this very moment, others were dying with Christ—and only last night Joey Doyle.

The sleepy-eyed dockworkers and sailors and truck drivers and bartenders and a few of their wives became aware that Father Barry was living this Mass with words and gestures that were spontaneous and not left over from other Masses. The Passion was his passion, the wine had tasted like blood and the wafer had pressed on his hand as heavily as the body of the crucified. In Father Barry's mind the Mass was beautifully, dangerously unified. The altar at which the sacrifice was offered and offered again had become Calvary on Market Street. *Et verbum caro factum est,* he said almost angrily. And the word was made flesh and dwelt among us.

As soon as he had finished saying Mass, unvested and made his thanksgiving, he hurried back to his room, changed into his street clothes and paced off the nearly three blocks to the Doyle flat.

At his knock, Katie came to the door with a dustpan. Then she stepped back in surprise, self-consciously moving her hands in a futile effort to smooth her wrinkled skirt.

'Mornin', Katie,' Father Barry said.

She hesitated whether to ask him in. She was still in the middle of her straightening up, and the kitchen into which he was looking was littered with the dirty glasses, dishes and ashtrays she had gathered from the other rooms.

'Oh, Father—if I had known you were coming I would've lit the hall light.'

'That's okay, Katie. Last night you lit a big light'—his hand tapped his temple nervously—'up here.'

'I'm afraid I spoke out of turn,' Katie said with conventual courtesy.

Father Barry hadn't come all this way for schoolgirl amenities.

'Listen, kid, you said what you meant. You belted me good. It kept me up all night, taking a long, hard look at what I've been doin'. What I began to see didn't look so hot.'

He watched her run her fingers through her long blond-brown hair in embarrassment.

'I walked. I looked up a lot of stuff. I thought about some of those saints you threw in my face.'

'Father . . .'

'A couple of hours ago I asked myself the sixty-four dollar question. Am I just a gravy-train rider in a turned-around collar?'

'*Father* . . .'

'Well, that's what you think I am, don't you?'

Her silence hurt them both.

'Don't you?'

'I—I wouldn't say *that*. I only thought . . .'

'I know. I know what you thought. You think I ought to live my religion, not just preach it. Am I right?'

Katie blushed. She was sorry for the young balding priest with his red eyes and his angry, pleading look.

'Okay. You don't have to talk. Last night you did the talking. Now it's my turn. So I asked the question, Katie, am I ready to take my lumps or am I just taking an easy ride?'

A look of doubt, of fear came into her face and he smiled sadly. 'Oh, don't look so surprised. There's plenty of those jokers in the Church. Always has been. The play-it-safe, play-it-smart boys who go through all the right motions and wind up as Monsignors or better. There's plenty of them uptown, I mean at the Chancellery. Katie, what I'm trying to say is, when I asked myself the question, the answer hit me—bang!' He paused and looked into her eyes, which were now frightened and believing. 'This is my parish. I'm going down to the docks. And I'm going to bone up on this. I'm going to talk to everybody who'll stand still for me. I knew it was there all the time, but you gave me the eyes to see it. I don't know how much I c'n do, but I'll never find out, I'll just be taking the easy out, if I don't go down and take a good look for myself. I'm no saint, Katie, I'm just barely gettin' by. But you nailed me on the button last night. Now I'm ready to throw some punches myself. Anyway, no more hiding in the Church for me.'

'I'll go with you, Father.'

'Down there?' He shook his head.

'Please."

'I get it. You think I'm giving you a snow job. You want to see if I deliver.'

'Father, you mustn't talk like that.'

'Well, maybe seeing you down there'll soften 'em up some.' His grin warmed his face for a moment, then quickly faded. 'Same way you did me.'

'I would never have thought a priest had to be . . .'

'A priest is a man,' he reminded her. 'A priest isn't holy because he wears this thing.' He flicked the collar. 'Last night you were blowing your stack because you believe something that too many of us—yes, I mean us in the rectory—only go through the motions of—and are willing to call it a day.'

'I just felt so—helpless.'

'We should all be so helpless,' Father Barry said.

When she smiled her eyes that had been crying and sleepless came to life again.

'Get your coat, Katie. We're going down and take a cut at the ball.'

9

THE LONGDOCK BAR and Grill, at the other end of the block from Friendly's on River Street, had served for years as the coffee-pot for the dock workers on Piers B and C who worked through Johnny Friendly's Local 447. By seven o'clock every week-day morning it was crowded with longshoremen grabbing cups of coffee and maybe some ham and eggs-over before drifting across the street to the shape-up. They were men of all sizes and ages, clean-shaven and unkempt, young war veterans in their service issue and weather-beaten men in their 50's in baggy denims, worn wool shirts and ancient windbreakers that looked slept in and lived in. It was a bitter cold morning, with snow in the air, and among the Irish caps and peaked ski-caps there were some black, round woolly jobs suggesting the headdress of Russian peasants. Some of the men were ex-cons and some were ex-pugs, with sunken eyes and flattened noses, trophies of battles not only in the ring but on the docks and in the bar-rooms. Some of them were mean and quick-triggered and surly with drink and some of the hardest-faced were simple, amiable men who liked to buy the beers and talk the day away.

Moose was one of these, a brawny, bull-throated roughneck on the outside but a gentle and sentimental do-gooder in his heart, a familiar Irish dichotomy. He led the way into the Longdock now, with Runty, Jimmy and Pop in tow. There were empty stools for a couple of them at the short-order counter across from the bar that wouldn't open until eight. Fred, a pink-faced old man with a cherubic expression under a few carefully combed wisps of hair, presided behind the counter with a carefully preserved brogue.

'Hey, Fred,' Moose's big voice rose above the clatter-chatter, 'how's about four cawfee's over here?'

'I c'n hear ye, Moose,' Fred said primly. 'We're not in Madison Square Garden.'

Coming up behind Pop was the little man they called 'J.P.' Morgan, the money lender, who had a way of slithering up to you without being heard, so that his big-nosed, bat-eared, prairie-dog face was always looking into yours before you were ready for it.

Runty caught a glimpse of the obsequious 'J.P.' over his shoulder and elbowed Pop.

'Don't look now but Mr. John Pierpont Morgan is breathin' down our necks.'

Pop and the other looked straight ahead as Fred served them their coffee while the loan-sharp leaned forward over Pop's shoulder.

'Condolences,' he said.

Pop sipped his coffee.

'J.P.' was used to this. 'How ya fixed fer cabbage this mornin'?'

Now Runty wheeled his stool around. 'Oh, me'n me chum is just rollin' in the stuff.'

'That's right,' Pop chimed in. 'Everybody knows we only woik down here fer a hobby.'

'Lookit all the fresh air we get,' young Jimmy Sharkey added with a grin. 'We're down here for our health.'

'Haw haw—you fellers tickle me,' Moose boomed, and they all laughed together.

'J.P.' Morgan gave a small, patient sigh. As the money-lender for the Friendly mob, whose beneficence was bestowed at wildly usurious rates, he had to absorb a good deal of abuse from hard-pressed longshoremen who dared vent their feelings on him while fearing to strike at Johnny Friendly himself.

'You'll be needin' a few dollars fer yer extras, won't ya, Pop?' The voice both needled and wheedled.

'Extras,' Pop muttered. Bitterness stopped him from saying more.

'You're three weeks behind on the last twenty-five but I'm willin' to take a chance.'

Pop sniggered and shook his head. 'Some chance—at ten per cent a week. And if I got too far behind ya get Big Mac to throw me a few days' woik—an' ya collect the check at the end of the week. Some chance.' Years and years of seeing 'J.P.' and other shylocks turn into the stevedore paymasters the metal work-tabs of longshoremen like himself piled up in Pop. 'Some chance. I oughta belt ya one.'

'J.P.' withdrew a few feet with an air of bored persecution. 'Raise a hand t'me and you're off the pier for good.'

'Listen, Pop's been woikin' these piers thoity years or more,' Runty reminded the money man. 'He don' need no scummy loan shark t' teach 'im the score.'

'Not so loud,' Jimmy cautioned the chesty old man. 'Look who's sittin' over there. The fifth stool down.'

It was Terry Malloy, flanked by a couple of young-punk admirers, Jackie and Chick. But Terry wasn't talking to them. He was chewing moodily on a powdered doughnut.

'Aah, he's nothin'—I c'd take him right now—all three of 'em,' Runty said, but he lowered his voice a little just the same.

'J.P.' Morgan had the money in his hand now, green, soiled and inviting.

'Now, Patrick,' he said, his voice soft and old like the money, 'how much will ya be needin'?'

'All right, slip me half a bill,' Pop said, ashamed. His voice tightened. 'And may ya rot in hell, "J.P."'

'J.P.' dealt the bills from a pack of tens. 'Insult me, humiliate me,' he whined. 'When I'm dead 'n gone you'll know what a frien' I was.'

'Drop dead now, why don'tcha,' Runty suggested, 'so we c'n test your theory?'

'Haw haw haw.' Moose coughed out his laughter like the motor of a big Mack truck turning over in the morning.

'Condolences,' 'J.P' said again, with a respectful little bow, and was on his way to the next transaction. There were longshoremen who need money to put meat on the table. And there were always a few who would borrow a sawbuck to put on the nose of a horse with Jockey Byrnes, the book for the mob. So the money would come from Johnny Friendly and return to Johnny Friendly, increasing itself as it flowed in a rising, uninterrupted stream.

'More coffee, fellers?' Fred wanted to know.

Lowering his voice, Pop said, 'If ya put a ball in it. I'm disgusted.'

Fred shook his head. 'You know the law. Eight o'clock.'

'In the cup,' Pop whispered. 'On the q.t. An emoigency.'

Fred looked at the old, lined face that he had known here at the counter over the years. He knew all about Joey. But he minded his business. It wasn't his war.

'Well, bein' it's you, Pop,' he said under his breath. He took Pop's coffee cup, lowered it to a shelf below the counter and poured a shot into it from the pint he used to help himself through what he called the Sahara stretch.

'I'm sorry fer yer troubles,' he said as he pushed the cup toward Pop. Pop downed it gratefully.

Men in business suits seldom ventured into the Longdock and when a pair of them entered, everybody was aware of them without looking directly at them. Some of the local officials and the shipping people went around in suits and white shirts and ties but they almost never came into the Longdock, which was strictly rank-and-file. Business suits nearly always meant cops. But most of the plainclothesers were familiar to the Longdock clientele and the two fellows who had just come in were strangers. One of them was a husky, square-jawed fellow in his middle thirties who looked like an ex-college football player still in pretty fair shape. The other one, slightly under medium height, was dark-complexioned, compact and professionally dour. He carried a brief case. This pair of outsiders walked along the counter until they came to the trio including Terry Malloy. Terry and his two buddies, Chick and Jackie, pretended not to notice that the two men had paused behind them.

'Any of you boys know Terry Malloy?' Glover, the ex-football player asked.

The three young men at the counter went right on eating.

'Did you hear him ask you a question?' Gillette, the smaller, and more aggressive of the two, cut in.

'Malloy? Never heard of 'im,' Jackie said over his shoulder.

'Me neither,' Chick quickly added, without looking around.

Glover and Gillette looked at each other and then Glover consulted a photograph he had taken from his overcoat pocket. He took a step closer to Terry, who was hunched forward in deliberate, brooding defiance of their presence.

'You're Terry Malloy, aren't you?' Glover said.

Terry still didn't bother to answer. Gillette was ready to repeat the question when Terry swivelled around on his stool as slowly as possible and looked them over.

'So what about it?'

'I thought I'd recognize you,' Glover said cheerfully. 'I saw you in St. Nick's a couple of years ago. I'm a fight fan.'

'O.K. O.K. Without the bird seed. Whaddya want?'

'Identification,' Glover said and he flipped his wallet open with a practised flourish. Terry regarded the flash of the badge and the I.D. card with studied contempt.

'State Crime Commission?' Terry waved the wallet away. 'Are you kiddin'?'

'We'd simply like to talk to you for a few minutes,' Gillette said.

'You're talkin' to me,' Terry said.

'He means over in a booth or maybe you'd rather step outside,' Glover said. 'So we can be alone.'

'I got nothin' I can't say in front of my friends,' Terry said. 'What's the deal?'

'The Commission is conducting an investigation of waterfront crime and underworld infiltration of the Longshoreman's Union.'

'The facts, ma'm, just the facts,' Chick cracked, and Jackie laughed.

'So go ahead and conduct it,' Terry said. 'Whaddya want from me?'

'Just a little information,' Glover said pleasantly.

'I don't know nuthin',' Terry said and swung back to the counter.

'You haven't heard the questions yet,' Gillette reminded him.

Terry slowly swung back again until he was facing them, took a good look, meant to be menacing, at the trim, business-like figure of Gillette and turned to his coffee again.

'The State's trying to root out labour racketeers,' Glover said.

'Look, who's kiddin' who?' Terry said. 'Nobody's gonna root out nuthin'. That suckin' Commission is just gonna get itself some headlines and maybe somebody'll run for Mayor or Governor or something.'

Chick and Jackie nodded. The waterfront had been investigated by Mayor's committees and grand juries and roving Senators for years. There had been headlines and more headlines, and when all the smoke had cleared away, there was the waterfront, the same old waterfront. Investigation: that was the dirtiest word in the harbour.

'We didn't look you up this morning to ask you your opinion of our work,' Gillette said. Terry had marked him right away as the nasty one. 'We came in to ask you a few specific questions.'

Terry was ready with another smart answer, but Glover was ahead of him, his voice still casual and pleasant:

'There's a rumour that you're one of the last people to see Joey Doyle alive.'

'You c'n go take your rumours . . .' Terry started to say.

'We're not cops, you understand,' Gillette explained. 'We can't do anything about the Doyle case. But we'd like to find out if there's any connexion between his death and the dock rackets in general.'

'We're not even serving you a subpoena,' Glover said. 'Simply inviting you to an executive session.'

'I told you guys—I don't know nuthin',' Terry said.

'All we want to do is ask you a few little things about people you may know,' Gillette added.

Terry swung his stool the long way around to face Gillette, wheeling as slowly as he could and making this a gesture of insolence.

'People I may know . . . you mean eat cheese for ya?'

'Slow down, boy, slow down,' Gillette said.

'The nerve of these guys,' Terry said for the benefit of his friends. Then he rose from the stool with his fists clenched at his side.

'You better get outa here, buster.'

Gillette was shorter than Terry but he had been a judo expert in the Army and he had the physical confidence of a small man who knows he is ready and able. He had judo in front of him and the State behind him.

'I wouldn't advise that, Mr. Malloy, unless you want to be booked for assaulting an officer of the law.'

'Listen, cop,' Terry said, relaxing his hands and having to make up for it with his voice. 'I don't know *nuthin'*, I didn' see *nuthin'*, an' I ain't sayin' *nuthin'*. Now why don't you an' your girl friend here take off? Go on, blow.'

'All right,' Gillette said quietly. 'We'll be seeing you again.'

'Never will be too much soon for me, Shorty,' Terry said.

Glover dropped his large hand on Terry's shoulder with a familiarity from which Terry flinched. All his life cops had been the heavies, pinching him for swiping apples and then winking at the real jobs. Only two ways to handle cops, outrun 'em or take care of 'em. His brother Charley never had no trouble with cops.

'Take it easy, kid,' Glover said. 'You have every right not to talk if that's what you choose to do.'

'Do me a favour 'n drop dead,' Terry wrapped it up.

The two intruders turned away. Terry shook his head at them and wolfed his doughnut to show his chums how little he had been affected.

'How do you like them two gumshoein' around, takin' me for a pigeon?'

Jackie laughed and mimicked them in a falsetto, using a paper napkin for a mock notebook. 'Gimme the names. I'll write 'em down in me little book.'

Terry laughed, with relief, and punched Jackie's arm approvingly.

'One more word 'n I would've belted 'em, badge or no badge.'

'Aah, them politicians is a joke,' Chick said. 'When they got nuthin' better t' do they pick on the waterfront.'

'C'mon, choke the coffee down,' Jackie said. 'Five minutes the whistle's gonna blow.'

'I hear ya sittin' pretty, Terry,' Chick said. 'A steady job in the loft. How's about fixin' us up now that you're a big shot.'

'The loft boss 'd bounce you the first day,' Terry said as he tossed a dollar on the counter to pay for the three of them. He was trying hard to push those Commission jokers out of his mind. 'You gotta have brains for the job I'm gettin'.'

'Or at least a brother with brains,' Jackie said.

Actually Jack and Chick, who had known Terry in reform school, stood in well with Big Mac. They were always ready to help things along on the pilferage and they worked steady enough to come out with around four thousand a year, aside from the personal loot. They weren't part of the regular goon squad like Truck and Sonny but Big Mac could count on them to throw a punch or a brick, when the situation demanded.

'Come on, girls, let's get over there,' Terry said, falling into his rolling, boxer-walk as he led them out.

The cold at the river's edge ate into their bones, the late November cold that blows off the river into the weathered faces of longshore-men. Now they were gathering at the pier entrance to wait for the summoning whistle of the hiring boss.

The great harbour of the world's most modern metropolis still hired its dockmen in the same haphazard way as in the days of the sailing ships when a transatlantic schooner would drop anchor off South Street and a chief would whistle for loiterers and hangers-on to leave their grog shops and pick up a good Yankee dollar or two for a four-hour turn as a human pack-horse unloading the coffee and tobacco and hemp that was making this upstart city of half a million people the greatest trading centre in the world. London and Liverpool and San Francisco had long since put away as a museum relic the hiring whistle, but here in Bohegan and all around the harbour the century-old whistle called the willing hands, called them not to work, but to offer themselves for work while the hiring boss looked them over and made his choices. In the clipper days he combed through them to separate the able workers from the rummies. Now he looked them over for signs of compliance. There were subtle devices an outsider scarcely would notice, a match over the left ear signalling willingness to kick back a couple of dollars on the job or a tiny American flag pinned to a windbreaker lapel identifying the wearer as a member in good standing of the kick-back club. This was the silent language of harbour corruption.

The men first to arrive at the Hudson-American pier operated by Tom McGovern's Interstate Stevedore Company had started a fire in a rusted metal barrel left there as a primitive heater for the frost-bitten dockers. Even through their thick gloves and heavy shoes the cold penetrated their fingers and toes, and they shifted weight from foot to foot and worked their fingers over the fire to fight off the numbness. From November until March it was chilling, thankless work, and half-frozen fingers and icy decks multiplied the accidents. And in the summer heat the bottom of the hold was airless and the hatch gangs felt as if they were being steamed alive. But the up-and-down fall tackle and the cargo sling knew no season. In January sleet or in sweating, bare-waisted July, you swung your hook, loaded that pallet. The pier superintendent has a bug up his rump this morning. He's yelling for twenty-five tons an hour! Let the bum load it hisself if he's in sech a fuggin' hurry.

The men around the fire-barrel blew little clouds of cold breath into the air and exchanged small-talk about how lousy the fight was the night before. They were careful not to mention anything too serious because the pier entrance was all ears, with the Friendly boys, Sonny and Truck and Gilly and Specs and Barney and the rest of them, wandering around on the Earie. And since the shape-up pitted every man against his neighbour one never knew when a fellow you trusted would go running to Big Mac or Specs Flavin, who held the title of shop steward, in return for the favour of regular work. Regular work—a chance to pull down your seventy-five, eighty a week every week so the money coming in balanced the money going out—that was the quest, the hope, the muffled cry of every one of the three or four hundred who offered himself to Big Mac's cynical double-o. A guaranteed minimum wage for every qualified longshoreman—that had been one of Joey Doyle's pet ideas as opposed to the surplus labour pool encouraged by the shipping companies and exploited by labour-racket boys like Johnny Friendly and Charley Malloy. Job security, that's what Joey had called it, instead of larcenous hiring bosses throwing jobs out into the crowd every morning like fish to hungry seals.

When Pop and his three cronies came up to one of the fire barrels they had an almost imperceptible but singular effect on the men already gathered there. These men felt they should say something to comfort Pop, but the words stuck to their tongues. Subconsciously they drew away a few inches as if Pop was death itself and the mere brushing of his windbreaker could be fatal. A killing on the docks always left the men edgy and withdrawn, sometimes for months. Even a year later the tensions would still be there. There was the time five years ago when Andy Collins was ready to take over as assistant hiring boss and was shot dead right in the office of 447. 'Elbows' Sweeney, who did the job for Johnny Friendly, had taken off for Florida and was seen at Hialeah every day betting in the money that Johnny sent him to keep him happy. Andy Collins had been a popular man who had done a lot for Catholic Youth in the parish. Everybody knew it was Sweeney. Every bar in Bohegan could tell you the story. Plenty of longshoremen in 447 hated Johnny Friendly and Charley the Gent for the Collins job. But what was a fellow gonna do? This was the only work you knew and this was the only place to get it. If you moved over to some other pier and another set-up, you'd have to start all over again as an outsider picking up the crumbs. And it was just as rough across the river on the midtown piers, or over in Port Newark, as it was here in Bohegan. You get the psychology? So with Pop here, the men felt deeply and at the same time had to be careful not to show their feelings. conflicting waves of emotion met in them like a rip-tide and made them dangerous below the surface.

Only Luke Tucker, a big Negro extra-man, came over and openly expressed his sympathies. There was a wall between the races that worked the docks; the Irish and Italians—the Micks and the Guineas —were clannish and held to their own. And of course the 'niggers' on the bottom were the lepers of the port. But Luke was, in the opinion of Runty and the rest of them, a proud, two-fisted, independent nigger who was honey-easy to get along with until you tried to push his face in the race thing. He was the acknowledged leader of the Negro minority that picked up the odd hatch jobs and the extra-gang work that was left at the bottom of the work barrel. As such, Luke had gained a certain status in the eyes of Big Mac who hated shines like poison but needed the black boys as extra men. Luke had come out of the Alabama share-crop country as a fourteen-year-old kid running away from home. 'I jest hopped me a choo-choo and sayed, "No'th here I comes",' Luke had told the boys. Luke had done a little cheap-circuit wrestling and a little time for some vague crime associated with strong, wandering, penniless boys who had never learned a trade. When he drifted to the docks he found a double-kickback system for the coloured. They not only kicked back five bucks to the hiring boss, double the head-tax of their white fellow workers, but an extra dollar or two to the Negro gang-boss who rounded them up. Luke was able to lick the coloured straw boss, a slickster called Hotstuff, and could have moved in on the dollar-racket and made himself fifty to seventy-five a week. But Luke had said, 'If I gotta rob the poor t' get rich, I'd ruther stay poor.' He was a rebel without quite knowing he was one. He came up to Pop now and slapped him on the back roughly, forever under-estimating his wrestler-strength, and he said right out, 'Ah feel bad about Joey. It ain't a right way.'

'Thanks, Luke,' Pop said. He knew in the Missal what they said about everybody bein' brothers, but it was askin' a lot for a Kerry man to brother-up to a garlic-smellin' guinea or some big buck yellow-streakin' nigger. Just the same Luke was half accepted, like Max the Jew, an old orthodox winchman, the only Yiddle workman Pop had ever heard of outside of the garment workers who rolled it up for Dubinsky.

'I took up a little collection among the brethren,' Luke said, meaning the two dozen Negro casuals who shaped up for extra work.

'Tell 'em thanks for me, Luke,' Pop said and took the money, though he didn't want to. 'I'll give it to Father Donogue to say Masses for Joey.'

'Looks like we all see a little change today,' Luke said, nodding toward the South-American freighter that had just docked. 'Bananas.'

Bananas meant hand labour, carrying the heavy stalks on your shoulders. Thousands of stalks, a whole deep hatch full of bananas.

This was old-fashioned unloading with hundreds of men moving in and out of the hatch doors like streams of ants.

'Bananers,' Runty said. 'I got a poimanent groove in m' shoulder from too many years of bananers. I wish I had as much money as I hate them bananers.'

'As long as it pays off at two thirty-four an hour, I'd carry manure,' Luke said cheerfully.

'For shit you should get double-time, like ammo,' Jimmy Sharkey said. 'Falls under the provision of "noxious cargo".'

'A lot Johnny Friendly cares what we carry,' Moose shouted. 'Lookit that caustic acid. That's noxious in every other port. Down in the hold it makes yer eyes water and ya feel like you wanna puke. But good old Interstate pays you the regular rate.

'Thanks to Johnny Friendly and Charley the Gent, those great labour leaders,' Runty Nolan laughed. 'Charley's really lookin' out fer our interests on the Negotiatin' Committee.' He drew his finger across his neck and the others chuckled.

Sonny, who was in on a pass because he was a brother-in-law of Specs Flavin, the hardware man, always kept an eye on this bunch and now he came over smelling trouble.

'Hey, better watch that talk. Whattid you say?'

'I was jus' sayin' how thankful we should be to Johnny Friendly fer bein' such a pisser of a labour leader 'n doin' so much t' improve our conditions,' Runty laid it on thick, grinning up at the big, stupid-faced Sonny Rodell.

'Don't get wise now,' Sonny warned.

'Wise,' Runty ho-hoed at him. 'If I was wise I wouldn't be no longshoreman fer forty years an' poorer now than when I started. Hell no, I'd be gettin' my six hundred a month from the International, wind-baggin' with Willie Givens, our esteemed president.'

'Whaddya mean, steamed?' Sonny demanded. 'Ya better not shoot ya mouth off about Willie Givens.'

Sonny was one of the hand-picked delegates to the Longshoreman's Convention, at a hundred bucks a day expenses, and he was annually impressed with the heights of oratory to which Willie Givens laboriously ascended.

'Anyway,' Sonny concluded, 'it ain't Willie Givens or Johnny's fault ya drink all your money away. Now ya watch yerself now.' He walked away with the air of a prep-school housemaster.

'Big bum,' Runty muttered when Sonny was out of earshot. 'If it wasn't for Specs and his cannon, he'd be beggin' handouts at the back o' saloons.' His friends, who looked to him as their own dock-side Durante, got a good laugh out of that.

Mutt Murphy came over and warmed himself by the fire. He never expected to work, but he almost always gathered with the others for the shape-up drawn here either by sheer habit or foggy-minded sociability.

'Mornin', Pop,' he mumbled. He was wearing a torn suitcoat picked up from a local mission and he looked as if he should have been chilled to the bone; his lips and hands were blue, but he seemed unaware of the cold. 'God bless ya, ya Joey was a saint.' He crossed himself elaborately and began to shout in his harsh, croaking voice:

'Joey died fer us an' Jee—sus'll save us . . .'

Truck Amon, whose two hundred and twenty pounds were pushed into five feet eight inches, and whose neck had the muscular thickness of a prize boar's, came waddling over to grunt at Mutt, 'C'mon, knock it off.' He shoved the one-armed drifter away from the pier entrance. 'They're gettin' ready to blow the whistle. You're a pimple on the ass o' progress. Disappear.' Truck's thick face pushed together in a grin of self-amusement. He was continually amazed at the comic sayings that popped into his head. His latest filled him with good feeling and he reached into his pocket and flipped a quarter to Mutt. 'Here, go drink ya breakfast,' he said, and his fat, muscular tub of a body shook with mirth.

Captain Schlegel, popularly called 'Schnorkel', an ex-German submariner who bossed the pier for Interstate, had just given Big Mac the cargo breakdown on the *Maria Cristal:* two loft gangs, six regular gangs and two hundred extra banana carriers. Captain Schlegel gave Big Mac a box full of metal tabs covering the number of jobs to be filled. There was bad blood between the pier boss and Big Mac because the German was a discipline-minded Prussian recruited by Tom McGovern when Schlegel settled in Bohegan after his sub was held there at the end of the first World War. Schlegel didn't like Big Mac's sloppy ways and the fact that he held his job because of his prison record and his influence with the mob and not through any particular loading skill. There was an art to loading, both as to speed and placement, and Schlegel was generally respected as a master at it, even though he was commonly regarded as an inhuman sonofabitch. It had been Captain Schlegel who had said arrogantly to the press, 'I have no special love for gangsters, but I can tell you one thing, you need a strong arm around here to keep in line the kind of working force we've got to deal with on the docks.' Captain Schlegel, on orders from Interstate, slipped a Christmas envelope to Johnny Friendly every Christmas, as well as to Charley the Gent and their subordinates, because Interstate was grateful for their co-operation. Oh, sure they shook you down once in a while, but it was quicker and cheaper to pay ten thousand on the line than to deal with the complicated demands of a genuine union. With a shop steward like Specs Flavin you didn't have to worry about the little everyday breaches of the contract that could run company savings into hundreds of thousands. Sure, if you had to have unions, Captain Schlegel preferred Johnny Friendly's kind to the real thing. Just the same he loathed having to deal with a 'getrunkener dumbkopf' like Big Mac McGown. Right now, for instance, Big Mac was still sweating off the effects of the load he always took on Friday evenings. It was only when he was on one that he referred to Captain Schlegel as 'You Heinie bastard.' Captain Bateson, Captain Schlegel's superior in Interstate, and Mr. McGovern could call the former U-boat officer a Heinie bastard because their position entitled them to this or any privilege. But Big Mac was just a vulgar red-neck who would have been an ordinary longshoreman if he hadn't risen to power as a henchman of Johnny Friendly. Captain Schlegel despised him, especially since he had no choice but to tolerate him as part of the Friendly set-up on the piers of Bohegan serviced by Interstate. In theory a hiring boss was an employee of Interstate and subject to Captain Schlegel's approval. In practice he was given the nod by Johnny Friendly. If Big Mac wasn't acceptable, Johnny could pull his men out and shut down the pier. Captain Schlegel had a horror of that as he tried to push his pier to the highest yearly tonnage rate on the Jersey shore. So he only reddened and pushed his lips together when Big Mac gave him 'Heinie bastard'.

A few minutes before, Captain Schlegel had been surprised when an Irish priest from across the park at St. Timothy's had come in with Joey Doyle's sister and asked if they could see a shape-up. Privately Captain Schlegel had considered Joey a trouble-maker, an agitator, the sort of smart-aleck who quoted back to you the union-stevedore agreement. But he hastened to assure the priest and the girl that her brother had been well liked by the company, a good worker, a fine boy. In behalf of Interstate Captain Schlegel extended his sympathies. Although the accident was off-hours, away from the pier and the company was in no way involved, Captain Schlegel was going to recommend that Interstate send Mr. Doyle a cheque for $100 as an official expression of company condolence. As to the shape-up that they wished to see, he frankly wondered why they should want to bother themselves watching a routine hiring practice. But if they wished to take the time, he would be happy to have a guard escort them to the entrance to Pier B where the morning hiring was about to take place. However, it would be better, he suggested, if they did not stop to ask Mr. McGown any questions, as he would be extremely busy with his morning duties. Captain Schlegel was anxiously unsure as to just what this priest and this girl were getting at, and Big Mac with a load on wasn't the man to satisfy their curiosity.

The shape-up is often criticized unfairly, Captain Schlegel explained as he walked them to the door of his office. Obviously men cannot be given regular jobs when three hundred are needed one day, only one hundred the next, and perhaps none at all the third day when the outgoing ship is gone and the in coming vessel not yet arrived. In practice our hiring boss tries to pick the most competent and deserving men, and the majority of them average out pretty well in a month. So the system is not quite as haphazard and inhuman as a few alarmists have tried to make it sound. 'Of course they have to sell papers and if it helps to exaggerate a little, who can blame them?' No system is perfect. He had been in nearly all the great ports of the world and this shape-up, as they called it, worked as well as any. Privately over beer at the Hofbrau Haus with his fellow-stevedore captains, Schlegel had said, 'When we call five hundred men for two hundred jobs and each fella sees with his own eyes there's at least two or three of 'em for every job, then by golly we can keep them toeing the mark like we want 'em.'

He didn't like this Father snooping around. He'd have to check into this. And the Doyle girl coming down was not a good sign either. Actually Interstate employees had been responsible for much of the dock violence in Bohegan, but the name of McGovern was a powerful one and Interstate had never been mentioned in connexion with waterfront crime. But Captain Schlegel knew how to be correct with a Roman collar and a young lady. He bowed and brought his heels together in a habit-hardened courtesy, and assured them of his eagerness to show them any phase of the stevedore operation they wished to see.

So Father Barry and Katie were looking on when Big Mac came out to the pier entrance with the cigar box full of brass tabs. The only reason the hiring boss wasn't swaggering or swaying was because he was a big-bodied man who could absorb a fifth a day with beer to wash it down and still walk a reasonably straight line, even if his movements became uncertain and his behaviour unpredictable from minute to minute.

McGown's cheeks puffed out as he blew on his whistle. Some four hundred men fell into a dutiful, silent horseshoe around him.

They shaped according to custom, with the deck men on the left, the hold men to their right, then the dock men, hi-low drivers and on the extreme right the longshore casuals, the extra men. Father Barry and Katie saw how they pressed forward, begging with their eyes for the coveted jobs as Big Mac approached them. First he called out the men for the loft, mostly old men no longer fit for the heavy work, but scattered among them a few youthful privileged characters to whom Johnny Friendly owed some favour. 'Hogan—Smith—Krajowski—Malloy—' Big Mac shouted. Terry caught his tab with a Willie Mays flourish and winked to Chick and Jackie as he started toward the entrance where he sang out his number to the timekeeper.

Then Big Mac began filling the regular gangs, looking for

106

familiar faces and the kickback matches, and saying, 'You—yeah you—okay you . . .' When he got down to the banana carriers the desperation mounted. Men jostled his arm in their eagerness, their frost-bitten faces challenging him, expressing an odd mixture of obsequiousness and defiance.

'C'mon, Mac, I need a day bad . . .'

'I got five kids home, Mac, I gotta work t'day . . .'

'Hey, Mac, remember me, you said next time you'd . . .'

And Runty, half begging but always saving his pride, 'Who d'ya have t' know t' get a tab around here, fat boy?'

Watching this, Father Barry felt ashamed. He had seen the shape-up from the distance of a block and a half when he had come out into the park for a breath of air after the 7 o'clock Mass. But he had never come close enough to look into these desperate faces. Here was depersonalization, here was indignity, across the park from St. Timothy's, under his very nose. It was one thing to hear abstract criticism of the shape-up. It was quite another to stand here, close enough to see the cold breath of the men, and to look into their eyes, pleading—for what? For a four-hour job, about nine dollars to lug two hundred-pound banana stalks in a late November wind. No wonder some of the faces were blank and defeated and some of them were already sodden with drink. He looked at Katie, who was staring in fascinated disbelief as she watched her father offering himself to Big Mac like the others. The priest thought again of Xavier and how the little Basque would've lowered the boom on a deal like this. Man is such a noble creature, his mind snatched from some familiar text, that only God is his master.

'—C'mon, Mac, gimme a break, I need a day bad, real bad,' a husky voice carried to him.

He looked at the girl staring speechlessly at a scene that might have been ripped out of some medieval sketchbook of enslavement.

'No wonder Pop never talked about it,' Katie said. 'And always warned me never to come down here.'

'You gotta be deaf, dumb and blind not to see that this set-up stinks to Heaven,' Father Barry said.

'Now you see some of what Joey was trying to change,' Katie said. Her face became taut. Her long blonde-brown hair blew about her in the wind. 'I still want to know—who killed my brother?'

Father Barry said, 'The least of mine. Oh, brother, are they giving it to the least o mine!'

10

EXACTLY HOW IT started a moment later was never clear. It was 'one of those things', a question mark to be raked over and argued in the bars for years to come. Big Mac was being crowded, jostled, heckled. Whether, tipsy and contemptuous, he deliberately tossed the cherished tabs into the air, or whether some over-anxious docker grabbed for a tab and upset the box, the fact remained that nearly two hundred tabs flew into the air. They scattered in front of the pier entrance and as they fell nearly four hundred men howled and scrambled and hustled and fought for them.

There were human snarls as vicious as any animal's and the sound of crunching bones and work-hardened fists making bloody wounds. Men who had had to rough-and-tumble on the docks all their lives fought with their heads, their knees, their feet.

Truck and Gilly looked on in amusement.

'Meatballs,' Truck grunted.

'Definitely,' Gilly said with his echoing chuckle.

It had begun to suddenly and was so unreal, even as it raged in front of them, that Father Barry and Katie experienced it as if it were a nightmare so terrible that they wanted to pull themselves awake to escape its horror. They saw Moose make a flying lunge at a tab, only to have a heavy boot stomp his hand to a bloody mess. In the melee they caught sight of Runty, bobbing up like a battered dinghy in a stormy sea. Blood was dripping from one eye but he wasn't taking a backward step to adversaries a hundred pounds heavier and a foot taller. Katie screamed as she saw him carried down swinging and kneeing into the swirling bodies, chopping and rolling against one another like the breakers of an angry sea. Pop, Pop, where was Pop! She couldn't bear the thought of her stringy-armed father over-whelmed and dragged down into that churning, bloodied tangle of bodies. 'Pop, Pop!' she cried out. Then she saw him, battling near the circumference of the free-for-all. He spied a tab on the ground near him, reached out to it, grabbed for it, was shoved aside, pistoned his fists into the nearest face and finally was ready to pick up the prize when the voice of the figure he had just knocked out of the way shouted:

'Hey, Terry, grab it fer me.'

Terry Malloy, standing just beyond the timekeeper, enjoying the fun, executed a quick-reflex reach for the tab and scooped it up.

'Here ya go, Jackie boy,' he sang out, easily body-checking the the old man. But Pop came at him with blood in his eye: *Hey gimme that* and swung a wild right-hand punch at Terry that looped harmlessly over his head as Terry slipped it neatly to one side.

Before Father Barry could stop her, Katie was rushing forward. She was too angry and panicked to know what she was doing. She had seen that young bully use his strength and his youth to block out her old man and send him sprawling. '*Give* me that, *give* me that,' she screamed at him, grabbing at the tab in Terry's upraised hand. Terry swung around, away from her hand, circling to her left as a boxer avoids a right-hand puncher. Light on his feet, amused, playing with her, he kept saying, 'Huh? Huh? What you want? Huh?'

'Give it to me! Give it to me!'

Terry laughed. 'Hey, things're lookin' up on the docks, hey, Jackie?'

'It belongs to Pop. He saw it first.' Katie was trying not to cry. Terry was grinning at her and she slapped at his face, but he pulled away, still grinning at her.

'Pop? I thought maybe you was gonna work—with all them muscles.'

'It's for Pop,' she said, lunging futilely again as Terry circled away from her, in his old boxing style when he wanted to spin an opponent into the ropes.

A real cool-looking broad, Terry sized her up as he clowned with her. Tall, young, firm, sweet, a lot of class. 'Your Pop, huh? What makes him so special?'

As Katie made another grab at the tab that Terry managed to

keep just out of her reach, it was Jackie Roche who said, "Don't ya recognize him, dopey? That's old man Doyle.'

Hey Joey, Joey Doyle—he's one of yours—I recognized the band.

Terry stopped circling away from her. He could feel something vague and bewildering, something falling away from him, like his stomach on the roller-coaster at Coney.

'Doyle . . . Joey Doyle's . . . you're his . . .'

'Sister,' Katie said, in a flat, direct tone, ' yes, I am.'

Terry looked at her, took off his cap, ran his hand through his hair and shook his head as if he was clearing it after a bad round. Then he made himself tough again. He turned to Jackie. 'Who the hell wants to lug bananas in the rain anyhoo? Am I right, Jackie boy?'

'Aah, give it to 'im,' Jackie said.

'Here ya go, muscles,' Terry said to Katie, and slapped the tab into her hand. 'It was nice wrastlin' with ya.'

He raised his left hand, boxer style, flicked a couple of quick jabs into the air and winked at her.

'C'mon, Jackie, let's go over to Friendly's and catch a few beers. I c'n check in any time.'

He and Jackie started across the street to the bar, walking tough. He was conscious of the girl's angry eyes on him. His side-to-side boxer's swagger was a little more exaggerated than usual. God-damn it, who dragged the Doyle broad into this? Just when he was ready to take life easy in the loft. In the loft you were out of the rat race, you were out from under the shape-up pressure if you had a regular job in the loft. He'd need three four five straight shots to get this out of his mind.

Katie watched him go, with his hands in his pockets, his shoulders slightly hunched, wise-cracking to his chum out of the corner of his mouth. She had been away from Bohegan most of her teen-age life. But Katie knew this type. The streets of her childhood had teemed with them. Dirty-faced, foul-mouthed, gutter-toughened little people drawn toward the strongest and most ruthless as nails to magnets. Slapped by the nuns, cuffed by the cops, whipped by their parents, beaten by bigger boys and each day challenged to be louder with their mouths and quicker with their fists; grabby, suspicious, loyal only to a few no-good cronies, sneering at authority, mean little twentieth-century savages—oh, Katie had known them all her life, had been warned by her father against them all her life, boys like the one who had just fought her for the tab, who could never stop proving to their pals just how tough they were. How little they knew, Katie was thinking as Terry headed for the bar. How they counted on force for everything and never suspected that no one is more the victim of force than he who thinks he must depend on it.

'Who is that fresh kid?' she asked Moose, who had come up out of the battle royal to see if she was all right.

'That was Terry Malloy, the kid brother of Charley the Gent,' Moose explained. 'Just a punk.'

'Charley the Gent?'

'He's our local representative on the District Council. A politician.' Moose didn't want to tell her any more.

Father Barry came rapidly toward them, half leading Pop, who was wiping the blood off his face with a handkerchief the priest had given him. Pop pulled himself free. He was in a sweaty rage, not so much at losing the tab. Nearly forty years on the waterfront had hardened him to the everyday setbacks. Even the fact that his nose felt broken didn't discourage him too much. He was a tough old man. No, the rage was for Katie's being down here where he had always forbidden her.

'Lemme alone, Father,' he said, and pulled himself free.

Katie held the tab out to him, ashamed at having to see his shame.

'Here—I got it for you.'

Pop grabbed it from her.

'Okay—I c'n use it.' He would have slapped her if it hadn't been for the presence of the priest. 'Now just as soon as we bury 'im you're goin' back to the Sisters where you belong.' He turned on the priest. 'I'm surprised at you, Father, if ya don' mind me sayin' so. Lettin' her see things that ain't fit fer the eyes of a decent goil.'

'She seems to know her own mind,' Father Barry said.

'Stubborn as an Irish donkey ya mean,' Pop said, glaring at her 'Stay away from here.' Then back to the priest, 'And if I wuz you I'd stay outa this too, Father.'

'She wanted to have a good look at it. Maybe it's time we all took a good look at it,' Father Barry said.

'I think the two of yuz is blowin' yer corks.'

'A time for patience and a time to blow your cork?' Father Barry said.

'Jesus, Mary 'n Joseph, everybody is got an answer,' Pop protested.

A bull voice broke in. It was Big Mac, drunkenly rebuilding the blocks of his dignity. 'Hey, Doyle, you got a tab?'

Pop held it up defiantly. 'Yeah.'

'Then knock off the chin music. Git in there. Number two hatch starboard gang. Puh-ronto.'

'Okay, okay, hold ya water,' Pop said. Specks of blood on his upper lip gave him the look of an embattled, straight-faced circus clown as he turned back for a final word to his daughter and the priest.

'You mind what I'm sayin' now. You too, Father. This ain't no surroundings for a man of God.' Then he started into the pier entrance, muttering to himself.

Captain Schlegel usually stayed in his office inside the pier, but this time the commotion brought him out to the entrance-way. When he saw Father Barry he hurried over to assure him that what he had just seen was in no way typical of the morning hiring. (That dumpkopf McGown, he was thinking. Maybe he could get Captain Bateson to shift him to the new pier so he could make life miserable for some other stevedore captain.)

Even without the scramble, Father Barry answered, it did seem to him as if the shape-up was a wasteful, callous inefficient way of hiring human beings. It seemed to be a system of no-system, with the men who were passed over having to get up and report for work just as if they had a regular morning job. That was hardly fair. And now, wasn't it too late for them to try their luck at other piers? Hadn't all the work-gangs been filled for the day, from Bohegan to Red Hook? And, Father Barry said, talking very fast as he always did when an idea seized him, was it wise to give one man such power over five hundred others as this Big Mac obviously had? 'A hiring boss would have to be a saint not to misuse this kind of power,'

Father Barry said. 'And that big fellow with the pot belly may not be the worst of them but he's not exactly my idea of a saint.'

'Father, I happen to be a Catholic myself,' Captain Schlegel said. 'Oh, maybe not the best one, but'—he paused—'but let me say to you frankly. We do not come over there'—he nodded toward St. Timothy's—'and try to tell you how to run your business. Is there any reason why you should come over here and tell us how to run the stevedore business? Hah? Hah?' Captain Schlegel's eyes twinkled with satisfaction that he had scored a direct hit.

'Captain,' Father Barry said crisply, 'I think the answer is *yes*. I'll be glad to drop in one of these days and give you the reasons.'

'At your pleasure, Father,' Captain Schlegel said, clicked his heels again and turned away, to take his feelings out on Big Mac, who was standing at the entrance with his cheeks sucked in, a habit that exaggerated his usual, well-filled expression of stupidity.

'Mac, we're losing time,' Captain Schlegel snapped. 'Get those men out of the way.' He meant the hundred or so left over, without tabs. 'We don't want to hold up the trucks.' There were thirty 10-tons lined up to cart away 60,000 pounds of bananas. Captain Schlegel hurried importantly into the pier again, the stem of his pipe held in the bulldog grip of his teeth.

Big Mac, with Truck and Gilly spread-legged at his side, turned on the hundred-odd men who continued to stand around in silent, submissive, resentful groups. The battle for the tabs in front of the nosey priest and the contemptuous looks from Captain Schlegel had put him in a black mood. For Big Mac a black mood was always a loud mood, and when he shouted at the rejected dockmen, the sound of his hard, foghorn voice filled the air and seemed to make it tremble for a moment as does the shattering blast from an ocean liner.

'The rest of yuz. Outa the way. Trucks comin' through. Come back tomorra.'

Big Mac waved the first of the trucks into the pier. The driver gunned his engine, counting on the left-over dockers to clear out of the way. And at the last possible moment they did, almost in a sleep-walking motion, inching out of the path of the procession of trucks without appearing to see them.

To one side of the pier entrance, along the ledge bordering the slip where the fruit boat rode at mooring, Luke, Runty, Moose and Jimmy stood in a disconsolate circle with a couple of other veteran dockers. It was a custom, this aimless waiting after the chosen gangs had already started breaking into the cargo. Sometimes the boss discovered that he needed a few extra men to fill out a gang. Often Big Mac worked short gangs with eighteen men pressured to do the work of twenty-two and the pay of four 'phantoms'—an easy hundred dollars a day—going to Big Mac, to be bucked up to Johnny Friendly and Charley Malloy, along with the kickbacks and payroll padding from other piers. It was no skin off Interstate as long as the work was done in time and the ship turned around and hurried back to sea. So Captain Schlegel would look the other way when Big Mac worked his short gangs—until he thought the hiring boss was pushing the racket to the point of serious interference with his quota of a thousand tons a day. Then he would get on Big Mac to fill the gangs out to normal strength. Anyway that was the hope of the men who loitered at the entrance another ten or fifteen minutes after the shape-up was over. Even after Big Mac had shouted at them the men lingered on in hang-dog groups, as if the morning's defeat had left them without the physical will to move on.

Father Barry, always intense and now wound dangerously tight as a result of what he had seen, strode up to the group. He had seen most of them at the wake.

'Well, what d'ya do now?'

The men didn't look at him. A sense of guilt pressed upon them, as if they had to atone for their helplessness. And the presence of Katie shrivelled them too. They were, most of them, Irishmen, never completely at east with women under the best of circumstances and double-troubled here to see this girl they all respected come among them and see them in their shame.

Father Barry held his ground. He knew they didn't want him down here any more than they wanted the girl.

'I said what d'ya do now?'

Luke shrugged. 'Like the man sayed. Come back tomorra.'

'T'morra,' Runty snapped. 'There's no ship t'morra.'

'And if he won't pick you the next day?' Father Barry asked.

Moose hunched his shoulders. 'Ya hit "J.P." Morgan fer a loan. A longshoreman spends the money t'day he hopes t'make t'morra. That's a fact, Father.'

'Not so loud,' Jimmy Sharkey warned, aware of Truck and Gilly looking on from the pier entrance.

'Moose, you try t' whisper somethin' and I swear t' Christ they c'n hear it clear t' the end of the next block,' Runty half laughed.

'I been standin' here the last five mornin's,' Moose shouted in what he thought was a confidential tone. 'I tell 'im I got four kids t' feed an' my wife is half crazy. But they got me down for a Bolsheviki 'cause they seen me talkin' too much in the Longdock with Joey. Hell, we're talkin' about fights an' ball games mos' the time.'

His conspiratorial shout assaulted the suspicious ears of Truck and Gilly, whose invisible antennae were constantly tuned to mutiny. Truck waddled forward, with Gilly mechanically falling in step with him.

'Anyway five days I'm standin' here,' Moose went on confiding in his booming voice. 'And that McGown bum looks right through me like I'm an open winder.'

Truck moved in on him. 'C'mon, get movin'. Y'heard d' boss.'

'Yeah, get movin',' Gilly chimed in, shoving Moose just a little.

Truck was a Catholic too, or he thought he was, and he was unable to pass on without acknowledging the priest. 'I'm sorry, Father, but 'ysee, there's no blocking the entrance-way.'

'Da's right. Definitely,' Gilly echoed.

Johnny Friendly's pair of muscle men hard-shouldered their way over to herd another group away from the pier entrance.

'C'mon, let's go get a ball,' Runty said. He was still breathing hard through his broken nose.

But Father Barry held them with his anger. 'Is that all you do, just take it like this?'

The men looked at one another with a what's-the-use shrug. Father Barry turned from one to the other. 'I thought you boys had a union. There isn't a labour union in the country that'd stand for a deal like this.'

Runty looked around to see if Truck and Gilly were still on the prowl. They were, and Runty took the priest's arm.

'Take a walk with me, Father.'

Father Barry nodded to Katie, who had sense enough to keep quiet. It was bad enough she was down here at all. She knew what Pop must be feeling. Mad enough to put the strap to her. And she had begun to worry into what uncharted shoals she was leading the priest. She followed along and said nothing, watching them with her innocent, critical, lively blue eyes.

'If I wuz you, Father,' Runty said, 'I wouldn't push my nose in this thing. I don' mean no disrespect. Fer yer own good I mean it. But if you want t' know, we don' have no union. We got these bums on top of us stickin' our dues 'n kickbacks in their pockets an' drivin' around in four thousand-buck convoitables.'

'You mean you fellers can't get up in a meeting and . . .'

Again they looked at each other with humorous shrugs.

Jimmy Sharkey said, 'You know what they call Four-Four-Seven? The pistol local.'

'I do remember hearing that,' Father Barry said.

'It's one thing to hear it. It's another thing to feel it with the pistol butts on yer noggin,' Runty said.

'You know how a pistol local works, Father?' Moose shouted.

'No—how?' Father Barry said.

Luke answered for them, speaking with a soft humour that could not sheathe the vicious edge of what he said.

'You get up in a meetin', you make a motion, the lights go out, then *you* go out.'

All the men laughed at the bitter accuracy of Luke's description.

'That's no lie, Father,' Moose's voice rose again. The subject always excited him. 'You get up in a meetin' and ask a question, you're lookin' t' get your brains knocked out. Like one time I got up an' tried t' make a motion about a pension fund. I was in order too. Runty read me how t' do it in Cushin's Manual. Well, I start talkin' and, boom, I'm rolling down the long flight o' stairs from the hall and I'm out on the sidewalk flat on my face.'

'That was two years ago,' Jimmy said. 'The last meeting we had.'

Runty grinned. 'Tha's the way it's been ever since Johnny and his pistoleros took over our Four-Four-Seven. When I got enough balls in me I go right up to 'em and tell 'em what bums they are. One time they hit me in the head with a pipe and threw me in the river. So me an' the river know each other pretty good. It was winter time an' the water was colder 'n a nun's—well, I mean it was ice water, Father, an' damn if it don't bring me to.' Runty went ho-ho-ho as if he had just told a funny story. 'So y'see, I'm on velvet, Father. I should worry, I'm on borried time.'

Father Barry felt himself being drawn in, deeper and deeper.

'Y'mean to tell me all this stuff's been going on and it never even gets in the papers?'

'The *Graphic* is the Mayor's sheet,' Moose shouted. 'You oughta know that, Father. And the Mayor 'n Johnny Friendly are like *this*, with Johnny Friendly on top. Hell, the Mayor pays off little political favours by givin' fellers in City Hall a note to Johnny or Charley to put 'em to work. It don't matter if we're regular longshoremen who need the work for the ice box and these bums who move in on us are just stinkin' ward heelers.'

Father Barry looked sceptical. 'You mean the Mayor and Johnny Friendly actually get together on who's to be hired down here?'

Runty laughed. 'Cripes, I thought everybody in Bohegan knew that, Father. The last Mayor walked out with maybe a million bucks. Where *you* been, Father?'

Father Barry looked at Katie uneasily. 'Maybe I've been hiding in the church.'

'An' if I wuz you I'd stay there,' Runty said. 'This set-up down here is a pisser, 'scuse me again. I tell ya there's nothin' like it in the whole damn country. An' God may kill me if I ain't tellin' the truth.'

'Okay, I believe you. But your ancestors must be rollin' in their graves. A fine bunch of Irishmen! Hell, the English slaughtered our families like pigs for eight hundred years and we never quit. We found ways of fighting back.'

Father Barry had memories, faded but precious as old flags in mothballs, of his father's glowing accounts of the O'Neills, Shane and Owen Roe, and Hugh, Earl of Tyrone, and of Red Hugh O'Donnell, that glorious lost-causer. They had figured in Pete Barry's boyhood dreams and he invoked them now as he felt himself more and more deeply caught up in a struggle he had been discreetly avoiding.

'It ain't so easy to fight back, Reverent,' said Luke, an occasional Baptist. 'Right now we couldn't even be talkin' like this if we didn't have you along for pertection. Those cowboys 'd be ridin' herd on us.'

Moose nodded. 'Name one place where it's safe even t' talk without gettin' clobbered,' he yelled. 'Name me one. Just one.'

'The church,' Father Barry said quickly.

'The church!' Moose shouted in amazement.

'Shhh, keep it down to a shout,' Jimmy cautioned. 'You mean that, Father?'

'I said the church. Use the basement of the church.'

This time Runty didn't laugh. 'Do you know what you're lettin' yerself in for, Father?'

Father Barry felt in his pockets for a pack of cigarettes. The pack was crumpled and empty. 'Anybody got a butt?' he asked.

Jimmy offered him a Home Run. 'Union made,' he said.

Father Barry took it and Runty snapped a match for him and held the light, looking at his face as if he had just come across him and was studying his features for the first time.

'You sure you know what yer lettin' yerself in for?' Runty held his question steady like the light.

'No—I don't,' Father Barry admitted. 'But I'm ready to find out.'

Father Barry and Katie left the men at the entrance to the Longdock. When they came down for work at seven-thirty and found nothing to do, what was there left for them except the companionship of the bar? Sometimes when a docker was hurt or they needed an extra hand, Big Mac sent somebody across the street to pull a man or two out of the bar.

Runty, Moose, Luke and Jimmy promised to show up in the church basement—used as an overflow chapel—at eight o'clock that evening. Father Barry hadn't even thought about the question of permission. It had seemed to him the moment for unqualified hospitality. He'd cross the next bridge when he got to St. Timothy's. He'd sit down with the Pastor just before lunch—no, maybe just after. Father Donoghue was a regular trencherman and was always in a better mood after he had eaten. 'How much more Christian and merciful the Pastor is after he's finished a steaming plate of corn beef and cabbage,' Mrs. Harris, their housekeeper, had once remarked, adding to the little repertoire of rectory jokes.

'I'll walk you back to your door,' Father Barry told Katie.

Katie shook her head. 'Thanks, but I'd like to stop in at the church anyway. There's something I want to pray for.'

'For Joey?'

There was some of her father's direct humour in her voice as she said, 'I think it's time I started praying for you.'

Father Barry laughed. 'Y'know, Katie, I was raised on a tough block. In the gang we had, two of the boys got the chair and at least three others are doing time. It almost seems like we had only two choices—to run with the mob or buck for the collar. Lots of those fellows could've gone either way. I fought 'em in the streets before they got into the heavy artillery. I'm not afraid to take them on again, if I have to.'

'I'm getting you into trouble,' Katie said.

'You can say that again,' Father Barry said. 'Every time you step outside the church in a neighbourhood like this, you bump into trouble.'

They were walking into the wind. The cold damp gusts of river air lashed at their faces. The Hudson was the colour of grey chalk, bleak and relentless. Ships were moving across and down river.

11

THE WATERFRONT WESTERN Union has no central office, no teletype machines, no uniformed messenger boys. Without them, news seems to flash around the harbour, from pier to pier, from bar to bar, from tenement to tenement. Each longshoreman approached for the meeting in St. Timothy's was cautioned not to invite anyone else unless he first made sure he was anti-Friendly. But the first leak soon grew to a trickling stream, and finally, in less than an hour, into a torrent of speculation and excitement. The Bohegan docks buzzed with news that Father Barry was calling a protest meeting to look into the job done on Joey Doyle. In the hold the stool-man whose task it was to set the stalks of bananas on the carriers' shoulders whispered into the ears of old Marty Gallagher.

'There's gonna be a meetin' on Joey Doyle in the bottom of St. Tim's t'night. Eight o'clock. Pass the woid along.'

Gallagher, hard-working except when he went on his periodicals, shook his head. He got a tab most of the time and he knew better than to mess with Johnny Friendly.

'Lemme alone. I'm an old man.'

Most of those approached said nothing at all. They just nodded and went on working. Some of them might sound off to a few trusted cronies about the way things were stacked against them, but they weren't going to commit themselves. And what the hell was a Roman collar butting into it for anyway? Nearly all of them were cynical and wondered what the priest was getting out of it. But one in a hundred felt strongly enough about Joey or about the whole stacked deal to take a chance.

Not Pop Doyle, though. When he came over to the Longdock for a beer and a cornbeef sandwich at lunch and heard what Father Barry was up to, he shook his head and muttered through a mouthful of cornbeef, 'I'm ag'in' it. Leave the dead sleep in peace. Ain't we had enough trouble?'

Runty had been on the bottle all morning, drinking on the cuff against his next pay-day. He was reviving again after sleeping off the effects of the wake. 'I don' even begin to feel like a human bean until I'm half gassed.' He laughed, and shrugged off Pop's surrender.

'I never yet seen the bunch that c'n stop Johnny and his respectable friend Weepin' Willie. But I say, hear the Father out. What've ya got to lose?'

'Just your life,' Pop said.

Runty grinned. 'If God wanted me He'd 've taken me a long time ago. I'm on borried time.'

Because he wasn't working and felt defiant, he ordered another thirty-five cent shot for Pop and himself.

'Here's mud in the eye of Willie Givens,' he offered the old, bold toast.

'You shouldn't be sayin' that so loud,' Pop cautioned.

Word of the meeting whipped along the waterfront like the wind from the river. It blew out of the Longdock across the street to Friendly's, along the bar and into the back room where Johnny Friendly was enjoying a high breakfast of pickled pig's feet and his Pale India ale. He heard the news from Charley Malloy who told it to him tentatively, as if in fear of the dark-age practice of destroying bearers of ill tidings. You don't get to be a leader by being frightened, and Johnny Friendly wasn't going to be bugged by any parish priest and a handful of cry-babies. The Monsignor, O'Hare, was a buddy of Willie Givens, always ready to speak glowingly of the Pres at Communion breakfasts and, if worse came to worst, he might be able to get the Monsignor to nudge the Bishop to crack down on this upstart priest's Pastor. But he was willing to bet it would never go that far. Most headlines blow over. Most rank-and-file beefs fall of their own weight.

Just the same, he told Charley, as he went to work on his second pig-knuckle, have somebody case the meeting. Get the names. Maybe frighten 'em a little as they come out. But leave the church alone. 'I don't want to get in bad with my mother.'

It had been left to Charley to decide how to once-over the church meeting. On the way down to the docks he had settled for Terry. It would do the kid good, he figured. Rein him in a little closer to the organization. Put some cabbage in his pocket. Give him a sense of responsibility. Charley had made it because he was an organization man, loyal as well as cute. But Terry was a loner without ambition, believing in nothing and nobody. He had some abilities, like being handy with his fists. He could dance, and make a good appearance when he tried. The boys liked him around because of his brief fame in the ring. But he never seemed to care about cashing in on any of his talents. Even when it had seemed for a short time as if he might have a chance of breaking into the big time, he had acted as if none of that mattered. Charley didn't know why. He just knew that Terry was a moody, go-it-alone, don't-give-a-damn kid who could watch Charley take a grand a week off the docks without ever thinking he could or should have some of the same.

So Charley, wanting to help his kid brother, had begun to throw a few things his way. The Doyle job the night before. Charley never liked it as rough as that, but if Joey had to go, he figured Terry might as well get what benefit there might be in it. Johnny liked the kid from the boxing days, but he wasn't giving anything away for nothing. He had a principle about paying off only for services rendered. It was the only way, Johnny knew, to run an organization.

So the next assignment for Terry, Charley saw, was the church job. Double-o it for Johnny. Actually, Terry was a good choice. Despite the blood relationship. he was known to be outside the mob. And so independent-peculiar that no one would be too surprised what he did. There were even those who thought he was just a touch punchy. It was imperceptible, but maybe it was there at that. A fellow like that could wander into a church and pretend he didn't know exactly what he was doing. And furthermore, Charley felt he could trust Terry. Even if the kid believed in nothing, not even money, and expressed enthusiasm for nothing except his pigeons and his poon, he had a son-father respect that amounted to awe for Charley. When their old man had staggered out on them and the Children's Aid had taken them to some strange barrack-like shelter there had been only Charley to say, 'Don't worry, kid. We'll handle it.'

The atmosphere of the pier loft was leisurely compared to the activity in the hold and on the deck. The closed-in upper floor was piled high with coffee bags, neatly stacked, and cases of olive oil, rolls of hemp, cylinders of crude oil set on pallets to be efficiently moved by the stubby, versatile hi-low trucks. Drivers, checkers, loft handlers worked quietly, expertly; most of them had been here a long time. These were the gravy jobs and every one on this top floor was a solid Friendly man. Johnny was Number One in their book, a square shooter, a guy who never let you down unless you crossed him. 'Johnny Friendly's done a lot of good around here,' you'd hear them say in the loft.

Here pilferage was thought of not as a crime but as a way of life. The loft was a gathering point for cargo from which 10,000 dollar hauls could be made simply by falsifying a single invoice. But a lot of expert handling went on here too. Even the stacking of coffee bags called for skill. A trained man could hoist a 165-pound bag bulging with coffee beans as if it were a child's coloured bean-bag.

Charley Malloy had hopped a hi-low truck cruising down the aisles between the hillocks of cargo. He stepped off when he came to the neatly stacked six-foot mound of coffee bags on which Terry was reclining, absorbed in the latest issue of *Confidential*. Charley raised himself on the outer edge of the bags, enabling him to look over Terry's shoulder.

'Working hard?' he asked.

Terry shrugged and answered without looking around. 'It's a living.' He wriggled his backside even more luxuriously into the space between the coffee bags, and turned the page to admire another beguiling torso. 'Wooo-oof,' he barked.

'You don't mind working once in a while?' Charley persisted.

'I finished the work. I counted all them bags.'

'Excellent,' Charley said. 'But we've got an extra little detail for you. That is, if you don't mind being disturbed or anything.'

Charley climbed up another rung of bags until he was almost on a level with Terry. His voice lowered to its familiar tone, habitually conspiratorial. 'Listen, this priest who took a hinge at the shape this morning, he and this Doyle girl are getting up a meeting over at the church tonight. St. Tim's. We want a run-down on it. You know, the names and numbers of all the players.'

Terry was studying a spectacular Latin type in a lascivious pose. 'Chiquita,' he read the caption longingly.

'Yeah,' said Charley. 'That means small. There's nothing small about that tomato.' He looked more closely over Terry's shoulder. Then he remembered his mission. 'Put that damn thing down a minute. Only one thing on your mind. Now listen to me. We need someone to cover this church meeting. You're nominated.'

Terry lowered the magazine reluctantly and raised himself on one elbow. This was the trouble with letting someone do you favours. You had to do favours back.

'Why me, Charley? I don't wanna go down in no church. I'd feel funny goin' in there.'

'You've got a nice little job here,' Charley said. 'I want Johnny to know you appreciate it. Now all you've got to do is plant your can in the back pew and keep your ears open. What's so hard?'

Terry frowned. How could he explain? To someone who had

drive and ambition and wanted a million bucks in a deposit box it couldn't be explained.

'It's stoolin', Charley. Don't you see? I'd just be stoolin' for you.'

Charley started to light a cigarette in exasperation.

'No smoking,' Terry said, thumbing toward the sign.

'Yeah, I know,' Charley said, and continued to draw until he was sure he had a good light. Rules were made for the other guys, for suckers. Smart guys made their own as they went along. 'Let me explain you something about stooling,' Charley said. 'Stooling is when you rat on your friends, the guys you're with.'

'Yeah, yeah,' Terry grunted his impatience.

Charley decided to drop the theorizing. 'When Johnny needs a favour, don't try to figure it out, just do it.'

Terry had picked up his magazine, and now he flipped a page and pretended not to listen.

'What right has this priest got poking his nose in our business?' Charley said, thinking this might be the pitch. It had always been a persuasive argument on the waterfront. He nudged Terry's elbow gently. 'Now go on—join the congregation.'

Terry's sigh was exaggerated. 'Okay, okay. Only this is the last thing I do for ya, Charley. I don't want nuthin' from Johnny except enough work t' keep me in coffee and doughnut money, an' I figure he owes me that much even if I don't run all these goddamn errands for 'im. He already made enough outa me to . . .'

'What's so hard?' Charley said again. 'You go in a church and you sit down. It's open to the public, free of charge. We don't want trouble. We just want to know what they're saying about us. That's only reasonable.'

'Charley,' Terry said, almost tenderly, 'you are the most reasonable son of a bitch I know. Now go away and leave me to my work.' He turned another page and gave himself up to an undraped, drooping-eyed blonde who beckoned.

Charley rode another hi-low back to the spiral staircase leading to the main floor of the pier. Terry was a broody, stubborn, hard-to-figure kid, he was thinking, but when the temperamental smoke blew away he usually did what Charley wanted.

12

WHEN HE STRODE into the overflow chapel in the church basement and found only a scattered handful of longshoremen on hand for the meeting, Father Barry felt a twinge of disappointment. There weren't more than a dozen, and with many sitting alone and leaving seats gaping between them as if not wanting the others to know they were there, the group looked even smaller. Father Barry recognized Runty, who made his presence felt in a chesty, defiant, yet sceptical way; and Moose and Jimmy and Luke. Sitting alone behind them was Katie, cool and reserved on the outside, but watching everything with a smouldering intensity that could be felt in the room, embarrassingly, insistently.

Father Barry had scrapped and scrambled all day not only to prepare himself for this meeting, but to inveigle permission to hold it at all. At first the Pastor, Father Donoghue, had been annoyed with his curate for leaping in with an invitation to longshoremen without first consulting him.

But it was an emergency, Father Barry had insisted, the sort of thing a waterfront church should be ready to jump into with both feet. Father Donoghue hadn't been so sure. President Willie Givens was known to be a good friend of Monsignor O'Hare. Might this meeting not offend Givens, and therefore the Monsignor? And if the Monsignor went to the Bishop? The Pastor stood in pretty well with the Bishop, Father Barry reminded him. Yes, Father Donoghue said, and I'd like to remain so. We have a serious concern with these men's souls as individuals, he pointed out. But is it our function to call them together as a social body? Aren't ,we overstepping our boundaries?

Father Donoghue asked his questions mildly enough. He was a pious, kindly man, sympathetic to the poor who made up so much of his parish, although not unmindful of the practicalities.

In answer, Father Barry quoted a statement of Pope Pius about the error of thinking the authority of the church is limited to religious matters. 'Social problems are of concern to the conscience and salvation of man,' Father Barry had roughly translated the Holy Father. 'It looks to me as if one of our parishioners was murdered for trying to establish a more human and moral social order on the docks. Does his own parish church say "it's none of our business"? Isn't that exactly what the Pope is talking about, brought right down here to the docks of Bohegan?'

· Father Donoghue sucked on his lips, said he would take the matter under consideration and let his eager, hot-tempered curate know by mid-afternoon. At three-thirty, with a daring that surprised even himself, he gave Father Barry a green light without first consulting the Bishop. His only qualification was that Father Barry made it clear that the dock-workers were simply using the church's facilities, but that St. Tim's would not be responsible for any decisions or actions issuing from the meeting.

'Any way you say,' Father Barry grabbed it. The main thing was, the meeting would not be cancelled, as he had feared when he first looked at Father Donoghue's undecided face. From that point on, Father Barry figured, he could play by ear. Eventually he might have to angle some way he could get a favourable nod from the Bishop.

Once the meeting was set, Father Barry called Frank Doyle, the old cop, to drop in for a little chat. Doyle was on the fence the first half hour. He wanted that pension and he was afraid he had already unburdened himself too freely to Katie. It wasn't until Father Barry promised him professional secrecy that Frank Doyle let go. After he got talking he found it a relief. Doyle told the priest it was on ice from the start that Donnelly's detectives would close the books on the Doyle case without a coroner's verdict of murder. Donnelly had no other choice. The whole Bohegan administration was so deeply involved with the waterfront rackets that you could say the Mayor, the Police Commissioner and the union dock bosses were partners.

Frank Doyle talked to Father Barry for over an hour. The priest took notes but filed it as the story of Mike X. Doyle told him of some earlier Bohegan murders, and of police blackout of clues and evidence. He agreed that pressing the case of his nephew was an ideal opening wedge for a better deal on the docks. But he had seen too much to believe that the priest, for all his good intentions, could get anywhere. The line-up against him, from the mob, through the stevedore companies, to City Hall had headed off tougher competition. Just the same, it took a load off his mind and his conscience to open up to the priest, almost like confession.

Father Barry thanked the ageing Sergeant for leading him deeper into the jungle of the Bohegan waterfront.

Frank Doyle shrugged. A lot of people knew the story. But that's as far as it went. 'As to getting much help from longshoremen themselves, I have me doubts. You take your dock worker, Father, he's a funny fellow. He's as tough as they come personally, but he seems to accept things as he finds them on the waterfront. Like me own brother. He's suspicious of any outsider and especially if they come in and try to help him. You better remember that, if you don't want your feelings hurt. Or your heart broken. Your dock worker, he knows how intrenched the union bosses are, and how they got the shippers and the police behind 'em. So he figures why jeopardize what little I got to point out some abuses that aren't going to be changed anyway. He knows there are too many ready to take his job if he bucks the dictatorship in the union. Or testifies. That's why this waterfront investigation is having such tough sledding. Sure it's lovely to swear on a Bible and get up and tell the truth, but who's going to look out for you once you step down? You've put your head in a noose. That's how the boys on the docks look at this new investigation. And you can hardly blame them. Why, there was a waterfront investigation in New York a couple of years ago, where it turned out in six Brooklyn locals every office was held by a member of the Genotta family, stooges for Benasio, and that's a fact. The investigation winds up with a demand for a new honest election. So what happens? You guessed it, Father. All the Genottas won the same offices all over again. See what I mean, Father?'

Sergeant Doyle laughed, in a special way the Irish have of laughing at the things that hurt them most.

By the end of the day, after Father Barry had been gathering facts from as many sources as possible, he was increasingly interested on the forthcoming investigation. A rank-and-file trade union revolt seemed impossible until public opinion was aroused and the evils spotlighted in the press in a way that would make it difficult for Johnny Friendly and his respectable supporters to continue running the show with medieval contempt for opposition. As the picture sharpened into focus through the busy afternoon, Father Barry began to plot the course of his usefulness.

Entering the basement chapel, Father Barry felt as keyed up as a boxer going down the aisle to his first main event. Father Vincent, a portly man of thirty-five, followed him in. Harry Vincent admired Father Barry, but he thought he was inviting ruin to a promising career by offending the Catholic lay powers in Bohegan and around the harbour.

'Pete, you've got a lot on the ball,' Father Vincent said, trying to be helpful when he heard about the meeting. 'Why throw your chances away on a wild-goose chase? Social justice is fine, but if I were you I'd wait until I had a little more rank. Pete, you're looking for trouble.'

Pete Barry's answer had been quick and impatient. 'That's right. And it's about time.'

Harry Vincent was a good priest and a good fellow, Father Barry thought, but he had carried into the priesthood some of his father's conception of material success-if-you-play-your-cards-right. Vincent senior had been a nominal Catholic who had been rather shocked at his son's decision to attach himself to the hierarchy of Rome rather than to that of H. J. Vincent & Sons, chain grocery-store merchants. Harry, Jr., was determined to prove to his father the rightness of his choice by eventually becoming a bishop. That was something H. J., Sr., could understand. Young Vincent had recognized that his colleague Pete Barry had the brains and the drive to wind up at the top, perhaps at the Chancellery—familiarly known to the younger priests as 'the powerhouse'—and it disturbed him to see his associate throw away his chance on an unprecedented longshoremen's meeting in the church. So it was with quizzical aloofness that he followed Father Barry into the sparsely attended meeting.

When Father Barry faced these men in their windbreakers and coarse wool shirts, some of them with their faces still grimy from moving cargo, he realized there was no sense of welcome, of gratitude for his effort, or even trust. Instead, he felt them looking at him through a silent, invisible wall of suspicion. He stood in front of the simple altar and looked out into the long bare basement room which had only the most basic adornments of a place of worship. The walls were of plaster, and the lighting was dim, as though the meeting did not want to call undue attention to itself.

He began in his rapid-fire, slightly nasal, East Bohegan way: 'Well, uh, I thought thee'd be more of you here, but we, uh, the Romans found out what a handful could do—if it's the right handful.'

He paused for some response, for some sign that he was on the target, but the men just looked up at him and waited. Go on, Father, play your hand, the poker faces seemed to be saying. Father Barry looked across them to Katie, in one of the rear pews. Even she seemed to be waiting, as if no longer sure what she had gotten him into.

So he plunged: 'Uh, I'm just a potato eater, but isn't it simple as one-two-three? One—the working conditions are bad. You got 40,000 men competing for less than 20,000 jobs. You've got a union that works against you instead of for you. Two—conditions are bad because the union is run by a mob—am I right?—and the mob does the hiring. Two-thirds of your hiring bosses have got criminal records. And three—the only way you can break the mob is to stop letting them get away with murder. When they knock off one of you they keep the rest of you in line. You've been letting them get away with murder.'

He looked at each one of them and saw in their faces only sullen resentment, They had come for help and his neck was way out to help them, but the waterfront silence was fathomless. Even a product of Bohegan who seemed to talk their language began to feel lost in the depths of their reticence.

'Now listen, boys,' the priest sounded angry, 'if one of you will just answer one question we'd have a start. And, uh, that question is: Who killed Joey Doyle?'

He tried to catch the eyes of his listeners again, but not one of them would be trapped. Moose was staring into his big lap and Runty leaned back and pulled his chin down as if sleeping off a drunk. Luke half turned in his seat to study the bare wall and Jimmy ran one hand over the knuckles of the other in front of his face. Who killed who was a taboo question on the waterfront. Father Barry should have known that.

In the silence Father Barry had cracked a match alive to light a cigarette. He looked over his little audience angrily. By God, if he was going to get into hot water with that Monsignor O'Hare and maybe even the Bishop, he'd like a little co-operation. Father Barry thought of Sergeant Doyle's words, 'Those dock workers are funny fellows . . .' and threw his hook again:

'Not one of you has a line on who killed Joey Doyle?'

The silence became oppressive. The wooden pews creaked as men shifted weight self-consciously.

'I've got a hunch every one of you could tell us something about it,' Father Barry said.

The men pressed their lips together and their eyes avoided his face.

'All right, then answer me this,' Father Barry tried again. 'How can we call ourselves Christians and protect these murderers with our silence?'

Silence seemed not only to hang in the room but to swell as if it were feeding on itself, wave on wave of silence.

'Can't you see?' Father Barry was shouting now. 'On this water-front, in a supposedly Catholic neighbourhood, murder has become a commonplace. There's something lousy rotten on this waterfront. And the entire parish—all of you—are conspiring in it.'

His loud, harsh voice, not so different in timbre from Johnny Friendly's, trailed away. In the silence the creaking of a door in the rear of the room was very loud. It was Terry Malloy, entering with an exaggerated rolling of his shoulders. He slumped down into the back pew just as Katie was turning to confront Jimmy.

'Jimmy Sharkey, you were Joey's best friend. How can you just sit there and not be saying anything?'

Jimmy started confidently. 'Sure, and I'll always think of him as my best friend. But . . . but . . .' He lowered his head again and was silent, withdrawing into the group apathy again.

Katie pushed the palms of her hands against her face and shook her head slightly. Jimmy saw the gesture of futility and felt miserable, helpless, ashamed. But what could he do?

Terry Malloy was slouched in his seat, leaning back with his hands clasped behind his neck. He could not have found a more appropriate posture for the scorn, superiority and boredom he was feeling at having to oversee these proceedings. A screwball priest and a bunch of meatballs. Lousing themselves up on the waterfront so that even a crummy loan shark wouldn't look at them. Charley would want to know their names. Hell, he didn't like stooling for anybody, even Charley, but if these clowns were stupid enough to throw themselves into the pot, maybe they had it coming to them. Just the same, Terry wished he wasn't here. He dreamily saw himself lying under a palm tree with a bottle of rum and a Latin broad ready to love him up like the one in the magazine. That priest should know what I'm thinkin', he thought to himself with an inward, satisfied smile.

Runty Nolan glared across the empty rows at Terry and then muttered audibly to Moose, 'Who invited him t' this party?' Moose looked around and expressed his feelings with a big-shouldered shrug.

Terry leaned back, looking smug. He felt out of place.

'Anybody in the harbour is welcome here,' Father Barry said, rebuking Runty. Then he spoke directly to Terry.

'I'm trying to find out just what happened to Joey Doyle. Maybe you can help.'

Terry kept his hands behind his neck and shook his head slightly, still wearing the mask of scorn and boredom.

'The brother of Charley the Gent,' Runty stage-whispered to Moose. 'They'll help us get to the bottom of the river.'

Terry had been instructed not to open his mouth. But he had a strong feeling about anyone's mentioning his brother. It was a mixture of pride and shame. So now he could not resist saying, 'You better keep Charley outa this.'

Runty never could keep his trap shut. It was an irrepressible, old-country trait, like never backing away from anyone, regardless of size. 'You don't think he'd be helpful?' he turned and asked the kid.

Terry hesitated a moment and smiled at what he felt was a smart answer. 'Ask him yourself, why don't you?'

'Maybe I will,' Runty said. 'One of these days.'

Terry snickered, and leaned back like a winner. 'One of these days.'

Katie, half-turned in her seat, had been watching the latecomer curiously. She recognized him as the boy who had given her the work-tab after roughly blocking Pop out to grab it away from him. And now, studying his face, she remembered him from earlier days, at parochial school on Pulaski Street before she went away to Marygrove. She remembered the Sisters shaking their heads at him, forever calling him a 'bad boy'. Then he had been sent away some place—a Catholic corrective school, she vaguely remembered. She had been going on thirteen then, and his swarthy, handsome, dirty, evil presence wasn't easy to define in the haze of early adolescence. He had been a dark spot to be avoided; that was almost all Katie could remember of him.

'Now *listen!*' Father Barry snapped them back to attention. 'Don't kid me. I've been talkin' to people about this thing all day. You know who the pistols are. Are you goin' to keep still until they cut you down one by one. Are you? Are you?'

Because Nolan had spoken up, and had a reputation for guts, Father Barry took a step toward him. 'Hey, Nolan, Nolan, how about you?'

'One thing you've got to understand, Father,' Runty said. 'On the docks we've always been D 'n D.'

'D 'n D?' Father Barry hadn't heard that one.

Runty nodded. 'Deef 'n dumb. No matter how much we hate the torpedoes, we don't rat.'

All the men nodded their heads or muttered an almost inaudible 'Tha's right, Father.'

Here was the nub of it, here was the code. Father Barry felt like a man trying to tear down a cemented stone barricade with his bare hands.

'Boys, get smart,' he shouted. 'I know you're getting pushed around, but there's one thing we've got in this country and that's ways of fighting back. If you'll use 'em. Like this investigation they're trying to get going. Sure you don't like the State butting in, I know all about that. But think of it this way, the State—which is after all only you and you and everybody else—is giving you a chance to get something out into the open that's been festering in the dark for years and years. You stand up and testify for what you

132

know is right and decent and democratic and Christian against what you know is wrong and evil and stinks like dead fish floating at the edge of the river. You do that and you start to make a new climate, a new soil where honest-to-God trade unionism can start to take root for a change. Boys, break the Joey Doyle case and you begin to break the power of the mob. Break the power of the mob and you begin to see a little daylight on the kind of job security set-up you deserve down here. You say ratting. What's ratting to them is telling the truth for you. Now can't you see that? Can't you see that?'

Again the same crestfallen, self-ashamed silence hung over the room. Father Barry lowered his hands, defeated. He started to raise his hands and then dropped them again in a gesture of despair. He looked over the heads of the silent men to Katie, as if to ask: Where do we go from here? She tightened the scarf around her neck and stared back at him.

Terry was leaning back with his hands still clasped behind his neck, enjoying the priest's discomfort. He could have told this round-collar joker how the men would clam up. It made him smile to think of this bunch of losers making trouble for real men like Johnny Friendly and his brother Charley.

There was a prolonged, awkward pause after Father Barry stopped talking. Father Vincent, who had shaken his head several times with impatience, seized this moment to take over the meeting. Smiling at Father Barry, and with a benign voice, he said, 'This seems to be just about all we can do at this time. I think you will agree with that, Father. And so may we close with a few words from St. Matthew, "Come unto me, all ye who are heavily burdened and I . . ."

Father Vincent's benediction was never completed. At this moment he was drowned out by an explosive wooden thunder outside on the sidewalk above the basement window level.

'Baseball bats,' Runty said. 'That must be our friends.'

Everybody was on his feet. Joey Doyle was forgotten now.

'There's a back way out through the inner courtyard,' Father Barry shouted. 'You better go home in pairs. Two's is two, you know.'

A number of men hurried to the side door to the inner courtyard.

'If they lay a hand on any of you I'll see they go to jail, I swear it,' Father Barry shouted.

'Fat chance,' somebody grunted.

'I'm walkin' out the front way,' Runty boasted. 'Let 'em have me. I don't hide from them bums.'

'I got a wife and kids,' Moose shouted. 'If I'm laid up they don't eat. I'm duckin' out the back.'

'And then you better run like hell,' Jimmy Sharkey said.

Outside the pounding of baseball bats on the sidewalk rose to a frightful crescendo—boom-boom-boom-boom-boom-boom. Inside people were shouting against the din. 'This way, Tim. Hey! C'mon, hurry . . .'

Father Barry was trying to restore order, but the group was out of his control now. Truck Amon and his goons had taken the play away from him.

'What did I tell you—sticking your neck out?' Father Vincent shouted at Father Barry. 'This is a police problem. Let them try to handle it.'

'These fellers need help, Harry,' Father Barry insisted.

'Okay, okay,' Father Vincent yelled back. 'I hope you're ready for the consequences.'

Father Barry laughed. 'I'm gonna go out and get those baseball bats.' But when he stepped outside, the Friendly muscle seemed to have vanished into the shadowy dampness of the night. He peered into the darkness, puzzled and disconcerted. Down the street from the park the blur of red neon lights beckoned men to drink, and to forget, to drink and to dummy up.

13

WHEN FATHER BARRY returned, the basement chapel was empty. During the moment he had stepped outside, there had been a brief, charged, almost wordless meeting between Katie and Terry Malloy that had brought them together and hurried them out into the night before she could focus her mind on what was happening.

Watching her, Terry had been quick to notice how she stood uncertainly at the side door, too frightened at the pounding of the bats to be able to follow Moose and Jimmy out when they had called her. In that instant of hesitation, Terry had grabbed her arm. 'Not that way. C'mon. I'll get ya out.' Obeying the rough grasp of his hand on her arm she had almost automatically started running along with him, out the back door and up the stairway to the main level, then through an emergency exit and down a fire escape that led into an alley.

They hurried across the street into Pulaski Park. A clammy mist floated over the empty benches and curled around the neglected, be-pigeoned statue of the old General, erected by the Polish Society just after the first World War. In the darkness the riding lights of the ships on the river were indistinct yellow sparklers.

It was not until they entered the park that Katie became conscious of his tight grip on her arm and pulled away.

'Thanks,' she said. 'Why did you do it?'

He shrugged. 'Why not?'

She looked back at the dark outlines of the church. 'Baseball bats!' She shuddered.

'Yeah, they play pretty rough,' Terry said.

They were following the central path through the block-square park that opened on River Street. She looked at him, puzzled. He was dark, with high cheek bones, and a strange puffiness around his left eye. He would have had a fine, Roman nose if it had not been dented in the bridge. He looked deliberately disreputable. He had a cocky, rolling, yet graceful way of walking. His manner was care-less, arrogant, uninvolved. Oh, she knew the type, hated the type.

'Which side are you with?' she asked suddenly.

He raised his shoulders cynically and tapped his chest. 'Me? I'm with me—Terry.'

She turned away from him. What was she doing out here, in a park, alone, with a—punk, Moose had called him that. 'I'll be able to get home all right now,' she said.

She started along the path that led through the middle of the park, past the forgotten Polish General who brooded over the empty benches with sad, metallic eyes. Terry followed behind her. Casually, with his hands pushed deep into his pockets, he trailed her. She glanced back questioningly and quickened her steps. What was he up to, protecting or pursuing her? Stay out of the parks after dark, her father always had warned her.

Near the River Street entrance a shabby form rose out of the darkness at her from a stone bench. She gave a short shrill cry and ran a few steps backwards, almost into the arms of Terry.

'A dime. Ya gotta dime? A dime for a cupa cawfee?'

The figure had one arm and a foul whisky breath. It seemed not only his breath but his whole, ragged, unkempt body was saturated with cheap whisky, as if he had slept and wallowed in it. Now she recognized him, Mutt Murphy, the wreckage of a human being who had staggered into the wake.

'Cawfee . . .' Mutt was cackling, his trembling hand outstretched. 'One little dime ya don't need . . .'

'Some coffee,' Terry laughed as he made the gesture of downing a shot of whisky. He raised his hand as if to slap Mutt away. 'G'wan, beat it, ya bum.'

Ignoring him, Mutt moved several steps closer to Katie, until his sodden face was staring into hers. The look and stench of him was horrible, yet Katie could not bring herself to back away. He screwed up his eyes as if trying to draw her into focus through the fog.

'I know you . . . You're Katie Doyle . . .' Quickly he crossed himself. 'Your brother's a saint. Oney one ever tried t' get me me compensation . . .'

'C'mon,' Terry said, pushing him away. 'Let's get outa here.'

Being pushed was so familiar to Mutt Murphy that he was no longer even aware of the indignity. Pointing a wavering, accusing finger at Terry, he started to say, 'You remember, Terry. You was there the night Joey was . . .'

'Aah, for Christ' sake quit ya gassin',' Terry said. 'Disappear! You're botherin' the lady.'

'You remember,' Mutt persisted, 'ya bumped inta me when ya was walkin' . . .'

'Yeah, yeah,' Terry said, stepping in fast. He reached into his pocket for a handful of change. 'Here's a couple of shots for ya. Go have yourself a ball.'

Mutt stopped talking to admire the coins in his hand. Terry had scooped them out of his pocket without even bothering to count them—quarters, dimes, nickels. Mutt stared at them incredulously. 'I can't believe it. A small fortune.' He reached down into his frayed jacket and pulled out a little tobacco pouch into which he deposited the coins one by one. Then withdrawing a few feet he raised his cap to Katie with incongruous formality.

'Goo-luck, Katie. Lord've mercy on Joey.'

Then he screwed up his face in an ugly grimace and his voice came out full and angry for the first time. 'You can't buy me.' He glared at Terry. 'You're still a bum!'

He staggered off along the path they had taken, stiff-legged, his chin upraised with a last display of dignity.

Terry looked after him, relieved that Mutt hadn't mentioned the pigeon. Lucky for him that the one witness who had stumbled on to Terry's rôle in the Doyle job was a goofed-up sour-belly that nobody would take seriously. He turned to Katie with what he considered his most debonair, light-hearted manner. 'I ask you to look at what's callin' *me* a bum.'

Katie watched the shaggy figure of Mutt fading back into the mist. At the statue in the middle of the park he seemed to be trying to engage General Pulaski in conversation.

'Everybody loved Joey,' Katie said, as if to herself. 'From the little kids to the old rummies.'

Terry was standing there wondering. Who boxed me into this? What do I have to be tailing after Joey's sister for? Last tomato in the world I oughta be seen with. 'Yeah,' Terry said.

She turned her head and looked at him a moment before asking, 'Did you know him very well?'

Terry tried to keep his tone casual. 'Well,' he shrugged, 'you know how it is. He got around.'

Katie frowned. She looked back along the path that seemed to have swallowed Mutt. 'What did that poor man mean just now when he said . . .'

'Aah, don't pay no attention to him.' Terry waved the rummy aside. 'He's fallin' down drunk all the time. Just a juice-head. Talks to himself. Don't pay no attention.'

She shivered slightly and pulled her cloth coat closer around her. 'It's cold. I'd better go home.'

She started at a rapid pace, making it clear that she was walking apart from him. But he loped alongside, drawn along with her. She veered away.

A *nice* girl, Terry thought. How long had it been since he had walked with a *nice* girl? Twenty to one a virgin even. Look how cool and quiet she walks. Melva would have been all over him. The park was a regular boudoir for Melva. What did you say to a nice girl? How do you break the ice? How do you get around to touching a nice girl?

'You don' hafta be scared of me,' he told her. 'I'm not gonna bite ya.' He had closed the gap between them to within a foot or so. She kept her eyes straight ahead. 'Wha's the matter?' He kept at her. 'They don' let you walk with fellas where you've been?'

She tossed her head slightly. She didn't want to be a prude. He was coarse, a roughneck, but he hadn't really done anything wrong.

'You know how the Sisters are,' she said.

She had lovely skin, smooth and fresh, like a—his clumsy mind groped—like a pink rose. He had noticed how her skin glowed in the light of the church basement. Rose hell, she was like a full fresh peach in the market at four-thirty in the morning. Sometimes he'd stop on his way home from the bars, pick up the best looking fruit he could find and take it back to his room under the roof of the tenement. Breakfast, courtesy of the Bohegan market.

'You training to be a nun or something?' he asked suddenly.

'No,' she said seriously, 'it's just a regular college.'

They were passing the section near the River Street entrance laid out as a children's playground. Impulsively Terry sat down on one of the swings.

'Care to join me in a swing?' His manner now was half courteous, half teasing.

'No, thank you,' she said gravely. 'It's getting very late.' But she lingered uncertainly.

He let himself swing a few feet back and forth. 'A regular college, huh? It's funny, I thought it was kinda like a nunnery.'

She smiled. 'It's just run by the nuns. The Sisters of St. Anne.'

'Yeah? Where is that? Where you stay?'

'In Tarrytown.'

'Tarrytown?' He wrinkled his nose. 'I'll bet that's a real corny joint. How far is that?'

'Just up the river about thirty miles. Out in the country.'

He made a face again. 'I don't go for the country. I was in a training camp once. The crickets made me nervous. What a racket!'

She laughed, for the first time. She was prettier than he had thought. His first impression had been of a nice-featured, rather plain girl. 'You know you've got a real sweet laugh,' he said, 'real sweet.'

The line, she thought. The roughneck under wraps. But there was something about him. Or was it simply that she hadn't been let out very often with unauthorized boys? That's what the Mother Superior called them at Marygrove. Unauthorized boys. She was a little frightened and excited. It was no better than a pick-up.

He swung back and forth slowly, a little too sure of himself. 'You come down here often?'

'Vacations,' she said. 'I haven't been here since Easter. I was away for the summer as a counsellor.'

'That's nice,' he said. 'And you spend all your time up there just learnin' stuff, huh?'

She nodded with a small smile. 'There's a lot of stuff to learn. I want to be a teacher.'

'A teacher!' he said. 'Wow. You know personally I admire brains. My brother Charley is a very brainy chap. He had a couple of years of college. He can talk as good as any lawyer. Very brainy.'

'It isn't just brains,' Katie said. 'It's, well—how you use them.'

Terry looked at her and nodded, impressed. Charley was brainy, all right, but he never talked like this. 'Yeah, yeah,' he said, 'I get your thought.'

His effort to look like a thinker made her smile. 'Now I *have* to be going,' she said. 'Pop'll be doing handstands. I'll be all right from here.'

She started walking toward the River Street entrance. There was a high iron railing on each side of the path leading to the street. Beyond them the banana boat was still being unloaded. The sound of the groaning winches carried to them. Fog horns moaned on the river.

Terry had jumped up from the swing to follow her. He knew Charley would chew him out, but he could not stop following her.

'You know, I've seen you lots of times before,' he said. Remember parochial school here on Palooskie Street? Seven, eight years ago. Your hair came down in . . .'

'Braids?'

Terry nodded. 'Looked like a hunk o' rope. You had wires on your teeth an' . . .'

'I thought I'd never get them off.'

'. . . an' glasses, pimples . . .' He suddenly interrupted himself with laughter. 'Man, ya was really a mess.'

Katie kept on walking. 'I can get home all right now.'

'Don't get sore, don't get sore now.' Terry trotted after her. 'I was just kiddin' ya a little bit. All I'm tryin' to tell ya is—well, ya grew up very nice.'

'Thank you.'

She tried to walk ahead of him but he stayed abreast of her. She was so quiet and *nice*. The word *nice* kept beating in his head.

'You don't remember me, do ya?'

'Not at first,' she said, 'but tonight I began to . . .'

He pointed proudly to his dented nose. 'By the nose?' He strutted a little. 'Some people just got faces that stick in your mind.'

'I remember you were in trouble all the time,' Katie said.

Terry was pleased. 'Now ya got me. Boy, the way those Sisters used t' whack me. Crack! It's a wonder I wasn't punchy by the time I was twelve.' He laughed. 'They thought they was gonna beat an education into me, but I foxed 'em!'

Katie looked at him as if she understood not only the young street hoodlum, but the whole foul-mouthed street-corner set she had watched grow up from ragged little boys dodging the cars and the blows of bigger boys. 'Maybe they just didn't know how to handle you.'

Terry was enjoying the turn of conversation. He was feinting her with his question to make her lead, 'How would you've done it?'

'With a little more patience and kindness,' Katie said. 'You know what makes people mean and difficult? When other people don't care enough about them.'

While she was talking Terry had raised an imaginary violin to his chin and started to hum a nasal, mocking version of 'Hearts and Flowers'.

'All right, laugh,' she said firmly.

'Patience and kindness,' he said. 'Now I heard everything.'

'And what's so wrong with patience and kindness?' she asked angrily.

'Aah—what—are ya kiddin' me?' Terry said.

'Why should I?' Katie asked. She looked at him so directly that Terry turned his eyes away, disturbed.

'Come on,' he said, 'I'd better get you home.'

They were walking along the high iron railing at the eastern boundary of the park. They could hear the river washing along the bank beyond them in the darkness. Terry felt good to be walking beside her. Right now he didn't give a damn what Charley thought.

'Ya see, I'm not gonna let ya walk home alone,' he explained. 'There's too many guys around here with only one thing on their mind.'

They were both silent then, and Katie followed him with quiet grace. He stopped abruptly. 'Am I going to see ya again?'

Katie looked at him with a guileless, blue-eyed expression unlike anything he had known. 'What for?' she asked simply.

Terry paused, shaken by her frankness, by her—the word eluded him—purity. He lifted his shoulders in a characteristic shrug. 'I don't know,' he admitted. 'But are ya?'

In the same gentle, matter-of-fact tone as before, Katie said, 'I really don't know.'

This was a new one, cool and refined, and yet on the level and warm. He walked ahead of her and turned to see if she was following. 'C'mon,' he beckoned.

She hesitated, with a tiny, mysterious smile that baffled him. When she walked slowly toward him, it seemed to him if she were floating in his direction.

They walked along silently, full of their own thoughts, listening to the river sounds. At the end of the next block, Katie said, 'Thank you. It's only around the corner now. I'll say good night.'

'It's been—nice talkin' to ya.' Polite conversation was like an awkward, sticky wad in Terry's mouth.

She smiled at him again, faintly, and an imperceptible shudder went through him. It didn't seem possible that the barest suggestion of a smile could communicate so much, patience and kindness and the far echo of physical love. Or was he only guessing and wishing as she hurried on? With a wry, pained look on his face he watched her melt away from him. Then he punched his right fist into the palm of his left hand so hard that it stung. 'God damn,' he said to himself out loud. 'God damn.'

The moment Pop heard Katie's footsteps in the hall he grabbed the knob from the inside and threw the door open. He was boiling mad. Having Katie up at Marygrove had been a strong rope to hang on to. It justified the back-breaking work, the anxious mornings in the shape-up and all he had to take from Big Mac.

'C'mere,' he said to Katie. With his braces hanging down over his pants and his upper body stooped in its dirty white long underwear shirt, he led the way from the kitchen to the cell-like bedroom. On the bed, next to Toesie, Katie's alley cat, was a small suitcase that had been packed in furious, careless haste.

'Ye're all packed,' Pop yelled. 'An' here's yer bus ticket. Ye're on yer way back to the nuns.'

'Pop, I'm not ready to go back yet,' Katie said.

Pop cursed privately, under his breath. 'Katie, for years we pushed dimes 'n quarters into a cookie jar t' keep ya up there with the Sisters, to keep ya from things like I just seen out the winder. Me own daughter arm-in-arm with Terry Malloy.'

'He was only trying to help me, Pop. There was—there was a little trouble down at the church . . .'

'I could of told ya,' Pop said.

'. . . and he was nice enough to help me get home.'

'Nice enough!' Pop shouted. 'Jesus, Mary 'n Joseph. You know who this Terry is?'

'Not exactly. Who is he, Pop?'

'Who is he?' Pop mimicked in an angry falsetto. 'The kid brother of Charley the Gent, that's all he is. Now go ahead, ask me who

Charley the Gent is. Johnny Friendly's right-hand man and a butcher in a camel's hair coat.'

Katie was stroking the ugly, heavily pregnant Toesie. 'Are you trying to tell me Terry is too?'

'I ain't tryin' t' tell ya he's Little Lord what's-his-name.'

'Sure he tried to act tough,' Katie said, 'the way they all do. But there's something in his eyes . . .'

'Somethin' in his eyes.' Pop's voice could be heard all the way down through the four floors of the tenement. 'Hold your hats, brother, here we go again. You think he's one of those cases you're always draggin' in and feelin' sorry for. Like that litter of kittens. The only one she wants to keep has six toes and it's cockeyed to boot. Look at her—the lazy bum!'

'This place would be crawling with rats if it wasn't for Toesie,' Katie insisted.

Pop, in quieter moments, had boasted about the hunting abilities of their odd-looking pet, but he was in no mood to admit anything. 'If only I knew what it was in ya that keeps pullin' you toward these goddamn misfits,' he went on shouting.

'Pop,' Katie tried to interrupt.

'Six-toed, cross-eyed cats! Well, don't think this Terry Malloy is any six-toed cock-eyed pussycat. He's a bum. Johnny Friendly owned him when he was a fighter. And when Johnny rings the bell he still goes into action and don't ya forget it.'

'He asked if he could see me again,' Katie said, drifting along some channel of her own.

Pop's anger propelled him forward, a taut, livid figure of wrath. 'See this arm . . .' He stuck his thin, stringy-muscled arm in front of Katie's face. The pitch of his anger made both his voice and the arm tremble. 'This arm's two inches longer 'n the other one. That's years of workin' and sweatin', liftin' and swingin' a hook. And every time I heisted a box or a coffee bag I says to myself—this is fer Katie, so she c'n be a teacher or somethin' decent . . .'

Katie put a restraining hand on his shoulder. 'Pop . . .' But he pushed her away. 'I promised your Mom, Katie.'

The sudden anger had swept through him and passed by, leaving an old, tired man full of aches and pains and disappointments. Katie thought of all the mornings he had pulled on the same worn work clothes and gone down to the pier, in frost-bite weather and suffocating summer heat, accepting the lowly hatch work when the hiring boss favourites copped all the rest. Lifting machine tools, bananas, hemp and bags of coffee, cocoa, cement . . . Lifting and waiting and borrowing and cutting down his smokes for Katie's education money. Katie could see how the years had worked their erosion in his face, in his fleshless chest and his stooped shoulders.

She put his arms around him, kissed his stubble cheek and said softly, 'Pop, don't think I'm not grateful for all you've done, for giving me the chance and keeping me away from all this.' She kissed him again, but hurriedly, as if to prepare him for what she had to say.

She backed away from him, for she knew his anger was quick and violent, especially when it was tied up with his ideas of right and wrong. She had felt the sting of it on her cheek when she was younger. 'I'm going to stay, Pop. I'm going to keep on trying to find out who's guilty for Joey . . .'

'You ain't gonna go to no more of them crazy meetin's,' Pop raised his voice. 'That Father Barry oughta have his head examined, encouragin' ya, stirrin' everybody up like that. For what—so Moose, or Jimmy or somebody else winds up in the river with a pair of cement shoes?'

He was shouting now, temper-shaken, frustrated, sorrow-racked. Afraid that tears might squeeze into his eyes, he stomped to the ice-box for a beer.

'Be a good goil, Katie,' he pleaded. 'On the memory of yer mother, God rest her soul, lissen to yer old man. I know as much about the waterfront as anybody. And I know it's something you don't fool with—if ya wanna keep alive.'

14

WHEN THE MEETING in the church basement broke up, Runty sprinted down River Street to the Longdock. In a few minutes, Moose and Jimmy, having chosen a more circuitous route, joined him. None of the customers around the bar had been to the meeting, but it was a live subject in their minds. Each one had decided for himself how he was going to handle it. Old man Gallagher, for instance, who knew and liked Moose, barely grunted a greeting and edged away so as not to be drawn into conversation. He lived in the same house with the Doyles and liked them; his big-hearted wife Mary would do anything for them; all the more reason for Marty Gallagher to be careful.

Runty, Moose and Jimmy felt themselves a three-cornered island connected to the others by underwater reefs of experience and even sympathy, but separated by channels of caution and self-preservation. As the three downed their drinks and talked among themselves they knew they were being both respected and resented, as anyone with the courage to stand up is respected on the waterfront, and as anyone who dares to tamper with the delicate status quo is bitterly resented.

The meeting of a dozen longshoremen with an agitating priest was a tiny pebble tossed into the river, but even a pebble can set up an ever-widening circle of ripples. Already it was all over Bohegan that Father Barry's pitch had been to urge the boys to co-operate with the Crime Commission as the only way to blast the corrupted union and clear the way for a new organization. In a few hours the name of Father Barry had become a dirty word to the waterfront bosses, and even the ordinary dock wallopers were wondering out loud why he had to go pushing his nose into their business.

Truck Amon and Gilly Connors, after beating their pavement chorus outside the church, had watched for Runty to come out and had tailed him to the Longdock. They took up a strategic position at the short side-section of the bar where they could keep an eye on Runty, Moose and Jimmy. On any ordinary night they were to be found over at Friendly's. The musclemen never entered the Long-dock unless they were tracking trouble. Runty caught them out of the corner of his eye and went right on making his jokes and laughing his chesty laugh. He was rebel Irish to his toenails, and the blood quickened in him, made him feel desperately, gaily alive at the prospect of a good scrap.

Moose was different. He had a family and his hulking, over two hundred pound physique concealed an unexpectedly nervous temperament. The needle of his courage swung the full arc from hurricane to doldrum. He had nights when, impulsively lion-hearted, he would get up and tell off his persecutors in loud heroics, be beaten down the stairs into the street, rise and try to fight his way back into the hall again. Next morning all the nerve would be out of him and he'd be riding the rim of fear, bruised and muscle-sore and terrorized by the possible consequences of his resistance. Nor would his wife, Fran, shore up his spine by bawling him out for messing himself in 'politics' when there were five mouths to feed, and healthy eaters all of them, no matter who ran the waterfront. Then big Moose McGonigle would be a good boy until the next time something set him off again.

Jimmy Sharkey was still another kind of fish. He was straight, tough, quiet, direct. He never went looking for fights like Runty and never exploded into them like Moose. He simply took them as they came, as hard, unavoidable facts of life in the harbour.

The two groups, goons and rebels, were like actors on a stage, laughing and drinking and small-talking and once in a while casually glancing over at one another, while the rest of the drinkers made up the audience, watching intently though pretending not to. The trio from the church meeting had three or four more drinks, kidding with Shorty, the night bartender as if this was just another good-time evening. Then they said their good nights and strolled out. Truck and Gilly finished their drinks, left a fat tip on the bar and followed them out.

Outside, Runty, Moose and Jimmy started down River Street toward their homes. Runty walked along with them although he lived in a furnished room only a few doors down from the Longdock. The footsteps of Truck and Gilly were behind them. The night was cold and Runty blew a little cloud of his own warmer air into it. Suddenly, in his best bravadeero manner, he stopped and turned around and waited for the well-named Truck and his rangy side-man to approach.

'Whad d'ya say, fellers?' Truck said, the bristle skin around his eyes crinkling into a slit-eyed smile. His tone sounded like a bass gargle but was meant to be friendly.

'Hiya, Truck, Gilly,' the three muttered.

'Lissen, we'd like t' talk t' ya a minute,' Truck said.

'Ye're talkin' to us right now, ain'tcha?' Runty said.

'Wise guy,' Gilly growled.

Runty was midget-sized alongside Gilly's six-foot-one. Gilly glared at his dwarf antogonist and then appealed to Truck: 'What's with this little bassard? Always has to be such a wise guy.'

'What do you want to give us so much trouble for?' Truck asked earnestly. Any defiance of power disturbed him. 'No kiddin', you better straighten yourself out, Runty.' Truck was almost pleading with him. 'You'd be working three-four days if you could only learn to keep that big yap of yours shut.'

'It's the fault o' the nuns,' said Runty, laughing.

'Nuns?' Truck grumbled. 'What the hell've nuns got to do with it?'

'When I was knee-high to a bar-stool,' Runty went on, enjoying this skating on thin ice, 'the nuns used t' say t' me in school, "Runty we can't understand a word you're sayin'. Ye're talkin' through yer teeth like you got a mouth full o' fish-cakes. When ye're talkin', Runty me lad," they said, "talk with yer mouth wide open." So tha's all I'm tryin' t' do—folly the advice o' the nuns an' talk with me mouth wide open.'

Runty winked at his friends and the three of them laughed.

'You better not talk so the boss c'n hear you,' Truck said, a little confused by Runty's eloquence. 'You know how Johnny is.'

Moose looked at Runty with a warning in his eyes. There were Fran and the kids home waiting for money he'd have to borrow off the shylocks. Johnny's shylocks. What was he doing here sticking himself out in front of all the rest of them anyway? What was he doing letting the priest get him all worked up? Why buck for the bottom of the river? Would the rest of the boys appreciate it when he took the knocks for them? Did they appreciate it when Andy Collins got himself killed or Peter Panto over in Brooklyn? Why couldn't he stay away from Runty Nolan, who was so brave he was crazy? Forget about Joey Doyle. Listen to Fran and make his peace like so many other longshoremen who had no love for Johnny Friendly or Charley the Gent but who went along to keep food on the table. There was no law said you had to like Johnny, but it sure made life simpler if he liked you.

'C'mon, Runty, le's go home,' Moose said.

'Good idea,' Truck said. 'Go home 'n *stay* home. Next time that priest calls his little prayer meetin', you stay home, unless you wanna eat cobblestones.'

'Definitely,' Gilly seconded.

Runty hated Gilly. He could almost taste it and enjoy how much he hated the whole stinking crew of them right up to Big Tom McGovern.

'Y'know why ye're so tall,' Runty shouted up at his towering opponent. 'Your mother was constipated the night she had you and you come out like . . .'

Gilly took a vicious swipe at Runty. Runty was hard to hit because he was so short. He had become a rough-and-tumble expert at fighting men who stood over him a good foot or more and out-weighed him a hundred pounds. He timed a short, mean uppercut to Gilly's groin and Gilly reeled back, holding himself.

'You dumb harp, you must like gettin' hit in the head,' Truck said, moving in heavily, feet apart to set himself to punch with his two hundred and fifty pounds swinging with him. Runty raised his knee and caught Truck. Truck bellowed like a wounded bull and made a club of his fist and swung it at Runty's head. From some-where behind them reinforcements arrived. Sonny and Barney came into it in time to clobber Jimmy and Moose. 'Run!' Runty yelled when he saw them out-numbered.

They took off down the street and around the corner. Runty lost track of the rest of them as he ran like a prairie dog into the park. In his youth he had been a sprinter for his neighbourhood club and at fifty-five he could still run with his knees high. But Gilly was known for his accuracy with a blackjack used as a hurling piece and he was on his target this time again. Runty stumbled and skidded forward. After a few seconds, like a dead game boxer, he started rolling over and crawling to one knee. But before he could gain his feet Sonny and Gilly were on him, holding him for the slow-moving Truck who went about his business with methodical brutality, working Runty over with those club-like fists while Sonny and Gilly held him in position.

Runty let out a yowl like an embattled tom-cat and kicked at Truck's shins and tried to bite Truck's hand slippery with Runty's blood. Then the little man was down on the ground, fighting a wounded animal's way, grabbing and biting at legs, kicking, scratching, while the heels of the Friendly boys came smashing down on him. 'Wise guy . . . son-of-a-bitch . . .'

The park closed in, around and over him like an ether cone. Then a sharp, nasal voice was saying, 'Here, use this.' He looked up and saw a white handkerchief. 'Where the hell did you come from?' The face looking down at him, lean and aroused, said, 'I could hear the yelling from my room, I figured this might happen.'

'Them dirty bastards,' Runty said. ''Scuse me, Father.'

'Hell, I agree with you,' Father Barry smiled. 'Open your mouth.'

Runty obliged and the priest looked in at the bloody mess. 'Not too bad,' he said. He wiped the blood of an extra mouth that had been cut into Runty's forehead, and like a boxer's second pressed the lips of the wound together. 'How's the rest of you? Your ribs?'

Runty tried to laugh. 'Could be worse. Considerin' they were usin' 'em for a football.' He spit into the priest's bloodied handkerchief, and chuckled. 'A hell of a thing to happen to a ladies' man.'

'And you're still D 'n D?' Father Barry said. 'You still call it ratting?'

Runty was sitting up now and he looked at the angry priest for perhaps five seconds without saying anything. Then he said slowly, 'Are you on the level, Father?'

'What do you think?' Father Barry tossed it back at him.

Runty shrugged. 'Don't get sore, Father. We've seen an awful lot of phonies on the waterfront. Politicians. Mayors. Police commissioners. D.A.'s. Even some priests.'

'I know,' Father Barry said.

Runty wiped the warm blood away from his mouth. The handkerchief was a bloody wet clot now.

'If I stick my neck out and they chop it off, would that be the end of it?' Runty kept after the priest. 'Or are ya willin' to go all the way?'

'Down the line, down the line,' Father Barry said impatiently.

'I wonder,' Runty said. Forty years on the waterfront, he had seen a lot of good men crumble. That's why Runty had stopped believing in anybody but Runty—and then only in Runty Nolan's ability to fight a lost cause to the losing, bloody end. 'They'll put the muscle on ya too, turned-around collar or no turned-around collar.'

'Come on across to the house,' Father Barry said. 'Get yourself cleaned up.' As he helped the battered, gnome-like figure to his feet, the priest said, 'You stand up and I'll stand up with you.'

'Right down to the wire?' Runty asked. He was a hard man to convince.

'So help me God,' Father Barry said.

Runty was on his feet now, a little unsteady, with blood still trickling down his chin from the gash inside his mouth. He nodded toward the rectory beyond the west entrance of the park.

'Ya got any beer in there?'

Father Barry nodded. He always kept a few bottles cached away for himself, to sneak into his room and drink before going to sleep. 'I think I can dig up a bottle or two,' he said.

Runty's grin was a smear of blood, but the thought of cold beer was reviving. 'What're we waitin' for?'

The tall, rapid-speaking priest and the battered featherweight docker kept the narrow, unadorned bedroom hot with talk until two in the morning. At first it was Runty's way to suck on his beer bottle and listen. This priest had made a good start, but Runty still wanted to see what other cards he had in his hand. Runty had played a lone game too long to trust himself to anyone merely because he meant well or sounded right. He wanted to see how savvy the priest was. After all, if he went along with what the Father had in mind he was putting his life in the man's hands. Sure, he always boasted he was on borried time and a bravadeero, but if he was going to go he wanted a voice in how and when. It was a deliberate game he had played with Johnny Friendly all these years. He was still alive because he was resourceful as well as almost miraculously enduring and lucky. No sense in letting a well-meaning amateur mess him up now.

The men felt each other out like boxers in the early rounds. The priest kept probing for the reasons behind the waterfront wall of silence. Runty told him it went deeper than simple fear. Everybody on the waterfront had a lining of guilt; it ran all the way from murder and wholesale pilferage to the petty, habitual filching of whisky, perfume, coffee, steaks, flight jackets. Runty's room, he admitted, was full of the loot he had lifted over the years. It didn't seem like stealing when you saw so much of it going by the truck-load to the boys on top. The stuff was lying around begging to be taken. Like the bananas all over the deck. Is it stealing to take a pocketful home when the sweepers would only have to clean them up if they were left behind? In the hold, on the dock, in the loft you lived among abundance, mountains of oil, sardines, imported cho-colates, portable radios, gloves, cases of Havana cigars. The pier was a giant grab-bag, Runty said, and you were either a big operator like Friendly or Charley the Gent, or a petty heister like Runty. 'But God c'n strike me dead if I ever in me life lifted anything t' sell,' Runty said righteously. 'That's what we call larceny down here. The stuff for your own house—we don't consider that stealin'. That's like a little extra bonus comin' to us.'

But, Runty explained, it all helped to keep them secretive, to feel that no matter how much they might hate the unequal way things worked out on the dock, their fate, their infinitesimal guilt was linked to the greater, blacker guilt of the big boys. That was as much a part of the code as the actual, physical fear. Take Runty's own case. Nobody hated the 'high-ocracy'—as he called them—more than he did. 'Tom McGovern, Willie Givens, Johnny Friendly, the whole, stinkin' high-ocracy, I hate 'em winter n' summer, all day 'n all night. The day I don't take some sort of poke at 'em I figure is a day lost. But Father, if you gotta know the truth, I did a little time meself once, when I was a kid an' even stupider 'n I am now. And Moose, same thing with him, when he was an overgrown kid. Get 'im t' tell ya about it one of these days. So we feel kinda funny runnin' to the State with our troubles. We'd rather just battle it out on our own.'

Father Barry opened another beer for Runty and told him a story. It took him back to a hungry time when the priest was twelve and his old man had been dead for a year or more. His mother was cleaning the police station, for a few dollars a week, and barely get-ting by on the little pension and some help from Family Aid.

Christmas was coming up and the kid brother, Connie, wrote Santa Claus for a big red fire engine. His mother read the letter and cried. December was a hard month, with the need for winter clothes the kids were always growing out of. And the need for good substantial food, meat and chicken broths to keep them from catching colds. So a big fire engine, or any toy over a few pennies, was out of the question. Connie would just have to be disappointed.

But little Connie kept asking about his fire engine. And every time he mentioned it, it made Pete wince. Pete felt bitter about it. Christmas had started out as the most joyous of all birthdays, but in Bohegan it looked more like a dirty trick played on the slum kids. Father Barry could still remember how he brooded about it more and more as the day approached. In this mood he hit upon a plan. By God, Connie was going to have his fire engine.

Two days before Christmas he went up to the toy department of the biggest department store in town. 'I figgered they could afford it better than some little joint,' was his rapid aside to Runty. 'I looked around until I saw just what I was looking for. A glittering red fire engine three feet long, with a ladder you could wheel up into the air—a beauty. I went up to the sales lady and priced it. Three bucks. Wow! My mother gave me ten cents a week allowance and I made a dime an hour helping in Mr. Kanzanjian's grocery store. Three bucks! Well, I went into the men's can and I waited until the store closed for the night. Then I came out and went over to the cash register. I knocked it hard with my fists on both sides, the way little Frenchy had taught me. He's away in Sing Sing now doing life as a three-time loser. We were raised two doors from each other. I always liked him. Well, anyway, the third time I tried it the gag worked and boom! out shoots the drawer. It looks like all the money in the world, right there in front of me. For a second, I've got to admit it, it crosses my mind to clean out the drawer. Boy, what we could do with that money! That's what I mean when I say a lot of us could have gone either way. That's why I feel for those fellers doing time. Yes, and even for Johnny Friendly. I know how it feels to want things so bad you c'n taste 'em. So you start grabbing with your own hands and the hell with everybody else. Isn't that Johnny Friendly?

'But I'm getting off my story. The cash register. The drawer open in front of me with all that cabbage. I finally decide to settle for the three singles. Then I try to get out of the store, but every door is locked, in some fancy way I can't unlock it from the inside. I'm scared to death. I find a phone and call the grocery store to send word up to my old lady I'm okay and staying overnight with a friend. Then I hide in the men's room for the night. I c'n hear footsteps coming. The night watchman. I go into the toilet partition and stand on the seat hunched down so he wouldn't see my legs if he looked under. But if he comes in there I'm a goner. My heart was going like a pile driver. Bam bam bam. But the watchman just took a leak at the urinal and went on out again to make his rounds. In the morning when the store opened I bought the fire engine. Then I asked the janitor to keep it for me in the cellar until Christmas Eve. I was afraid my old lady would guess what happened and make me give it back.

'Christmas morning I got my reward. Connie just about split a gut, he was so happy. But I could see my mother looking at me. I kept looking away. Finally she told me to follow her into the kitchen and she put it to me on the line. "Where would you get the money for a toy like that?" I couldn't tell her. "All right," she said, "as long as you tell Father Meehan. You'd better make a good confession."

'Waiting to see Father Meehan—I always call that my first visit to Purgatory. What if he made me give it back? It was Connie's now. The best Christmas present he ever had. I made up my mind waiting in line—I'll never forget it—if the priest gives me too much hell I'm through with the Church. I couldn't believe it was such a terrible sin if it made Connie so happy.

'Well, Meehan was okay. Oh, sure he warned me not to do it again and he threw the seventh commandment at me pretty hard, but he didn't say anything about my having to bring it back. Just six Hail Marys and three Our Fathers. Whew! I walked out of there with both feet off the ground.' Father Barry laughed his sudden, hearty laugh.

'So Runty, I'm in no position to sit in judgement on you when it comes to taking something home that doesn't belong to you. I know

153

the temptations, plenty. I know how it feels when they push you into a corner and lean on you until you feel you've just got to break out. That's how a lot of these neighbourhood punks feel. I figure our job isn't to judge them, high and mighty, but to help 'em. I don't want to act for you—but maybe I can fill the vacuum your union leaders would've filled if they were legitimate. I don't want to try and lead you, but maybe I can give you a little more confidence to help yourselves.'

Runty could feel himself slowly coming over to the priest. The first one he had ever known man to man. Father Barry was sitting on the bed with his collar and his jacket off, in his undershort and braces, his balding head glistening with perspiration from the excitement of the talk. Runty told him of his lone-wolf efforts to spike the intrenched union mob. Like the time Willie Givens came down to the local to sit in on one of 447's rare meetings. When it came time for 'Good and Welfare', President Willie was a master at chewing up the time with long-winded assurances of how much he loved the men and of the extent of his devotion to their welfare. The men would begin to yawn and get thirsty. By the time Willie was raising his voice to an eloquent peroration, most of his audience was in the saloon on the corner raising their whisky glasses. Johnny Friendly would bang his gavel to adjourn the meeting and the pension, vacation and overtime ideas would be out the window for another year. No wonder the shippers were so fond of Weeping Willie.

So, Runty was saying, this particular time he heard Willie through to the last flowery, whisky-blown phrase. Whereupon Runty got the floor by saying he wanted to put in the form of a motion a brief tribute to President Givens. Johnny Friendly winked at Charley. So this little bundle of trouble was learning his lesson at last!

'Mr. Chairman,' Runty began. 'Our esteemed international president has only one fault. He gives too much of himself. He is so devoted to our interests that he don't hesitate to stand on his feet to the point of exhaustion, ours as well as his, tellin' us about it. So I'd like to make a motion, to protect the voice and strength of our esteemed president, that he never be allowed to talk to a meetin' of Four-Four-Seven for more than five minutes at any one time.'

The high-ocracy on the platform had been caught off balance.

The fifty or so who were still present couldn't help laughing and there were spontaneous cries of 'Second the motion'. Charley the Gent, always the diplomat, tried to out-parliamentary the motion but Runty had boned up on his Rules of Order. On a point of order, he called for a vote. The question then had to be put and all in favour carried by a shouted vote of Aye! 'It couldna gone through nicer 'n smoother if it had all be rehoised by a Commie fraction,' Runty chuckled. As Runty was well aware, Willie Givens was particularly unpopular in Four-Four-Seven, even among Johnny's supporters, because he had gotten his start in this local. Old-timers like Runty knew what a four-flushing windbag he was. Plenty of them respected Johnny Friendly for being tough and competent. But Willie, the International president, was just a blarney boy, a suck-around the higher-ups who had nothing but a lot of Irish oratory and some opportunistic good-time-charleying to go on. He needed the executive power of a Tom McGovern above him and the naked strength of a Johnny Friendly below him to prop him up to his exalted position as nominal head of all the dock-workers from Bangor to New Orleans.

Runty told his story with relish. 'So it's still on the books of Four-Four-Seven that Willie Givens is limited to five minutes. Every time he speaks I take a seat in the front row and hold up the biggest Elgin I c'n find. Ho ho ho. Every time Willie looks down he gets poiple in the face. After it's over his boys usually folly me out 'n beat the bejesus outa me. I tell 'em it's worth it jus' t' see the poiple look on Weepin' Willie's face.' Runty laughed again and felt the coagulated blood on his forehead.

Father Barry had a good laugh too at the way Runty, like a flea, had worked his way under Willie Given's oratorical armour. Runty's staggering up on to his feet and asking the big boys to knock him down again was real comedy, of the bloody, gadfly kind the Irish have a knack for understanding.

'But Runty,' Father Barry asked, 'when it's all over what'll you have done to Johnny Friendly, or Willie, or Big Tom? Won't the murders still go on at the bottom and won't McGovern keep soaking up that million-dollar gravy off the top? That's why it seems to me your best bet is to break the silence and testify. The Crime Commission is willing to unlock the door for you. But what's the good of opening a door if nobody's willing to walk in?'

'If you testify, you might as well stick your head in the cement yourself and save them the trouble,' Runty said. 'You wouldn't have the chance of a snowball in a blast furnace.'

But, Father Barry argued, if Runty had defied the waterfront powers all his life, if he was on borrowed time as he was always saying, why not strike a single, effective blow that might add up to more than all the bravadeero escapades put together? 'If you really hate those fellers, here's a chance to make 'em look bad in the papers, where it really hurts,' Father Barry said. 'Baiting them in a bar and getting your head staved in, what good does that do?'

'In me own soul it does me good,' Runty laughed. That one was hard to answer. 'What makes you so hot for this investigation?' the old longshoreman asked.

'Because I can see the Joey Doyle case will wind up a hush-hush job. This whole mess down here is being smothered in silence like a —a pillow held over the mouth of the harbour. And on the other hand here is the State setting up machinery and begging you to come forward. If it worked, if enough of you put the story together it could change the whole direction of this thing. The mob would be publicly discredited—instead of hiding behind a phony trade union respectability.'

'I know enough to send Tom McGovern and Willie Givens away for years,' Runty boasted. 'I go all the way back to when Tom was hijacking meat trucks with his own hands. Yes, and killing with them too. Now he's got a manicurist come up to his penthouse to paint his nails and he's chairman of the Mayor's Harbour Improvement Society, God help us all. I seen him come up from the gutter. I seen how it happened.'

'Runty, get your story down,' Father Barry said excitedly. 'I think you've got a hell of a chance to knock Johnny Friendly out of the box. Maybe Willie and McGovern too. And Donnelly and the Mayor over here. This investigation is a stick of dynamite. And you guys are too stupid to light the fuse.'

'God Almighty, Father,' Runty said, half-impressed. 'You make it sound like the second comin'.'

'Look, why don't we do this?' Father Barry said, talking fast. 'I'll get in touch with the Commission. Set up an executive session for you. You can testify on the q.t. The Commission doesn't want to come out in the open anyway until they're sure they've got enough stuff to make a case. By that time you've got them on the run. I'm going to bring a lawyer in on this. I c'n see a petition in the courts for an on-the-level election. The rest is up to you. Only don't back away from this and come crying to me that you want my help. I'll probably catch enough hell as it is. I'm thumbing you into the game, Runty. You c'n take it or leave it.'

Runty said, 'Cripes, I oughta have me head examined.'

Father Barry prodded him. 'Listen. I'll line it up for you in the morning. I don't like big government any more 'n you do. But in this thing I can't see any other way. Without government implementation, you boys haven't a chance.'

'Balls to government impleme—whatever that is,' Runty said. 'Don't give me any of those ten-dollar-Willie-Givens' woids. I'll buy the rest of it.'

'Amen,' Father Barry grinned. He took a good look at Runty's bruises. 'You're sure you're okay now?'

'Hell, lemme outa here,' Runty said. 'It's a quarter after two. I gotta get to the Longdock before they close.'

Father Barry had to choke back the warning—How can you go back into the streets and ask them to clobber you again? He gulped the words down because he knew the man who would go back on to River Street, not to be brave but just for another couple of shots of thirty-five cent whisky, was the same man who might have the spirit—with Father Barry's help—to get the waterfront on the side of decency.

'Take it easy now,' Father Barry said as he walked Runty down to the front door of the rectory. 'You're gonna be valuable merchandise.'

Runty looked out into the cool, moonless night. There were snow flurries in the air. General Pulaski was a brooding shadow of iron in the park.

'Don't worry, Father. I don't think they're gonna folly me no more t'night.' He tapped his wounded head humorously. 'They had their fun.'

'Tomorrow we get our turn at bat,' the priest said. 'Take care now. Stay out of the gin mills.'

'I ain't afraid to go anywhere in Bohegan,' Runty boasted.

'I know that,' Father Barry said. 'But if you don't mind, I'd like to keep you in one piece, at least until we get this thing on the road.'

Runty went boldly out into the night, his hands pushed deep into his windbreaker pockets, his hard, bantam chest thrust defiantly forward.

A noble little lush, Father Barry thought to himself as he watched him go.

Father Barry felt pleased with himself all the way up the stairs and into the bathroom he shared with Father Vincent. It was rather a primitive bathroom, with an old-fashioned tub. Father Barry had been trying to promote a stall shower ever since he reported to St. Tim's. He liked his bracing morning shower. When the Pastor had turned this down as an unnecessary luxury he had gone so far as to pray to St. Jude to intercede for him. Only the Saint of the Impossible, Father Barry had decided, could work such an innovation in habit-set Father Donoghue's rectory. The Pastor had spent his boyhood in the old country and was not at all sure that hot water, stall showers and the like were necessary to salvation. In fact it was one of his notions that Americans were too clean. 'Rub all the natural protective oils off their skins, they do for a fact.'

Father Barry was leaning over the sink and staring at his hairline in the small mirror, wondering if his hair was indeed receding as alarmingly as it seemed to be, when Father Vincent came in, in his plaid bathrobe, sleepy-eyed and grouchy.

'Pete isn't it bad enough to drag this thing into the church?' Father Vincent began, standing at the toilet and continuing to talk over his shoulder. 'Are you going to start dragging these drunks in at all hours of the night?'

'That's no way to talk about our parishioners,' Father Barry tried to joke it.

'We see enough of the parishioners at the Masses and Confession,' Father Vincent said, going to the sink to wash his hands.

'I'm not so sure,' Father Barry said.

'Peter, I hate to see you do this to yourself,' Father Vincent said.

'You've got a lot on the ball. You can go places. But not this way. You're cutting your own throat.'

Father Barry shook his head. 'I'm just trying to keep a few throats from being cut.'

Father Vincent shrugged. 'That's a problem for the laity. I don't think a priest has any right butting into it. All you'll do is get yourself out on a limb the Monsignor will be very happy to chop off,' Father Vincent said. 'But go ahead, if you want to be a curate all your life.'

'Damn it, there are people out there getting clobbered,' Father Barry said. The long, strenuous day was catching up to him now and there was no reserve of patience for the argument. Anyway he could throw the entire Encyclical of Pius XI at Brother Harry and it would make no difference.

On his knees for his night's-end prayer, Father Barry begged God to help him repair his weaknesses so that he'd have more strength to follow the path he had set for himself. 'Lord, give me the strength to climb out on this limb,' he prayed, 'and please God, try to keep the Monsignor from going to the Bishop and getting him to chop me down.' He reinforced this request with fifteen Our Fathers.

15

TERRY'S FLOCK WAS aloft again that next afternoon, a fluttering, swiftly moving cloud against the sun-brightened sky. Terry watched them parentally, occasionally swinging his long pole to keep them exercising. At their deceptive rate of nearly a mile a minute they could sweep far out over the river and circle back across the squat buildings of Main Street in a few seconds. Billy Conley, attached to Terry like a pilot fish, enjoyed the sight too—one of the three experiences in Bohegan he gave himself up to with enthusiasm. The other two were girls (from the age of eleven) and block battles against the rival Dock Street Dukes.

'Will ya look at them beautiful goddamn birds?' Terry said.

'The ones you stole off the Army sure rounded out the flock nice,' Billy said.

'Wait'll we get the squabs from these Army slates and our Belgian blues next spring,' Terry said. 'We'll fly them other bums into the ground.'

Billy laughed and then, looking across the roof, frowned when he saw Katie Doyle making her way along the roof through the forest of television aerials and clothes-lines.

'Who ast that broad up here?' Billy said.

Terry tensed at the sight of the girl approaching across the next roof level. He wanted to see her again, but he knew there was no percentage in it.

'Okay, I guess they got enough exercise,' he said, no longer bothering to follow the sweeping flight of the birds. 'Let 'em come in.'

He handed the pole to Billy and waited for Katie. She had a graceful, ladylike walk, he was thinking; it seemed almost as if she were floating toward him. His chance meeting with her, his walk through the park with her the night before, her soft way of talking and the unfamiliarly kind things she said belonged more to the world of adolescent day-dreaming than to the hard reality of the Bohegan riverfront.

'What're you doin' up here on the roof?' Terry asked gruffly.

'Just looking,' Katie said.

She was startled. She felt out of place, though she had been up a few times with Joey when he was exercising his flock. She lingered a moment, just now, to look at Joey's coop three roofs away. The birds were still there, unconcernedly eating from the self-feeder. The sight of them, all alive and waiting for Joey, made her brother's absence unbearably intense. Then she hurried on to Terry—why, she didn't know exactly—perhaps because he was a pigeon fancier too.

Now that Billy had lowered the pole the birds were circling closer to their loft. Terry hailed them with an encircling wave of his hand.

'You're looking at the champion flock of the neighbourhood. Everyone of 'em bred 'n raised 'n trained by yours truly.'

'I love seeing them fly out over the river,' she said.

'They'll fly anywhere,' Terry said. 'Over the ocean. As far as fifteen hundred miles. They'll keep coming all day. And they won't even stop for food or water until they're back in the coop.'

They were coming in for a landing one by one and pushing trustfully through the movable bars into the coop.

'Joey raised pigeons,' Katie said.

Terry frowned. 'Yeah. He had a few birds.' He glanced at her and then seemed to be studying the tar-paper flooring of the roof. 'I went over and fed 'em this morning.'

'I wouldn't have thought you'd be so interested in pigeons,' Katie said.

Terry shrugged. 'I go for this stuff. Ever since I was a kid. I like the feel ya get when ya spot 'em in the sky comin' home from Wilmington or somewheres. Makes ya feel big'—he snickered—'almost like ya done it yerself.'

'Do they always fly home?' Katie asked.

'Well, sometimes they get lost or hit a wire or somethin',' Terry admitted. 'And then of course the hawks get 'em.'

'Oh.' Katie shuddered.

'Ya know this harbour's full of hawks?' Terry said. 'That's a fact. They hang around on top of the big hotels. The Plaza over the river is full of 'em. When they spot a pigeon in the park, *swoosh* right down on 'em. They c'n tear a pigeon's throat open in a second, right in the air.'

'The things that go on,' Katie said, shutting her eyes for a moment.

'Yeah, ya c'n say that again,' Terry said. 'Hawks is a pain in the . . .' He stopped abruptly. 'What good is a hawk?' he wound it up.

Katie noticed one bird on the landing platform with a long string attached to its leg. When she asked what that was for, Terry looked across at Billy, who had turned aside disapprovingly.

'Well, that's kind of a funny thing,' Terry began. 'Y'see, a bird from some other flock or a lost racin' bird sees the string and—it's somethin' about pigeons—right away he's got to find out what it is. So he comes over 'n joins the flock and next thing he knows he's followin' 'em right into the coop. Kinda like hypnotism.'

'Isn't that stealing?' Katie asked in that disconcertingly unemotional way she had of asking hard questions in a soft voice.

'Well—it's sort a like a sport. See what I mean?' Terry apologized. 'Everybody does it.'

'And that makes it right?'

'Yeah—yeah,' Terry muttered uncomfortably. Then he called to Billy, 'Better check their water, kid. Looks like the can run dry. Get on the ball.'

Billy glared at the two of them and swallowed a profanity as he entered the coop.

'The Golden Warriors?' Katie read the emblazoned inscription on Billy's back.

'Yeah. I started them Golden Warriors.' Terry swaggered a little. 'You might say I was the original Golden Warrior. This little bum here'—he thumbed toward Billy inside the coop—'he's my shadow. He thinks I'm a big wheel because I used to box pro for a while.'

'Aah, I couda licked ya,' Billy said.

'Ha, ha. Ya couldn't lick a postage stamp,' Terry said, and flicked his left a couple of times.

A large blue-checker pigeon with a thick white wattle around the eyes and a proud carriage flew through the movable bars and took his place on the highest perch, where he moved about and cooed authoritatively.

'You see that one,' Terry said. 'Now what do you think of that hunk a stuff?'

'Oh, she's a beauty,' Katie said.

Billy had filled the self-serving watering can and was dexterously tipping it right side up.

'She's a *he*,' the boy said furiously. 'His name is Swifty.'

'He's my lead bird,' Terry explained. 'He's always on that top perch.'

'He looks so proud of himself,' Katie said.

'He's the boss,' Terry said. 'If another bum tries to come along 'n take that perch he really lets 'im have it.'

Katie sighed. 'Even pigeons . . .'

'Well, there's one thing about 'em though,' Terry said, more in earnest than usual, 'they're faithful. They get married just like people.'

'Better,' Billy said out of the corner of his mouth.

162

'They're very faithful,' Terry went on, ignoring Billy's interruption. 'Once they're mated they stay together all through their lives until one of 'em dies.'

Katie lowered her head. 'That's nice,' she said.

He put out his hand to touch her and then, still afraid or in awe of her, he drew it back again. Terry noticed Billy grinning malevolently at them from inside the coop. 'Okay, okay, now get outa there and fix the roof. Make yourself useless,' Terry ordered.

Billy made an obscene sibilant sound under his breath, but did what he was told. Katie continued to keep her head down.

'You like beer?' Terry asked irrelevantly.

Katie looked at him. 'I don't know.'

He wanted to touch her, touch her gently. He had never felt tender toward anybody in his life and he was fumbling for words or gestures. 'I bet you never had a glass of beer,' he said. 'That's what I bet—you never had a glass of beer.'

'Once, my father . . .' she began to say.

'How about you come 'n have one with me?'

'In a saloon?'

'Well, yeah. I mean I know a little dump—a place that's very nice, with a side entrance for ladies and all like that.'

'I really shouldn't,' Katie said.

'Come on, it won't hurt,' Terry begged. 'Come on . . . Okay?'

He took her by the hand and drew her along. She told herself a better acquaintanceship with Terry might be a way of cutting into the dark horror of waterfront murder. But it was actually something about the hurt in Terry Malloy, the defensive toughness like the scar tissue over the wounded eyes, that drew her on.

Terry guided Katie to the ladies' bar of the Bellevue, which was the second-best hotel in town and prided itself on being off limits for local whores. An elderly Irish biddy, Mrs. Higgins, well known in the neighbourhood for chronic, noisy insobriety, was being ejected by the bartender as Terry and Katie approached.

'Take your hands off me, I'm only after havin' one more . . .' Mrs. Higgins was protesting.

'You and your *one-mores*,' the bartender said, pushing her out. 'Go home.'

Katie hung back, and Terry took her arm.

'Come on—don't be ascared. See what I was tellin' ya? They run a nice quiet place. I mean the drunks get the heave-ho'.

Inside, the Bellevue bar had a nineteenth-century flavour, with its time-worn mahogany bar and elaborate chandeliers. A merchant sailor nearing the end of a long drunk was singing *Rose of Tralee* to a middle-aged women who had come in for lunch and had lost track of time. To Terry's chagrin a plump over made-up young girl was at a corner of the bar with Terry's chum Jackie. Terry tried to look away, for it was Melva, but she caught his eye and called over, 'Hiya, Terry?'

Terry barely nodded.

'A friend of yours?' Katie said.

Terry winched. 'Just a—passin' acquaintance,' he reached for the phrase he had heard somewhere. 'What're you drinkin'?'

Katie hesitated and in the pause the sailor at the bar gave up *Tralee* to tell the bartender. 'Hit me with another Gluckenheimer.'

'I'll try a—Gluckenheimer,' Katie said.

'Two Gluckenheimers,' Terry called. 'And draw two for chasers.'

Katie looked bewildered. 'Come on, give a smile. You're beginnin' to live a little,' Terry tried to reassure her.

'I am?'

'Hey, Terry,' the bartender called over from the bar. 'See the fight last night? That new kid Ryff. Both hands. A little bit on your style.'

'Ha, ha,' Terry said. 'I hope he gets better dice than me.' To Katie he shrugged the bartender's compliment off. 'Comedian.'

'Were you really a prizefighter?' Katie asked.

'Aah, I used to be. I was goin' pretty good for a while. But—I didn't stay in shape. I had to take a few dives.'

'A dive? You mean into the water?'

Terry laughed. 'Yeah. Into the water.' He laughed again.

'What are you laughing at?'

He pointed to her. 'You. Miss Square from Nowhere.'

She blushed slightly but she wasn't put off. 'What made you interested—in fighting?'

Terry raised his shoulders again in that gesture of casual disgust.

'Aah, I don't know. I had to scrap all my life. I figured I might as well get paid for it. When I was a kid my old man got chopped off' —he saw the question rising in her eyes and added quickly—'never mind how. Then they stuck Charley 'n me in a dump they called a Children's Home.' The sore memory of it made him screw up his nose. 'Boy, that was some home. Well, anyway, I ran away from there and peddled papers, 'n stole a little bit and fought in club smokers and then Charley hooked up with Johnny Friendly and Johnny bought a piece of me . . .'

'A—*piece* of you?'

'That's right,' Terry said, without bothering to explain. 'He was a piece man. Tied in with Mr. T.'

'Who's he?' Katie asked.

'Forget I mentioned him,' Terry said quickly. 'Well, anyway, I won about twelve straight and then . . .'

He stopped and took a good look at her. What was he, punchy or something? Telling this Doyle broad all this stuff. He never talked about dives, or Mr. T., or the connexion with Johnny F. What was he doing—getting soft in the casaba?

'Yes—and then?' Katie said, leaning forward a little and looking into his eyes.

'Aah, what am I runnin' off at the mouth for?' Terry said. 'What do you really care?'

'Shouldn't everybody . . .' Katie hesitated.

'Come again?' Terry said.

'I mean, shouldn't everybody care . . .'

Terry shook his head in disbelief. 'Boy, what a fruitcake you are!'

'Well, I mean . . . the Mystical Body . . . brotherhood . . . I thought . . .' Katie was groping.

'Gee, thoughts,' Terry said, both mocking and impressed. 'Alla time, thoughts. And the funny part is, you really believe that drool.'

'Yes, I do,' she said quietly.

The bartender had set their drinks down on the table. Terry was relieved to have something to do. This kid gave him a funny feeling when she looked at him, almost through him, and said crazy things like that, saying screwball things like she believed them, things that lower your guard and feint you wide open.

165

'Well, here we are,' he said, picking up the thick jigger with the familiar false bottom, handing it to her and then lifting his own with an air of festivity. 'One for the lady and one for the gent. Here's to the first one, I hope it ain't the last—Dink—' He touched glasses with her, lightly ceremonious, and then waited in amusement as she sniffed the rim of the glass suspiciously and allowed the surface of the sharp-smelling liquid to touch her lips.

'Mmmmm,' she murmured non-committally.

'Not that way,' Terry said. 'One hunk. Down the hatch. Like this.' In a practised gesture he poured the shot down his throat. 'Wham!' he said.

Challenged, Katie raised the formidable ounce of whisky to her mouth and gulped it down. Her eyes opened wide and she coughed as it burned all the way down. 'Wham . . .' she whispered with amazement.

'Not bad, huh?' Terry was grinning at her. He felt better when he had her on his own ground.

'It's . . . quite . . .' was all Katie managed to say.

'How about a repeat?'

'A what?'

'Once around again.'

'No *thanks*.'

'Mind if I do?'

'Of course not,' Katie said. 'You do what you want to do.'

'Hit me again, Mac,' Terry called out, feeling a little more confident with the first ball in him. He drank half the glass of beer and leaned closer to her across the table.

'You wanna hear my philosophy of life?' Terry said, still bothered by her 'brotherhood' pitch. 'Do it to him before he does it to you.'

She looked at him a moment before she said, 'I like what our Lord said better.'

'Maybe,' Terry said. 'But I'm not lookin' to get crucified. I'm lookin' to stay in one piece.'

'I must be crazy to have come here with you,' Katie answered.

He put his hand on her arm to hold her. 'Hang on a second. Gimme five minutes. I don't get a chance to talk with a kid like you every day.'

She shook her head angrily and pushed his hand away. 'I never met such a person. Not a spark of feeling—or human kindness in your whole body.'

'I wouldn't know about them things. Whatta they do for you excep' get in your way?'

'And when things get in your way'—Katie's voice was rising—'or people, you just get rid of them. Is that your idea?'

'*Listen*,' Terry said, suddenly taut, suddenly dry-mouthed, 'don't be lookin' at me when you say them things. It wasn't my fault what happened to Joey. Fixin' him wasn't my idea.'

'Why, whoever said it was?'

Hell, he had been asked a lot of tough precinct questions and punched around by cops, but this was worse, these goddam soft-voiced innocent questions.

'Well,' he began lamely, 'I didn't like the way everybody was puttin' the needle on me. You and them bums in the church. And this Father Barry. I didn't like the way he was lookin' at me.'

'He was looking at everybody in the same way,' she said.

'Oh yeah? I thought he was givin' me the business. Anyhow, what's with this Father Barry? What's his racket?'

'His *racket*?'

'Yeah, yeah, his racket. You've been off in daisyland, honey. Around here everybody's got a racket.'

'But he's a priest.'

'Are you kiddin'? So what? The black suit don' make no difference. Everybody looks to get his.'

'You don't believe anything, do you? You don't believe anybody?'

He reached over and tried to touch her hand again, but she drew away. 'Katie, listen to me. Down here it's every man for himself. It's keepin' alive. It's standin' in with the right people so you c'n get a little change jinglin' in your pocket.'

'And if you don't?'

'If you *don't*?' he looked at her wisely, arrogantly, yet with a certain inexpressible sadness. 'If you don't, right down—chop.' He shook his thumb savagely toward the floor.

Katie shuddered. 'That's no better than an alley dog.'

Terry drained his glass of beer and wiped his mouth with the back of his hand. 'All right. I'd rather live like an alley dog than wind up like——'

He caught himself. Who was baiting him into this trap? It was a sucker play and he knew it. Something about this straight-talking, freckle-faced, cool little broad.

'Like Joey?' she was saying. 'Are you afraid to mention his name?'

'Naah,' Terry said quickly, but it sounded more like a cry of pain than a denial. 'Only why do ya have to keep harpin' on that? Come on, drink up. You gotta get a little fun outa life. Come on, I'll stick some music on.'

She shook her head without looking up at him. What she was feeling inside spread over and around him like an ocean roller before it breaks, when you know any second it is going to change from a smooth gathering swell to plunging foam. He was like a swimmer trying to ride it over, up and over easy. But it wasn't easy. He was over his head. And yet, as in drowning, there was something hypnotic about it, something that numbed his will to strike out for his old line of survival.

'What's the matter with you?' he sighed. 'What's the matter?'

He had risen to push a nickel into the gaudy coloured juke-box. 'What kind of number you want? You like her nibs Georgia Gibbs?'

She lifted her head to look at him and just as he had feared, the wave broke in her, catching her more by surprise than it did him. The words rose out of her and broke over the dam before she knew what she was saying. 'Help me. If you can. For God's sake, help me.'

Terry was caught between the table and the juke-box with the coin cold and damp in his hand. She made it sound so easy. He wished it were! But there was Charley and the steady work and respect for Johnny and their trust in him. What kind of rat would he be if he went back on rock-bottom things like that? Johnny and Charley's world was built on standing with your own. You just didn't walk out on a fella like Johnny, a natural leader like Johnny. And here was this *nice girl*, this fugitive from daisyland begging *him* for help, *me!—Terry*, whose only interest in a girl like this should have been to catch her against the wall of a dark tenement hallway.

He turned back from the juke-box and swung his hands loosely against his sides.

'I'd like to—Katie—but—I don't know nuthin'. There's nuthin' I c'n do.'

Katie started to rise. She felt listless now, tired. The effect of the drink spun her deeper into bewilderment. 'All right . . . All right . . . I shouldn't have asked you.'

She picked her coat up off the chair.

'You haven't touched your beer,' he said. 'Go on, drink it. It'll do you good.'

'I don't want it. But why don't you stay? You stay and drink it.'

'I got my whole life to drink,' Terry said.

She gave him such a look of understanding, sympathy, disapproval, that he could not help blurting out:

'You're not sore at me?'

'What for?'

Again the innocence, the misplaced trust was sharper to take than the back of a copper's hand.

'Well, fer—fer not bein' no help to ya?'

'Why, no,' Katie said softly. 'I know you would if you could.'

There had been one fight when Tony Falcone, who could hook very strong to the body, had caught Terry under the heart. Terry copped the decision but he could feel that punch in his body for weeks. He still carried the memory of it. They say a punch like that and you are never the same, never quite the same. Katie's *would-if-you-could* was a punch like that.

As Katie turned from the table toward the exit, she found her way blocked by a couple of muscular men in rented tuxedoes who were snarling at each other, 'Don't tell me I didn' see ya, I *saw* ya'—'The hell ya saw me'—'The hell I didn' see ya, ya dirty . . .' Then they started swinging at each other. Katie backed away in fright while the bartender hurried over apologetically.

'There's a weddin' inside in the private room. These fellas 're just feelin' good. Celebratin'.'

'Yeah,' Terry said. 'Don' mind them. In two minutes they'll be huggin' 'n kissin' each other. Come on. I'll get you out through the lobby.'

169

He led her down a narrow panelled corridor which passed the small ballroom rented for private parties. A local five-piece orchestra was playing, as a somewhat corrupted two-step, that good old Irish jig 'The Washer Woman'. The room was darkened, and shifting beams of red, green and purple lights moved across the bodies of the dancers from a cheaply ornate balcony.

As Terry and Katie paused to look in, the bridal couple dashed past them, escaping from their guests in the semi-darkness. The bride was small and not very pretty. Terry recognized her as the eldest daughter of Joe Finley, a minor City Hall grafter who had a piece of the loading on Pier B. The kid was Freddie Burns, a checker, moving up in the world. The bridal gown was lacy white and beautiful, and Katie, bemused by the drink, the confusion, the music and the rainbow effect of the moving lights, was touched by the rented hall romance of it all. She had no thought, as Terry did, that the groom was a cutie marrying City Hall to beat the rap of an eight-hour day. 'I love weddings,' Katie said.

'The car's in the side alley,' the groom was saying.

'Give me a cigarette,' the bride said, as they hurried away.

'Later. You smoke too much anyway,' the groom said, and the couple disappeared down the corridor.

The five-piece semi-pro band had swung into an oldie, 'Avalon'; the sound of the sliding of feet on the wooden floor was hypnotic. The men were mostly heavy muscled petty officials who looked too big for their tuxedoes. Most of the women had gone to fat. Many had yellow, shellacked beauty-shop hair. This was a gathering of the minor politicians and straw bosses of Bohegan, spiced as usual with members of the local mob, not the goons, but the loan sharks, shop stewards and delegates who fed on and fed the local politicians.

Katie stood at the threshold, lost in the music. Terry wondered what she was thinking. 'I met my love in Avalon—beside—the bay: I left my love in Avalon—and sailed—away . . .' the song crooned its simple, heartbreaking logic.

'Guess they forgot to send us our engraved invitations, huh?' Terry tried to arouse a spark in her.

She smiled faintly and he was encouraged. He indicated, in the grand manner, his brown corduroys and red-and-black checked wool shirt. 'I'm glad I wore the tux. I hate to feel outta place.'

She smiled at him and he slid his arms around her, careful not to come too close.

'Come on—you wanna—you wanna spin a little?' He made a pair of dancers out of his index and middle fingers and spun them around in front of her face, closer and closer until they danced along the bridge of her nose. She laughed, and before she could say no he was dancing with her in the corridor. He swung her around, expertly; she followed easily, instinctively.

'Ah, you dance divinely,' he said with borrowed elegance, and she laughed again. With more confidence now he led her to the edge of the darkened ballroom where they began to whirl among the other dancers.

'Hey, we're good!' he said. 'Mr. and Mrs. Arthur Murray.'

She let him hold her tighter. The music was soothing with its simple-sweet lilt and its saxophone croon. 'The Sisters oughta see ya now,' he said with his mouth close to her ear. When she closed her eyes he let his lips touch her hair and slowly move down to her cheek.

'Oh, I'm just floating, floating,' she murmured. 'Just floating . . .'

The saxophone player had lowered his instrument and risen to his feet to do the vocal in a thin, true, Rudy Vallee voice. Terry joined in with him softly:

> *'And so I think I'll travel on—*
> *To Av—a—lon . . .'*

The band hit a final, conventional chord and the overhead lights came on in an intrusive glare. Terry and Katie were still holding on to each other, caught in the crooning, tin-pan-allegorical mood of the song, when Truck came up to them. Gilly was with him. Truck and Gilly weren't there for any wedding, Terry could see that. They didn't say, Hiya, kid, or anything like that. None of the back-slapping and clown-sparring. They were all business, solidly, heavily business.

'I been lookin' all over for you, Terry,' Truck said.

One thing about Bohegan, you couldn't hide. It was a mile long and a mile deep and everybody watched everybody else.

'Well, okay?' Terry said.

'The boss wants you,' Truck said.

'Right now?'

'Definitely,' Gilly said.

Truck bent his bull neck toward Terry's ear. 'He just got a call from Upstairs. Something's gone wrong. He's hotter 'n a pistol.'

'Well, I gotta take this—this young lady home first,' Terry said.

'I'd get over there, Terry,' Truck said. 'If I was you I wouldn' waste no time. Gilly c'n take the little lady home.'

'Definitely,' Gilly said.

'Look, you tell 'im—tell 'im I'll be over after a while,' Terry said.

Truck looked at Gilly, scandalized. 'O-kay,' he said, the inflection on the last syllable making his meaning unmistakable, 'O-kay . . .'

The two Johnny Friendly boys shrugged to each other and left Terry standing there.

Katie crossed the threshold into the corridor and watched them walking rapidly toward the lobby. Terry joined her, shifting uncomfortably.

'Who are those . . .' she started to ask.

'Aah, just a couple of—fellas around,' Terry said, troubled.

'What was that short, thick one whispering to you?' Katie asked. 'Why does he have to whisper?'

'Listen, Katie, for your own good,' Terry jumped ahead of her questions. 'You gotta quit askin' things. You gotta quit askin' so many questions. You gotta quit tryin' to find out things. Lay off. Lay off.'

'Who were those two?' Katie said.

'It ain't safe,' Terry continued. 'Now I'm tellin' you for your own good. It just ain't safe. I tell you, lay off.'

'Why worry about me?' Katie said. 'You're the one who was just saying you only look out for yourself.'

'Okay, okay,' Terry said harshly, feeling some relief from guilt and his frustrated attraction for her in being able to lash out at her. 'Go ahead, get in hot water. Just don't come hollerin' to me when you get burned.'

'Why should I come hollering to you at all?' Katie asked.

'Because . . .' Terry said resentfully, 'because . . . I think you and me are gettin' . . .'

He looked at her angrily, and guiltily, and hung his head.

'I won't let myself,' Katie warned him. 'Not me!'

'That goes for me double,' Terry said.

Inside, in the private room, the overhead lights were dimming again. The band swung into a Lombardo version of a Dick Rodgers waltz.

'I'm leaving,' Katie said.

'Yeah, let's cut outta here,' Terry said. 'I'll see ya home.'

It had grown colder as the sun ducked behind the massive ridge of factories marking the western outskirts of the city. They no longer had anything to say to each other. They walked rapidly down Dock Street. Approaching Terry's stoop, a half dozen doors down from the Doyles', Katie was just about to tell him there was no need for him to accompany her any farther when a man in a brown tweed overcoat and a dark brown hat stepped quickly out of the front hallway where he had been waiting 'Mr. Malloy?' he called out to Terry.

Terry swung in surprise at the *mister*. He frowned as he recognized the Crime Commission joker, the tall, broad-shouldered one who had asked him too many questions at the Longdock.

'Yeah, yeah?' Terry said.

Glover approached with a pleasant smile. 'I've been waiting for you, Mr. Malloy. You're being served with a subpoena, Mr. Malloy.'

He handed the unprepossessing sheet of paper to Terry. Terry didn't look at it. He crumpled it into a ball in his hand.

'Be at the State House. Courtroom Nine, at ten o'clock Monday morning,' Glover said.

This was too much for Terry. 'Listen, I already told ya. I don't know nuthin'. I don't *know* nuthin' about that.'

'You're entitled to bring a lawyer with you,' Glover went on. 'And you're privileged under the Constitution to protect yourself against questions that might incriminate you.'

'Are you kiddin'?' Terry said, suspended somewhere between anguish and anger. 'Y'know what you're askin' me to do?'

'Mister Malloy,' Glover said in a practised voice, as if he had spoken this line a thousand times, 'all we're asking you to do is to tell the truth.'

173

'*All*,' Terry said bitterly. 'That's all, huh?' He shook his head scornfully. 'Boy, what you don' know.'

'See you Monday morning,' Glover said. 'And of course failure to appear means a warrant for you and an automatic contempt of court. Good day, Mr, Malloy.'

'*Mister* Malloy,' Terry said with his hands on his hips, disdainfully, as he watched Glover walk away. 'Cop!'

'What are you going to do?' Katie said.

Terry had forgotten she was still there. 'Tell you one thing,' he said viciously. 'I ain't gonna eat cheese for no cops, and that's for sure.'

It was hoodlum talking, pure hoodlum and it aroused a sharp, pure reaction in Katie. 'It was Johnny Friendly who killed Joey, wasn't it?' she said.

Terry clenched his fingers around the subpoena. He looked down at his feet. He felt like running, as if he just swiped some stuff off a push-cart and should be getting out of there in a hurry. 'Katie . . .' he started to say.

But now Katie was pressing. 'He had him killed or had something to do with it, didn't he? He and your brother Charley? Isn't that true?'

'Katie, listen . . .'

'You can't tell me, can you? Because you're part of it. And as bad as the worst of them. Just as bad. Aren't you? Tell me the truth, Terry. Aren't you?'

She was raising her voice, on the verge of tears, and Terry took a step backward and put a hand out as if to calm her.

'Shhh, take it easy, take it easy. You better go back to that school out in daisyland. You're drivin' yourself nuts. You're drivin' me nuts. You're drivin' everybody nuts. Quit worryin' about the truth all the time. Worry about yourself.'

Katie lowered her voice, so as not to scream at him. 'I should have known you wouldn't tell me. Pop said Johnny Friendly used to own you. I think he still owns you.'

'Please. Don't say that to me, Katie . . .'

Katie looked at him and wanted to cry. Then she said, as gently as she could, 'No wonder everybody calls you a bum.'

174

'Don't say that to me, Katie. Don't say that to me now.'

'No wonder . . . no wonder . . .' Katie kept repeating softly.

'I'm—I'm tryin' t' keep ya from bein' hurt. Don't you see? What more d'ya want?'

'Much more, Terry,' Katie said. 'Much much much more.'

She turned away abruptly and ran up the street toward her tenement stoop so as not to let him see her crying.

Terry watched her hurry up the steps into her hallway. Then he looked at the crumpled paper in his hand. 'Son of a bitch,' he said fervently, 'son of a wall-eyed bitch. Son of a lousy joint-chewing wall-eyed bitch.'

Then he remembered Johnny Friendly. He must be getting light in the head to follow a broad like this and disobey a direct order from Johnny Friendly. With his head down, trying to think, and the stinking subpoena burning a hole in his pocket, he turned the corner toward the docks and the back room of the Friendly Bar on River Street where Union Brother John Friendly was waiting for him.

16

Big mac and Gilly and Truck and Sonny and Specs and 'J.P.' and the rest of them stared at Terry when he entered the back room of Johnny Friendly's bar. They looked at him as if they had never seen him before. Even Charley barely mumbled 'Hiya, kid'. They were waiting for Johnny Friendly to make the move.

'Well, it's nice of you to drop around,' Johnny said as Terry approached. Friendly's eyes were feared around here for their cold-blue dead-pan stare when he was crossed. His lips barely moved when he talked. There was more than anger in him. There was a studied withdrawal that made men who incurred his enmity come close to collapse when he fixed them with this look. It was known and dreaded on River Street as 'The Friendly freeze'.

Terry was on his guard because he could feel all their eyes watching him for sign of geezer. How tough was the tough kid now? their eyes were asking.

'I was comin' over,' Terry said carefully. He glanced at Charley, who was standing near Johnny. Charley was with him, but he kept a stern face on him so as not to weaken himself with Johnny. These were make-or-break moments in this business. Johnny's was a terrible authority, beyond appeal. There was no hedging, no uncertainty. Mercy or punishment was dealt from the top of the deck, slapped on the table for all to see, irrevocable.

'Just comin' over here,' Johnny said mincingly. Then he made his voice coarser and louder. 'How? By way of Chicago?'

Big Mac and one or two others laughed obligingly. Terry tightened his mouth at them and tried to stop Johnny from jabbing him silly with words.

'No kiddin', Johnny, I was . . .'

'Shut up, you shlagoom,' Johnny said. The seventy-five cent H. Uppmann clenched in his mouth was like the muzzle of a .45 fixing Terry at point-blank range. 'How many times you been knocked out, Terry?'

There was scattered laughter again, but this time Terry didn't turn away from Johnny's ice-blue eyes.

'Knocked out? Uh . . .' Terry thought back, over the good nights and the tough ones. 'Only two times. And one was on cuts that night . . .'

'Shut up,' Johnny said. 'Two times. That must've been once too often. Your brains must be rattling. What you got up there, Chinese bells? Huh? You got a bunch o' Chinese bells up there where your brains useta be?'

There was another claque-like chuckle, and Johnny said over his shoulder, 'All right, turn it off. This ain't no comedy hour. Because of this—genius here, we're in a squeeze.'

'What's a matter?' Terry said. 'What I done wrong?'

Johnny turned to Charley the Gent who was trying to play it cool. 'I thought he was gonna keep an eye on that church meeting? I thought you said he could do the job?'

Charley said nothing.

'Johnny, I was there,' Terry said. 'I cased the whole thing. There was nothin' happened.'

Johnny turned to Charley again. Charley managed an expression for his face that was no expression. Johnny Friendly pushed the needle in deeper. 'Nothing happened, the kid says. Some operator you got yourself there, Charley. One more like him and we'll all be wearing striped pajamas.'

This time nobody laughed. The silence in the room was like a sudden lack of oxygen. Behind him in the front room Terry could hear the indistinct buzz of bar talk and the senseless laughter from the television. He longed to be out there, tanking up and shooting the breeze. He touched his forehead with his fingers and the skin was cold and wet. He hated to give himself away in front of these other punks. You could hold on to yourself inside, but those sweat glands kept pumping fear on to your face.

Terry turned to Charley for solace, for support. 'I told ya, Charley, it was a big nothin'. The Father did all the talkin'.'

Johnny looked around at the group whose indignation was a bare-faced copy of his own. 'All right, you fellas, beat it,' he said. 'Everybody but Charley. I want to talk to this shlagoom alone.'

They filed out dutifully. Johnny chewed forcefully on the end of his cigar.

'The Father did all the talking,' Johnny kept taking Terry's words, crumpling them into hard balls and throwing them back in Terry's face. 'Well, this afternoon your goddamn priest took a certain Timothy J. Nolan into a secret session with the Crime Commission and Nolan did all the talking. Now whaddya think of that?'

'You mean little Runty Nolan? The old-timer? Half gassed alla time?' Terry shrugged. 'He don't know much.'

'He don't, huh?' Johnny said. Reaching into his inside pocket he pulled out a thick manuscript bent lengthwise, and slammed it down on the table.

'You know what this is?'

Terry shook his head, worried.

'Just thirty-nine pages on the way we operate, that's all.'

'How'd you get that?' Terry was impressed.

Johnny gestured with his thumb in the direction of some higher connexion. 'None of your goddamn business. I got it.'

'Never mind, he got it,' Charley seconded. 'The complete works of Timothy J. Nolan. Hot off the press. Thank Christ it was an executive session and can't be used against us until he testifies in public.'

'Charley,' Johnny said, 'you got the brains to talk but sometimes you haven't got the brains not to talk. You know what I mean?'

Charley knew what he meant. When the pupils of Johnny's eyes were the size and hardness of buckshot even his intimate friends were cowed.

'Nolan!' Terry couldn't get over it. 'I knew he had the guts, but . . .'

'Guts!' Johnny stood up with both fists shaking. Charley had seen him like this perhaps a dozen times and each time it had signalled an execution. 'A crummy pigeon who's lookin' to get his neck wrung.'

He turned his back on Terry, whose face was an expressive composite of fear, resistance and resignation.

'Charley, you should've known better than to trust this punched-out kid brother of yours. He was all right hanging around for laughs. But this is business, important business. We're chopping up ten G's a week. I can't afford to have goof-offs messing in my business.'

'Now listen, Johnny, how could I tell . . .' Terry tried to cut in.

'I told you shut up. It's too late now. You should've kept an eye on 'em. Every one of them cudsuckers. You should've asked for more troops if you needed help.'

He turned to Charley again. 'Charley, do you realize what this means?' He flipped through the pages of the transcript. 'The stuff Nolan's got in here is dynamite. He was around when Willie Givens and Big Tom were gettin' started. He knows where a couple of bodies are buried.'

'For Mr. Big it's forty years ago,' Charley said. 'Statute of limitations.'

'Sure, sure,' Johnny said. 'But it'll be all over the papers. Even if they can't indict him, it won't do Willie Givens any good. And the big guy'll be pissed off at us for not cutting this Nolan down. And the bunch we got over here in City Hall is pretty shaky. A bad stink now could blow the lid off.'

'It's still only one fella,' Charley said. 'And we've been investigated before.'

'Sure, sure,' Johnny said. 'And rode 'em out fine. And we will

178

again. They ain't gonna pry me loose just because they blow on me a little. I worked too hard. Only remember, the last time we had an investigation, it was a city job and they weren't pushing too hard. So it was all a lot of headlines and recommendations and when all the smoke and the bullshit blew away we was still in solid, just like before.' He chuckled hard to himself. 'Was that funny, in Brooklyn the investigation found out that the Genotta family was the officers of all the locals. So they recommend there's gotta be a new honest election. So all the Genotta boys win every office agin. And the city certifies this is now okay because there was a new election like they recommended.'

Charley joined, tentatively, in the laugh on reform futility. 'Yeah, its pretty hard for a city to investigate itself.'

'But this is a State job, Charley, a bi-state job. There's already been some stink in the papers, and the Governors and the City Halls got no love for each other. I tell you, Charley, I don't like this investigation. I don't like this Father Buttinsky. I think it's time Willie Givens tries to get the Monsignor to stick a towel in his mouth. Slap him back in the church and make him shut up, for Christ sake. I'd be willing to make a nice contribution if this Barry would only get lost.'

'Gee, Johnny, I thought I done what I was . . .' Terry tried another half-hearted lead. This time it was Charley who cut him off.

'What the hell are you going around with his sister for?'

'I'm not, I'm not. I was only . . .'

'Johnny, it's that girl,' Charley interrupted. 'He meets that Doyle broad in the church and whammo, he can't find his way back to his corner.' He turned and raised his voice to Terry. 'It's an unhealthy relationship.'

'Move away from her, stay off her,' Johnny ordered. 'Unless you're both tired of living.'

'Crazy kid,' Charley said.

Johnny said, 'Charley, the next week or two is gonna be very touchy. We better have a meeting with Willie Givens tonight, and our legal eagle and some of the other—officials around the harbour. Sort of close ranks.'

'We've got to make this investigation look like a union-busting conspiracy,' Charley said. 'It's a dangerous precedent for the State to investigate or try to control a bonafide labour union.'

'Right,' Johnny said. 'You keep working on that. Talk to some of the reporters friendly with the shipping companies. We want to get this into the best papers. As for this Nolan—that dirty stooling bastard, we got to find a way to put the muzzle on him or he might start a whaddya call it—when it gets going faster 'n faster.'

'An avalanche,' Charley said.

'Yeah,' Johnny said, 'a pebble gets rolling and then a few rocks and whammo the whole goddamn mountain is coming down on top of us.'

'Don't worry, we'll ride it out,' Charley said. 'There's too much money on our side. Too many connexions.'

'And thank God we got the best muscle on the waterfront,' Johnny said. 'The time to use it is now, pronto, before that phony priest talks any more of these screwball Nolan bastards into singin' on us.'

'How can a little barfly like Runty . . .' Terry started to say.

Johnny Friendly walked over to him until his mouth was shouting in Terry's face. 'The only time you talk now is when I ask you something. You know where you're going? Down in the hold. No more cushy jobs in the loft. It's down in the hold with the sweat gang until you learn your lesson.'

'It's nice of him to give you any job at all after you goof like that,' Charley said.

'Yeah . . . I guess so,' Terry said miserably.

'On your way out tell Specs Flavin to come in,' Johnny dismissed him. Terry tried to keep his chin up as he walked out. Charley looked worried and Johnny said to him, 'I guess once a bum, always a bum. Same reason he never made a great fighter.'

When Terry passed through the front room nobody called to him to stop for a shot. He kept on walking. He walked down to the foot of Dock Street and along the river to a burned-out pier. The blackened, fire-chewed pilings stuck up out of the water, some of them barely rising above the surface, others nearly as tall as their original height. Terry sat on a charred stump near the river's edge and stared into the murky, refuse-littered surface of the Hudson.

Near-by a plump girl of about eleven in a dirty dress and a younger brother in an oversized torn sweater were fishing for coins, just as Terry used to do when he was a kid. You used a long stick and a piece of string and a stone with chewing gum on the bottom. Out in midstream a tug was towing a lighter with three freight cars on it. How many times Terry had stowed away in one of those boxcars to beat the ferry out of a nickel. Terry stared down at the dark, brooding reflection of himself in the filthy water.

Miss Square from Nowhere, he thought. Hell, the way he was going, they were a pair from nowhere.

17

RUNTY NOLAN LEANED on the bar at the Longdock conversing with his friends Moose McGonigle and Pop Doyle. He was wondering whether or not to show up for the night shift in the hold he had been tabbed for at the shape-up that morning. After seeing Charley the Gent's brother at the church meeting, he had been rather surprised that Big Mac had given him the nod for anything, even the hatch gang. The hold was a kind of longshore slum usually reserved for the more recently arrived foreign-born, the ship-jumpers, the Negroes and the Johnny-come-latelies without influence on the docks. It was a studied insult to offer a hatch job to a veteran docker. Most of the American-Irish on Big Mac's pier would have spit in the hiring boss's face at the suggestion that they help lift the hatch covers, break into the top-compartment cargo and gradually work their way down into the bowels of the ship.

Runty even wondered what was behind Big Mac's thumbing him into the hold. He had approached the Crime Commission office by as roundabout a route as possible and he was fairly sure he had not been followed. Just the same there were ten thousand eyes on the waterfront, and you never knew.

Well, he wouldn't stay out of the hold for that reason. He was on borrowed time, he always said, and if they were going to get him they'd find him anywhere. The hell with them! He could use that time and a half, thirty-five dollars for the gruelling, ten-hour shift, bread and beer money, of which he would need all that he could get if he was really going to stick his neck out and testify in public. But there was an extra incentive tonight, a come-on absolutely irresistible to an Irishman fond of his whisky and fonder of it still when he doesn't have to pay for it. The ship being unloaded was the *Elm*, out of Cobh, Ireland, and the cargo was Irish linen and lace and hemp and a hatch compartment full of cases of Jameson's whisky.

Laughingly Runty reminded Moose of the time the *Ash* had come in with ten-year-old whisky in hundred gallon hogsheads, to be bottled over here. Runty had tapped the key and then hollered 'Fire!' Then the hatch boss and a few willing lads had run for the pails. Two hours later the shop steward had found Runty and most of the others sprawled on the hatch floor sleeping it off. 'What's the matter with these boys?' Barney Backus, the steward, had asked. Runty had gained sufficient consciousness to mutter. 'It's the water. Must be somethin' in the water made us all sick as dogs.'

There was a pail next to Runty. Barney went over and peered into it. The fumes would have knocked over a smaller man. 'Yeah, there's something in that water all right,' he laughed. Barney got the shop-steward job because he was one of Johnny's muscles, but he was a good-natured fellow and got along well with the rank and file and even with the 'insoigents' like Runty, though he had to hit them in the head once in a while on Johnny's orders.

The sound of a whistle carried to them from across the street and Runty pulled his old cap a little more to one side, as if it were a tam.

'Well, time t' go t' work. The dear old *El-em*, loaded to the gunnels with sweet Irish whisky.'

'Now, Runty, you don't be liftin' any o' that,' Pop said severely. 'You wouldn't be breakin the law now?'

'I should say not,' Runty said emphatically. 'O' course if a case should fall 'n break and a bottle or two roll out on the deck, it would be a shame to see that fine old stuff go to waste, wouldn't it now?'

Runty downed a quick one. He threw a dollar and a nickel on the Longdock bar to cover the last three whiskies, threw his pals a 'see ya tomorra' and swung into his rapid, chesty walk on his way to the Jameson's.

Luke was on the hatch gang that night with a couple of other Negroes who got the left-over work in the hold if they kicked back enough, and several Italians who couldn't speak English and probably just came over on some deal Johnny worked. They were given union cards right away and in return most of their pay was funnelled into the back room of Friendly's. These men had their lives in hock because one squeak out of them and Johnny would turn them over to the Immigration Department. There were also a couple of old Irishmen who were on Johnny's s-list, but they had to be thrown some crumbs so they could repay the loan shark the fifty-five they owed on the fifty they borrowed that week. But the fella Runty was really surprised to see down there was Terry Malloy.

'Well, well, don't tell me a member of the high-ocracy is comin' down here and gettin' his hands dirty,' Runty rode him. Terry stared at him sullenly. Old Runty didn't seem to know he had one foot in the cement. Terry had been sweating out whether or not to smarten him. One wrong step now and he'd be S.O.L. with Johnny. And that L stood for life, not luck. But he liked Runty. He got many a laugh out of him. He bought the way the little guy got up. He could sure sop up the punishment. Once they even threw him in the river for a corpse and he swam out. He was like a scrawny undersized tomcat everybody tosses a brick at and nobody can kill. Aah, screw, Terry thought to himself. If he wants to get his balls in a ringer, that's his business. I didn't ask him to go spill his guts to those stinkin' investigators. That's his business. My business is stayin' alive. And I got my work cut out for me doin' that, the way things been goin'.

The temperature had been dropping throughout the evening and the damp cold lashed at the faces of the hatch gang as they worked their way through the top layer of packaged linen. The up-and-down fall tackle, worked from the winches on the dock and the pier, lowered the pallet down and the men loaded the cases on to it with the help of their curved, pointed hooks. Now and then Luke would hum or sing a snatch of a song as he laboured.

> *'Mississippi water taste like sherry wine.*
> *Yes, Mississippi water taste like . . .'*

he sang for the amusement of the gang.

> *'North River water taste like turpentine . . .'*

Runty laughed. 'To hell with that sherry wine. Let's get down to the Jameson's.'

Old man Gallagher, the hook man, attached the tackle hook to the cover of the third level and when all the covers were lifted off, swinging dangerously across the deck in the imperfect light of the overhead 100-arc, there were the whisky cases, as handsome an invitation to pilferage as Runty had seen in many a day. But Big Mac was prowling around the lip of the hatch, so the men had to bide their time. Except for one case that accidentally slipped off the pallet and broke open, rationing each man in the hatch a single bottle, the men were circumspect until they had unloaded their way down to the bottom of the third level. There they could work on cases under the deck, away from the hatch opening and the prying eyes of Big Mac.

'You see, fellers, the good Lord does watch over us, after all.' Runty grinned at his mates as he went to work expertly on the bottom slats of the whisky case with his cargo hook. The trick was to open the case from the bottom, remove its contents and then close the empty case again, load it on the pallet and send the intact-looking case up out of the hatch.

'Now doesn't this call for a bit of a party?' Runty said happily. 'We'll drink to God 'n Ireland, its whisky and its women, to Joey and Andy Collins, all the good ones gone. An' death to tyrants everywhere.' He held a bottle to his lips a moment, then lowered it with a chuckle. 'We'll even let these wallios drink to Ireland and Old Jameson. That's how good I feel tonight.'

He began stuffing the bottles into the deep pockets of his windbreaker. 'Now you see the beauty of a little man in a big coat.'

'That sure is some swag jacket,' Luke said admiringly.

Runty looked across the hatch at Terry, who was working listlessly, loading the cases on to the pallet.

'Hey, Terry, what you doin' down here?' he called out, the

alcohol warming the bravadeero in him. 'Keepin' an eye on us so we don't make off with any of Mr. Friendly's precious cargo?'

'Aah, go ahead, drink yourself into the shakes for all I care,' Terry said.

Runty laughed and raised the bottle in a general toast. 'Up Kerry! Where me lovely mother first saw the glint in me old man's eye.' He talked d-dropping Boheganese most of the time, but the brogue seemed to come on him a little more with each swig. 'I wonder if I can walk with a couple of these down my trousers,' he said.

'Runty, you're a walkin' distillery,' Luke laughed.

'God bless the *El-em*,' Runty said. 'And God bless Mr. Jameson. And God bless the Irish. And God forgive us for breedin' bums like Willie Givens and Tom McGovern and Mac McGown up there an' . . .'

Almost as if Big Mac had been eavesdropping on the impromptu party at the bottom of the hatch he shouted down, 'Now don't be walkin' off with any o' that cargo. Ya know how the boss feels about pilferage down there.'

'Why, Brother McGown,' Runty called up to him, 'you wouldn't be accusin' us of stealin'. I never stole anything in me life.' Then he whispered to Luke, 'Except Irish whisky . . .'

'I want every one of 'em cases on the dock—puhronto,' Mac cupped his hands to bellow into the hatch.

Runty pretended to clean out his ears. 'Talk louder. I can't hear ya.'

Mac shouted down, 'If ya kept ya ears open once in a while instead of your big mouth . . .'

'It ain't that my mouth is so big,' Runty grinned up at him irrepressibly. 'It's just that the rest of me is so small.'

The hatch gang stopped their work and roared with laughter.

'Okay, okay, more work 'n less lip,' Big Mac shouted, remembering not to get into a word-wingdo with this trigger-phrased little bat. 'We gotta get this ship out tomorra night. Get the lead out down there, you drunken bums.'

'That drunken bum can't talk to us drunken bums like that,' Runty said, sitting down now and leaning against the bulkhead to work on his bottle.

Oh, brother, what a pushover he'll be, Terry was thinking. One little push. Splash, and it's deep six for Runty Nolan. They must've known this job on the Jameson's would set him up. They ain't so dumb. They work pretty cute. Once more he even tried to edge over to Runty, to warn him to take it easy, but Runty was full of flit and real sassy now.

'You don't fool me,' Runty put him off. First they send you in the church and then they stick you down here to keep an eye on us. You're lucky we don't run this hook in one side of you and out the other.'

'Runty, I'd take it easy if I was you, if I was in your shoes,' Terry tried to warn him again.

'Well, you ain't,' Runty said, feeling better and better on the Jameson's. 'You're up there with Charley and Mac. I'm down here with Joey and fellas who stand up.'

'Man, you ain't standin' up, you're sittin' down,' Luke said good-naturedly. 'An' one more swallow o' that bottle an' you'll be layin' down.'

'I gotta stand up,' Runty said. 'Because I feel the singin' o' The Green Above the Red comin' on me. An' you'll never find an Irishman who's worth a damn who won't stand up for The Green Above the Red.'

Terry shrugged and went back to the other side of the hatch. Luke helped Runty to his feet and he sang all three verses of the sweet anthem of the trouble days in a wavering, dedicated voice:

'. . . an' freely as we lift our heads
We vow our blood to shed
Once 'n forever more t' raise
The green above the red . . .'

By two in the morning he was trying to teach the words to the bewildered Italian immigrants. In the next two hours Runty passed through his entire repertoire from the potato song to Galway Bay. By four o'clock he was beyond singing. Staggering from case to case, he groped his way to the hatchway ladder, his sexagenarian nimbleness hindered by the liquor in him and on him. Weighted down by the half dozen bottles in his deep pockets, he somehow managed to climb the long narrow ladder and scramble out over the side of the hatch on to the deck, deliberately careful to protect his own cargo of Jameson's.

The hatch gang had called it a night and he felt proud of himself for having resisted Luke's repeated offers to take him home. Hell, nobody ever had to take Runty Nolan home. He stepped off the gangway on to the stringpiece, balancing himself with the grace of a tightrope walker—he thought—and went into the pier shed. A hundred yards in he could barely make out the backs of the last hatchmen as they walked slowly down the pier to the street.

'An' fleely azh we . . .' he tried to sing, gave it up and flopped down to rest on a convenient hand-truck. He reached into his pocket for the bottle he had been drinking from, but just as he raised it to his lips it slipped from his hands and smashed to the floor. Inside the entrance to the pier Specs Flavin and Sonny Rodell heard the sound of the breaking glass. They looked at each other and kept on walking forward. 'He'll be blind,' Specs said. 'Take him out quick with the jack. Now don't miss him, goddamn it.'

Specs had been over at Friendly's most of the night, getting ready for this. Every trip to the can, to sniff up the junk, added an extra layer of confidence. He was just a small, nervous, pasty-faced man, but by four in the morning he had grown ten feet tall. Truck and Gilly and the rest of them, they were supposed to be tough guys, but a job like the Joey Doyle job or this one was too much for them. It needed Specs Flavin. It took guts to go all the way. It took a real man. Specs wore thick glasses and sometimes they kidded him about his astigmatism and the fact that he had to pay for his gash because he wasn't good-looking enough. Well, he'd show 'em, he'd show 'em all. The viciousness rose and rose in him until he could feel it boiling in his head, ten feet tall. Sonny wasn't on the junk, but he had had about a dozen snorts to steady himself. He wasn't a natural killer or a psycho or anything, and he only did this out of a certain awe for Specs and to prove he was tougher than Truck and Gilly figured.

When they came up to Runty he had passed out cold on the hand-truck. He was stretched out on his back, snoring irregularly through his broken nose.

187

'Jesus, he sounds like the winch is still working,' Sonny said.

'Christ, he's a homely little bastard,' Specs said.

'How could one little guy give us so much trouble?' Sonny said.

'He won't give us no more,' Specs said. 'What a rummy he was!'

'He could sure take a beatin',' Sonny said with admiration.

'Maybe you better hit 'im in the head with the jack once for luck,' Specs said. 'I don't trust that little bastard not to come to.'

Sonny did as he was told.

It takes a big man to do this, Specs was thinking, lifted on the nose candy. It's like you're God or something. He's dead and don't know it, but I know it because I got the power in me.

'See that bailing wire over there,' he said to Sonny. 'Wind it around him and under the truck.'

Sonny did as he was told, but he did it hastily. He was anxious to get it over with.

'Now grab the handles and push the damn thing out to the stringpiece.'

For a moment they stood together on the stringpiece ten feet above the level of the river. The night was still dark, but the eastern sky held a promise of morning. Below them they could hear the water washing against the pilings.

'Give it a good hard push,' Specs said.

It was almost like a formal burial at sea, the two of them standing there with their heads bent. The hand-truck trundled to the edge of the pier and plunged Runty Nolan into the depths of the black river. No longer was Runty on borrowed time. Specs Flavin had called in the I.O.U. The good old North River, Johnny Friendly's silent partner, had done it again.

'I'll bet it's plenny cold down there t'night,' Sonny said.

'Not where he's goin',' Specs laughed nastily.

Specs Flavin turned from the stringpiece and Sonny followed him back into the pier shed. The stuff was slowly wearing off and Specs was uncomfortably shrinking back to his own self-despising, nondescript size.

18

ONLY A FEW blocks away the light was still on in Father Barry's room. He had been up all night working on a report for the Crime Commission hearings. More and more clearly in these few days he had come to see that the shape-up, depending on a surplus of man-power so the hiring boss could pick and choose, was the seat of infection poisoning the labour relations of the harbour. The shape-up had been abolished years ago in Liverpool and London, in Seattle and Portland.

Why did it still fester in the greatest harbour in the world? That the waterfront racketeers should cling to it for the power it gave them over the rank and file was understandable. But now Father Barry had been reading reports proving conclusively that the association of shipping companies and the leading stevedore companies favoured the shape-up too, and, not only that, were closely tied to the mob elements around the harbour through a deeply imbedded system of personal bribery.

At the Crime Commission offices, when he had escorted Runty to the secret session, he had seen the charts. The most respectable shipping and stevedore companies in the harbour had been handing out regular monthly bribes for years to known hoodlums like Johnny Friendly and Charley Malloy, to the mob on the midtown piers across the river, to the Benasios in Brooklyn, to Danny D., to Slicker McGhee on the Lower West Side and the rest of the tribe. On the walls of the Commission office Father Barry had seen the truth: two hundred of the most notorious hoodlum 'labour leaders' in the harbour were on the payroll of the great luxury and freighter lines and their stevedore subsidiaries. Looking over those charts and remembering that an overwhelming majority of the executives and dock bosses as well as working hands were Catholic, Father Barry could not help thinking again of Xavier and his problem in India four hundred years earlier—his appeal to the King to send out honest officials. The ones who were wielding temporal Christian power in India, he wrote, were wolves and jackals who preyed on Mohammedans and Christians alike, and were so depraved, so greedy, so selfish, so lacking in every Christian virtue, that they were making a daily mockery of Xavier's tireless efforts at conversion.

The harbour was crying out not only for a thorough house-cleaning of a corrupted union, not only for a new, modern, humane, efficient method of hiring, but actually for a moral revolution that would prevent prominent Catholic laymen like President Willie Givens and king-maker Tom McGovern from mouthing pious speeches at Communion breakfasts while providing respectable coloration for convicted criminals masquerading as union delegates, shop stewards and hiring bosses.

Father Barry took heart from the knowledge that he wasn't the first priest in the harbour to raise his voice against the moral rot that permitted the underworld to sit at the partnership table with shipping magnates and political leaders. Old Father Mahoney on Staten Island—where Vince Donato ran the docks—had been delivering fiery sermons against this jungle for decades. If Father Barry were called to testify at the waterfront hearings, as had been suggested, he wanted to quote the old priest's warning: 'When the Church and the community cease to be interested in the men that labour, both the Church and the community die.'

But Father Mahoney was a pastor over there and had established his right to speak his mind through two generations of service. He had baptized the grandchildren of the parents he had married. He could defy Donato even though that padrone, with the docks in his pocket, was a big political wheel on Staten Island. Here in Bohegan, Father Barry was still a young curate, and already his Pastor had stopped to talk to him that afternoon about the danger of committing himself too deeply on an issue that might first require discussion with the Bishop. Father Donoghue did not want to discourage his curate's interest in the plight of the parish dock workers, not at all. Perhaps it was time to apply a little Christian charity to what did seem an unfortunate, un-Christian state of affairs. But sometimes it was better to walk carefully than to rush ahead and stumble. However, as long as Father Barry confined his guidance to local communicants from the docks who came in for assistance, Father Donoghue could see no objection. He too regretted the brazen self-interest of certain prosperous Catholics and he was more than willing to remember at Mass Father Barry's campaign against the evil spirits of profiteering and self-aggrandizement. 'Just go easy, lad,' the ageing Pastor advised. 'Easy, easy. Like mountain climbing. Make sure one foot is securely dug in before you try raising the other.'

Father Donoghue was a good, mild man and Father Barry took his remarks both as mild rebuke and mild encouragement. Saying his office that morning, the curate promised to be circumspect and to lend the men as much support as he could without embarrassing his Pastor or needlessly exposing himself.

He had just finished the eleven to twelve confessions and was on his way to lunch in the rectory dining-room, wondering if Mrs. Harris, the housekeeper, was going to serve her meat loaf again, when Moose ran up, out of breath, his big, deceptively tough-looking face livid with anxiety.

'Father, Runty . . . Runty Nolan . . .' he gasped.

'Yes, yes, what happened?'

'His body just washed up to the surface off Pier B. The propellers of the *Elm* churned it up. The sons of bitches, Father.'

'Okay, okay, I'll go down with you,' Father Barry said. The two men hurried toward the docks.

Runty Nolan was lying under a tarpaulin on the stringpiece. The word had flashed around the bars and up the mouldy tenement stairwells and four or five hundred people had quickly gathered. Pop and Jimmy Sharkey and Fred the counterman from the Long-dock, and Katie with Mrs. Collins and Mrs. Gallagher who mothered their tenement, and Luke, and Billy and Jo-Jo and some other Golden Warriors, and a sprinkling of the mob, Big Mac, and Truck and Gilly and 'J.P.' Morgan and cops waiting for the coroner, and Captain Schlegel and some of the stevedore officials and Mutt Murphy still muttering to himself and a couple of hundred tight-lipped longshoremen from the day shift.

Terry Malloy, in the middle of the crowd, tried to make himself inconspicuous. He spotted Katie, noticed that she looked pale and frightened, and purposely avoided her glance. He had nothing to do with this. Hadn't he even tried to warn the little guy? And the fresh little bastard would have no part of him. He had nothing to do with this. He wished it hadn't happened. He'd miss little Runty and his wise-cracking sass, his clownish face except for the flattened nose. his crazy courage. A little man with balls big enough to bowl with, he had heard somebody describe him in a bar. But what the hell! He went the way he wanted to go. Defiant and up to his eyebrows in good Irish whisky. Terry could only hope he'd be that lucky when his number came up.

Father Barry came thrusting through the crowd angrily, muttering staccato orders, 'One side, gangway, lemme through.' When he reached the tarpaulined figure of Runty, he quickly gave him the last rites conditionally. Then he started to speak loudly and rapidly. He sounded more like a man engaged in fierce argument than a priest attending the dead.

'I came down to keep a promise,' he began. 'I gave Runty Nolan my word that if he stood up to the mob, I'd stand up with him. All the way. Now Runty Nolan is dead. He was one of those fellers who had the gift of getting up. But this time they fixed him. Oh, they fixed him for good this time. Unless it was an accident, like they'll be saying. Yes, and I'll lay you two to one the police'll go along. Just another accidental drowning for Port Bohegan.'

His voice was full of anger. A ferry let go a warning blast in mid-river, but nobody looked around. A cold wind was whipping up off the water and the priest's cassock, which he hadn't had time to change after Moose's hurry-up call, billowed out and swirled around his legs.

'Some people think the Crucifixion only took place on Calvary,' Father Barry continued. 'They better wise up. Taking Andy Collin's life a few years ago, the very morning he was supposed to blow the whistle as hiring boss on Pier D, that was a crucifixion. Taking Joey Doyle, to stop him from organizing an honest opposition, to stop him from testifying, that's a crucifixion. And when they give Runty Nolan the river treatment, because he was ready to spill his guts next Monday to the Crime Commission, that's a crucifixion. Every time the mob puts the crusher on a good man, tries to stop him from doing his duty as a union man and a citizen, it's a crucifixion.'

The angry word 'crucifixion' crackled in the air and hung over them a moment like dangerously close lightning. Father Barry glared at the crowd as if he was accusing every one of them.

'And anybody who lets *this* happen'—he gestured fiercely toward the tarpaulin—'and I mean *anybody*, from the high and mighty shipping company interests, the Police Commissioner and the DA down to the lowliest worker in the hatch—anybody who keeps silent about something he knows has happened—or strongly suspects has happened—shares the guilt of it just as much as the Roman soldier who pierced the flesh of Our Lord to see if he was dead.'

In the midst of the crowd, Terry thought, 'He's lookin' at me,' and lowered his head to hide himself in the anonymity of the clustered longshoremen. *Why the hell does he have to keep lookin' at me?*

From farther back in the crowd, Truck's gravel voice called out, 'Go back to ya choich, Father.'

Father Barry pivoted, almost like a fighter, in the direction of his heckler. 'Boys, this is my church. I took a vow to follow Christ wherever He might lead me. And if you don't think Christ is down here on this waterfront, you've got another guess coming.'

He shouted it in the tone the pier cowboys understood. Now he lowered his voice to speak to the rest of them.

'Every morning when the hiring boss blows his whistle, Christ stands alongside you in the shape-up. Okay, I know that may bring a cynical smile to some of your faces. Don't try and kid us, Father, a few of those faces are saying. Well, if this is kidding, so is the fact that Christ earned His meat 'n potatoes with His own muscle and sweat. It's only kidding to those whom Christ Himself described as "Having eyes, they see not. And having ears, they hear not." That takes in too many of you fellers. Sure you have eyes and ears but you'd rather wear earplugs and look the other way.

'But take my word for it, Christ stands with you in the shape. He sees why some of you get picked and some of you get passed over. Chances are, He gets passed over Himself because He won't kick back and He won't play ball with the boys who don't have to work because they've got those strong backs of yours working for them.

'So Christ is left standing in the street with the other rejects. He sees the troubled look in the eyes of the family men worried about getting up the rent money and putting meat on the table for the wife and kids. He sees them driven to the loan shark, who's happy to help 'em out—at the rate of ten per cent and up. He drove the money changers out of the temple—and where do they wind up?—here on the docks!

'How do you think He feels when He sees His fellow workers selling their souls to the mob for a day's pay? How do you think He feels when He walks into a tenement kitchen and talks to Mrs. Joe Docks, who's red-eyed with grief because her man isn't working steady? She can't figure where she stands from day to day. Right now she needs a five-dollar food ticket because her old man talked up for his rights and is being starved off the dock.

'How does He feel when He goes to a union meeting—one of those rare, rare union meetings—and sees how it's run? Sees how few show up, and even fewer dare to ask for the floor, unless it's to second a motion from the boys on top. Sees what happens to the one or two stand-up guys who haven't had the last shred of human dignity—yes, dignity in Christ—beaten out of them.

'How does He feel when He walks our neighbourhood and counts the number of bars and the horse-rooms and money lenders and looks around in vain for a playground or a community centre? How does He feel when He sees the ragged kids of honest longshoremen wearing hand-me-down clothes and playing stick-ball in narrow, filthy streets, jumping our from under the wheels of the speeding trucks?

'How does He feel when He finds out what these kids are saying and doing, what they're up to in their wised-up ignorance by the time they're eleven? Ready to fight the world at eleven in the Catholic Protectory. He who said, "Whoever causes one of these little ones to sin, it were better for him to have a great millstone around his neck and to be drowned in the depths of the sea."

'What does Christ think of the easy-money boys who pose as your union leaders, sell you out every day in the week and twice on Sunday, and wear two hundred dollar suits and sop up the beef gravy at Cavanagh's on your union dues, your vocation fund and your kickback money? Yes, and what does He think of His respectable followers, the shipping executives and the city officials who drop a fin in the basket during Mass and then encourage or condone the goons and the dock bosses who learned their stevedore technique at Sing Sing and Dannemora?

'What must He who established the dignity of work not with words, but with His hands. think about a set-up like this? And how does He who spoke up with fear against every evil feel about your silence?'

Again he seemed to be staring through the other listeners into the lowered eyes of Terry. Terry pressed forward as close as he could against the broad back of the fellow in front of him. Goddamn the priest and his big mouth. Goddamn Charley and his big ideas too. Goddamn everybody and everything that drew him into this. The prolonged bass whistle of an ocean-going freighter competed for a moment with the angry blast from Father Barry. Maybe Terry ought to ship out, get away while the getting's good. Maybe Charley had connexions to fix him up with a sailor's card and ship him out.

'You want to know what's wrong with our waterfront?' the priest began slowly when the sound of the ship's whistle faded away. 'It's love of a lousy buck. It's making love of a buck—the fat profit—the wholesale stealing—the cushy job—more important than the love of man. It's forgetting that every fellow down here is your brother, yes, your brother in Christ.'

The word *Christ* wasn't spread over them softly as a balm. It was hurled at them as a gauntlet, as a furious challenge. It might have been in this manner that the first-century revolutionists had brought their dangerous faith to the market places and temple squares of Antioch and Philippi, stirring, converting and scandalizing. Most of the people gathered around Father Barry were accustomed to think of Christ only as a pious abstraction, a grey figure in the Missal illustrations. For them it was a hell of a shock to be urged to make room for a living Christ who stood among them in a windbreaker, carrying a cargo book in His hand, a Christ Who wondered how He was going to meet His rent and His grocery bill, a Christ crucified by loan sharks and strong-armers, a Christ on a North River cross, dumped like garbage or Runty Nolan, tied up with bailing wire, into the muck of the Hudson.

'Fellows,' Father Barry seemed to be speaking to each one personally, 'no matter how tough it gets—and it looks to me like it's gonna get tougher before it gets better—remember, Christ is always with you. He shapes with you every morning, in winter rain or ninety-degree heat. He's in the hatch. He's in the union hall. He's in the bars. He's kneeling here beside Nolan. And He's saying to all of you: If you do it to the least of mine, you do it to me. What better slogan could an honest union have? What they did to Andy Collins, what they did to Joey Doyle, what they just did to Runty Nolan, they're doing to you, and you, and you. All of you! And only you, with God's help, have the power to knock 'em out of the box for good!'

Then he said an Our Father and announced, 'There will be a requiem Mass for Timothy J. Nolan at ten o'clock Saturday.' He turned to the covered figure, silenced at last under its tarpaulin. 'Okay, Runty?' He made the sign of the Cross, looked around at everybody and, still angry, gave voice to a harsh, loud 'Amen'.

Pop Doyle hurried up to shake his hand. Katie followed her father silently. The blood was drained from her face. This second killing so soon after Joey's had carried her into a state beyond her fresh-eyed militance of a few days earlier. But the loss of Runty had an opposite effect on Pop. Joey was a born martyr. He had known what he was doing, the deep chance he was taking, and Pop had warned him and feared for him and unconsciously prepared himself for bad or worse. But Runty was a gadfly, a mischievous clown, a lifelong drinking and talking crony, and Pop found it painfully impossible to believe that Runty would not be over at the Longdock in a few minutes, bending an elbow in his everlastingly cheerful and malicious toast, 'Here's mud in the eye of Willie Givens . . .'

'Father, I'm with ya,' Pop said. 'I don't care what they do to me now. I'm takin' my chances with ya.'

'Good boy,' Father Barry said. 'I think we better have another meeting to keep things going tonight. The Longshoremen's Committee of St. Timothy's. I got an idea for putting out a leaflet on Joey and Runty. We c'n use the office mimeograph. Maybe we c'n keep enough pressure on Donnelly so he won't be able to close this one out as an accident. Maybe we c'n get up a petition of protest.'

He looked sharply at Katie. 'Okay, Kate?'

'Father, I'm frightened,' she said.

'My old man used to give an old Irish toast,' Father Barry said.

' "May the Devil chew the toes—of all your foes—so you'll know 'em by their limping." If this movement of ours can really get rolling, there'll be a lot of tough guys limping around here before we're through.'

Moose and Jimmy and Luke and the widow of Andy Collins and half a dozen others who were standing around chuckled or smiled appreciatively.

'Got a smoke on you?' the priest said.

Pop offered him one. 'Father, you and Mutt Murphy are a pair—a couple of scrounge artists,' he said.

'The Lord looks after his own,' the priest said lightly. Then he nodded toward the tarpaulin, which was being lifted toward the waiting door of the police emergency wagon. 'And I hope that goes for Runty.' He felt heartsick at what had been done to Runty, and yet strangely exhilarated. Men have felt that way on a battlefield when their buddies spin in and they have to keep going. 'See you later,' he saluted them sharply, then turned and swung into his rapid pace along the stringpiece.

'Man, a few more like him and I quit the Baptists,' Luke announced.

'Like Runty'd say, a bravadeero,' Moose shouted.

'Jesus, I haven't seen things so hot down here in thoity years,' Pop said.

'The waterfront's a funny place,' Jimmy agreed. 'All quiet for years and then whammo, it goes off like a bomb.'

Half an hour later Terry was sitting at Hildegarde's bar.

'Wha's a matter you so quiet today, you no luff me no more,' the outrageously fat proprietress tried to joke him.

'Again,' Terry said, tapping his empty jigger glass. 'Double it up this time.'

'You want I play you a new record, very saxy?' Hildegarde offered.

'Lea' me alone,' Terry said.

'I know you feel bad about little Runty. Such a rascal. He always came in kiddin' me about us gettin' married. "Hah, in the bed I won't be able to find you," I useta tell 'im.'

'Okay, okay, stick the goddamn record on,' Terry said, and as she did so, his mind played a dirty trick on him and he heard the trusting, quiet agony of Katie's voice, all mixed up with the musky voice of the vocalist, crying, 'Help me, help me, if you can, for God's sake help me . . .'

'Here, kid, haff a drink on Hildegarde,' the hefty proprietress said.

He nodded okay. But he heard himself answering Katie, 'I have my whole life to drink . . .'

19

FATHER BARRY BEGAN his day with the six o'clock Mass. The attendance was better than usual because the priest had won new allies when he pulled no punches in his send-off to Runty on the docks. Most of them had held back from joining Father Barry openly, but now they got up an hour early and joined the early Mass as a way of showing silent approval of Father Barry's guts. 'He's stand-up,' they said to each other as they drifted into small groups from various tenements on their way to the old brick church through the bone-cold semi-darkness. 'Stand-up' was the highest praise in the waterfront book.

Father Barry was still feeling nerved up from the dumping of Runty and the bitter wrath that had surged in him on the dock. When he made the gesture of washing his fingers after offering the chalice he spoke the Latin words so angrily that many of the longshoremen who usually let the unintelligible chant pour over them now bothered to check the English text on the facing page of their missals.

'O Lord, I love the beauty of Thy house and the place where Thy glory dwells. Destroy not my soul with the impious, O God, nor my life with men of blood. In whose hands there is iniquity, whose right hand is full of bribes. But as for me, I will walk in my innocence, rescue me and be gracious to me.'

The words bit hard into the issue facing nearly all of them sharing in the sacrifice that morning. Dozens of longshoremen had pliantly paid their bribes to the hiring boss for years, or joined in the phony walk-outs when the mob wanted to shake down a tulip bulb cargo or a delivery of furs. Once more Father Barry was able, without launching into a sermon, to make the Mass not a cut-and-dried ritual but a living experience rooted in the soil of their lives. 'And converts to reconvert,' Father Barry recalled his own thought, remembering Xavier's experience with the predatory Portuguese captains in India. Now as he turned from the altar which was Calvary, and looked into the attentive faces of men who had made their peace with rottenness, he wondered if the apostleship of tough-mindedness was beginning to pay off at last. Once more Christ had offered Himself to the sharp nails and the hard Cross, and through the lips of Father Barry He had made His crucial promise to redeem them with His blood.

The men went out into the pale winter morning to get some eggs and coffee in them before showing up at the piers. There was scattered talk of a wildcat one-day strike to protest the push-off of Runty Nolan. Runty had been around so long that even fellows who thought he was a goddamn nuisance found themselves missing him.

Father Barry was removing his vestments in the sacristy when Father Vincent handed him the Bohegan *Graphic*. 'You made the front page,' the priest said to his fellow curate.

A reporter from the local tab had been in the crowd when Runty's body was recovered. Father Barry's attack on the 'evil triumvirate' of shippers, city officials and union racketeers was spread over two columns. 'I haven't seen the Manhattan papers yet, but I hear they covered it too,' Father Vincent said. 'Well, you asked for it, kid. You're a celebrity.'

Father Barry shrugged. 'I called it the way I saw it. They can't hang me for that.'

'Not with a rope, no,' Father Vincent agreed with him. 'But where's Father Coughlin these days? A few more of these'—he waved the *Graphic*—'and you'll be a left-wing Coughlin.'

'What's left-wing?' Father Barry said. 'You call the Missal left-wing? You call the dignity of man left-wing? You call the Encyclicals left-wing?'

'Don't waste your ammunition on me,' Father Vincent said, lowering the sleeveless white chasuble over his head. He was to say the next Mass. 'You better save your strength for the Vicar General.'

'What do you want to bet the Pastor backs me up?' Father Barry said.

'And what do you want to bet the Monsignor will be in there steaming up the Bishop inside of an hour?' Father Vincent countered. 'When you step on the toes of the Police Commissioner, City Hall, the longshore headquarters and the Interstate Stevedores you're treading on some powerful digits.'

'The bigger they are . . .' Father Barry shrugged.

'The harder *you* fall,' Father Vincent warned as he muttered the last of his vesting prayers.

When Father Barry returned to the rectory, all hell was breaking loose. Reporters from the metropolitan newspapers were calling for interviews. A delegation of longshoremen from the West Side, across the river, had come over to ask for advice on how to organize opposition to the criminal clique that had their local sewed up. There were even a few callers from the Jerry Benasio preserve in Brooklyn. There was an assistant hiring boss from the East River, another Italian-mob territory, who had worked with the boys for years, but was uneasy with his conscience. At nine-thirty an assistant counsel from the Crime Commission called to make an appointment. He wanted to discuss the possibility of Father Barry's appearing as a friendly witness at the waterfront hearings. The priest could testify as to what the deceased Nolan had told him of corruption and violence in Bohegan. Also, a Commission investigator had informed the counsel that Father Barry was working on a plan for harbour reform.

Father Barry made dates to meet the press and the Commission counsel, and was conferring with Jimmy Sharkey, Moose and Dino Lorenzo, a tough Jersey City recruit, on the leaflet plan, when word came that the Pastor wanted to see him.

Father Donoghue was having a cup of tea in his old-fashioned sitting room when Father Barry came in.

'Pete, I'm troubled by these headlines,' the elderly Pastor said. 'I feel you have, well, not exactly disobeyed my orders, but chosen to ignore my advice. As you know, I am not at all opposed to what you are doing. I have come to agree that the waterfront workers in our parish do need our help. But there are ways to do these things. Discretion is often the better part of valour. And I could hardly say you were discreet in these remarks of yours on the docks.' He nodded towards the *Graphic* and the black headlines on the tea table. 'Before you went so far as to impugn the character of our local officials I should have liked to prepare the ground a little bit with the Bishop. We're only a small church, one of the poorest in his diocese. But I must say he has always treated me very decently. Now I'm afraid Monsignor O'Hare, whose position I realize is diametrically opposed to your own, will undoubtedly have a chance to influence the Bishop against you. I might even say *us*—before we have a chace to explain what we are trying to do.'

'Father, believe me, I never intended to buck your authority, or your good advice,' Father Barry said quickly. 'It's just that events got behind me and started pushing me faster 'n faster. I had no idea they were going to get Runty when I promised to do my work from inside the church yesterday morning. And when I got down there, Father, and thought of the stinking evil of this thing, men who have turned away from God, juggling the lives of human beings like so many Indian clubs—when I thought of the so-called leaders of the community who are even worse than the goons because they ought to know better, well, I guess I did blow my cork and I hit 'em with that stuff about Christ in the shape-up.'

'And very moving it was,' Father Donoghue agreed, sipping his tea. 'I think it would have made an excellent sermon as part of the Mass, a special Labour Day Mass, for instance. I'm simply not sure of the propriety of involving yourself so directly in the temporal affairs of the port.'

'Father, the men were telling me of a big wildcat strike five or six years ago that the Communists were able to move in on,' Father Barry argued. 'Nearly all of these men are Romans. How could the Moscows get any hold on them? Well, now I begin to see why. These men have a problem, economic insecurity, physical safety, their lives. They're generations behind the average American working stiff. But their leaders are nearly all racket guys, really company-union stooges on the take from the shipping companies.'

'On the take?' said Father Donoghue.

'Accepting bribes,' Father Barry explained. 'Playing footsie with the boss stevedores.'

'I quite understand,' Father Donoghue said.

'What the Commies did was to move into a leadership vacuum,' Father Barry went on. 'There are thousands of honest, decent men working the docks, our people. It's simply that they're divided, leaderless, helpless—terrorized. To accept their fate with a shrug and a shot of whisky has become a way of life. The best way to keep out the Commies and give these men back their God-given dignity is to stand up for the real issues and interests of the rank and file. Murders that go unpunished—not occasionally but year in year out—isn't it time we took an open stand on that? And this thing affects the home, the home life. Demoralized longshoremen get drunk, sink into debt, fight with their wives, the kids go hungry, they stop going to church. That's right, Father, they stop believing in us because they see Monsignor O'Hare breaking bread or lifting a whisky with their mortal enemies. Sure the Monsignor raises a lot of money for his church and I suppose one of these days he'll make Bishop. But he's not my idea of the one, true, universal Church. I don't see him "walking without blemish and working justice".'

'I understand what you mean—yes, deeply,' Father Donoghue said. 'Just the same I'm worried for you. I want to see you continue this work. I think you can help us build a strong, more meaningful parish, closer to God. But, Pete, I am worried. I am once again as old as you are. I never had any particular ambition to "get anywhere" in the Church. I wasn't interested in a wealthy parish and making a reputation as an able money raiser. I know we have that kind. It's our strength that we have every kind, from the most selfless, the true saint whose feet ache whenever his fellow man stubs a toe—to the shrewd makers of power plays, the politically astute——'

'Father, I took an oath of obedience, and I never intend to back away from it,' Father Barry cut in, 'but I think I can speak to you frankly. I didn't accept this calling to follow the O'Hares. I can't play ball with these ecclesiastical climbers who go where the money is. We've had them as Popes and we know the disgrace. It's to our everlasting glory that we somehow survived some of those Medici

202

Popes, that we fought our way back to our Leo XIII and Pius XI. In this last week I've begun to see the moral battle we've got on our hands here in Bohegan. I'd like to try to slug it out, inside the sanctions of your authority—that goes without saying.'

'What I'd like to do,' Father Donoghue said frankly, 'is to preserve the quality of your fervour within the bounds of—well, not expediency—shall we say practicality?'

'You don't want to see me take such a lead off first base that I get cut down and blow my chance of sliding home with the winning run.' Father Barry grinned.

'I believe that expresses the idea,' Father Donoghue smiled, 'although I still think hurling has baseball beat a mile as a national sport.'

'You foreigners have strange ideas.' Father Barry grinned.

'Now to get down to cases,' the Pastor said, wiping his lips and pushing the tea tray away. 'I'm afraid I will have to forbid you to form a Longshoremen's Committee of St. Timothy's. I understand that was to be the name of it. I feel that would involve us far too directly in the inter-union conflicts of the waterfront.'

'Check,' Father Barry said. 'How about the basement chapel? Can we still use it for the protest meeting on Runty Nolan the boys are getting up for Sunday night? It's the eve of the Crime Commission hearings. Runty wasn't the most conscientious parishioner we ever had, but he did manage to show up for Mass whenever he was sober enough to find his way.'

'If you can put the proof in my hands—in case the Bishop should call for it—that such a meeting cannot be held safely any place else in Bohegan. In that case I'll go along.'

'And our mimeograph machine? The boys want to hand out a leaflet on Runty. He was popular with a lot of the fence sitters. They want to run off what I said on the dock yesterday—and pass it out along the waterfront.'

Father Donoghue sighed. 'Since you have said it, I suppose they have a right to circulate it. As far as you are concerned it is a calculated risk. You'll find longshoremen and the business and political interests lining up for and against—er, Barryism. I think it would be best if our church was not associated with that. In other words, I want to make it very clear what you are forbidden to do, what you are permitted to do with my authority and protection, and what you may do on your own as an American citizen expressing your own opinion.'

'Thanks for laying it on the line,' Father Barry said.

The careworn but oddly boyish face of the old priest lit up with a faint smile. 'If some of our parishioners want to borrow the mimeograph machine to run off something on their own, I don't believe I would have any objection.'

'Father, I couldn't ask for more than that,' Father Barry said. 'You're solid.'

'I'm a feeble reed leaning on the mercy of our Lord,' said Father Donoghue. 'But I'm an old reed. I've weathered some storms.'

'And you're shoring this house against the next one,' Father Barry said.

'Which reminds me,' the Pastor said. 'Be sure you don't slack off on any of your parish duties. You'd better not leave yourself vulnerable on any count right now. Arm yourself against the charge that you're shirking your regular responsibilities in order to interfere in a labour dispute.'

'Which reminds *me*,' Father Barry said. 'I only have five minutes to wash up before hearing confessions.' He took his leave of the old Pastor, who would never be more than a poor parish priest, and for reasons that Father Barry was beginning to appreciate.

'Take your time with the penitents.' Father Donoghue's cautionary humour-touched words followed Father Barry into the hallway. 'Don't brush them off with a snap judgement because you're in a hurry to get to other things. Hearing confession can either be an art or a routine.'

In the stuffy confession box Father Barry tried to lose himself in the frailties of the poor sinners who mumbled through the dark screen their misdeeds and wrong thoughts, their mortal and venal commissions and omissions. An old man had pinched a plump middle-aged buttocks on a stairway. 'It was right in front of me, Father. God help me. I just couldn't resist it, Father.' Three Hail Marys and one Our Father. A teamster had stolen a side of beef. Father Barry tried to make of himself a scale to weigh these sins.

'Six Hail Marys and three Our Fathers and make a really good act of contrition.' Adultery. Failure to attend Mass on three successive Sundays. Calling your wife a bad name. Shoplifting from a Jewish department store. And a girl of eleven who had persuaded a little neighbour boy to lower his pants so she could examine the difference.

As Father Barry doled out the penances and prayed with the penitents for the cleansing of their immortal souls, he was guilty of a slight venal sin of his own. Instead of giving himself fully to the confessional experience, as the Pastor had cautioned him, he found his mind wandering back to the sins of the waterfront that seemed to him a graver lapse from the plan of God, for it involved more than the sins one commits against oneself. The sins against humanity on the docks were chain-reaction sins, turpitude on a wholesale, community, harbour-wide and even nation-wide scale. While the frightened child with her natural, Eve-like curiosity must learn the wonder of sex in some deeper, later way, still her vice seemed to Father Barry a tiny one compared to the brazen denial of Christ's love that raged on the docks. Johnny Friendly was proud of his attendance at Monsignor O'Hare's Church of the Sacred Heart. He and his mother were a familiar pair at every Sunday Mass. How much did Johnny Friendly bare of himself when he made confession? How much of the black worldliness filtered through the screen of the booth? To what extent did the priests under O'Hare over at the Sacred Heart, in the newer section of Bohegan, press men like Friendly to confess their crimes of extortion, plunder and intimidation? To rob a man of his dignity is to rob him of the glory and mystery of his birthright; surely no less a sin than the more traditional plucking of a girl's virginity. That is what Father Barry was thinking as he listened to the young voices and the old voices reciting their ageless imperfections.

He still had a great many things to do before lunch, including a call on Mrs. Glennon to find out if her wayward husband Beanie was bringing the money home. Otherwise Father Barry would have to track him down and get it off him before he spread it around the bars. To gauge his time, Father Barry stepped out of the box a moment to see if the line of penitents was reaching its end.

Sitting in an empty pew was the young tough who had shown up at the basement meeting for Joey—Terry Malloy. He was crouched down, his face lowered and his hands pressed against his head. He seemed jumpy and rose quickly when he saw the priest. 'Hey, I wanna talk to ya,' he said gruffly.

'You mean you're waiting to be heard in there?' Father Barry said, thumbing toward the booth.

'Yeah, yeah. I guess so,' Terry said uncomfortably.

'Wait a few minutes,' Father Barry said. 'That old lady's ahead of you.'

He bent his head to pass through the black curtain into the box. With his ear against the screen he listened to the feeble voice struggle to think of a sin worthy of absolution. 'Bless me Father, for I have sinned,' she mumbled. 'I lost my temper with the janitor for not coming up to fix the toilet. I scolded him something terrible.'

Father Barry reminded her that a tenement janitor in the winter time can be a very busy man and that a little Christian understanding of his daily trials might get the faulty plumbing repaired more rapidly than angry words. He gave her one Hail Mary, absolved her in God's name, and dismissed her with a 'God bless you, and pray for me.'

Then he stepped quickly out of the almost airless booth, wiped the perspiration off his forehead, and hurried back to Terry.

'Lissen, I wanna talk to ya,' Terry said impatiently.

Father Barry stared at him. The boy looked grimy, as if he hadn't shaved. The arrogant composure, the familiar, cocksure, street-corner smirk he had carried into the basement chapel the other evening were gone.

'That's no way to talk to a priest,' Father Barry said. 'I don't care for myself but . . .' He touched his stole.

'Okay, okay, but I gotta talk to somebody. I need a——. How's about your stick your head back in there'—Terry nodded toward the confessional—'and listen to me a minute.'

'How long has it been since you've been in this church—any church?' Father Barry asked.

Terry shrugged. 'I dunno. I think I come in with Charley Easter a year ago.'

'You've been pretty far away from us,' Father Barry said. 'I don't think you're ready to go to confession. Why don't you get back in the swing, and start examining your conscience?'

'Lissen, Father, do you have to make such a big deal out of it? I got somethin' I wanna tell ya.'

'What brought you here, Terry? Can you tell me that first?'

'I'm here, ain't that enough? That stuff you was sayin' on the dock yesterday about Runty. Sure, I know Runty was gettin' ready to stool but'—he hunched his shoulders in an expressive helpless gesture again—'but he had balls. He got a lot of kicks out of life. And then this Doyle broad. And those goddamn pigeons of Joey's.' He wiped across his mouth and nose with the back of his hand in the defensive gesture of a boxer trying to smear the blood off his face. 'I tell ya, Father, it's got me so I gotta come in here and sit down to find out what gives with me.'

'Kid, I've got to change into my street clothes and make a call,' Father Barry said. 'Sure, something's eating you. That's your conscience. It's been buried in there pretty deep. It's like a clean white tooth covered with green scum and grit. You don't brush that away in five minutes.'

'You mean you won't buy me in there, huh?'

Father Barry shook his head. 'Not yet. I've got to run now. Why don't you stay here and pray? Try St Jude. He's sort of a specialist on fellers who've got evil deep-rooted in 'em. He converted plenty of barbarians.'

'Yeah? And how did he wind up?'

'Beaten to death with a broadaxe,' Father Barry said. 'Stay here and think about him. Pray to him. He's a saint of desperate cases. Ask him to intercede for you. Maybe something'll happen.' He started rapidly toward the sacristy. 'I'll see you later.'

'Hey,' Terry called after him, but Father Barry was hurrying down the side aisle.

A few minutes later, when Father Barry came down the steps of the church, two at a time, on his way to the Glennons', Terry was outside waiting for him.

'What is this, a brush-off?' Terry said.

'That was a real quickie of a prayer,' Father Barry said, crossing

207

the street into the park. A common pigeon was perched on General Pulaski's head, which was turning a mottled green with oxidation. Father Barry had long legs and was moving them in such rapid strides that Terry had to trot occasionally to keep up with him.

'Lissen, Father, I don't wanna pray. Hell, why kid ya, I'd be fakin' it if I prayed. But I got somethin' that feels like it's bustin' me open inside—like a fist was in there beltin' me from the inside . . .'

Father Barry kept walking.

'Lissen to me, goddamn it, don't pull that high-and-mighty stuff,' Terry half begged, half bullied. 'Hell, the other night you was beggin' for someone to give you a lead on Joey Doyle.'

Father Barry stopped and studied him.

'Oh? You got a lead?'

'Lead, hell.' Terry almost shouted. 'It was me, understan', it was me!' He grabbed the priest so fiercely by the arm that Father Barry thought for a moment he was going to attack him. Father Barry wrenched the arm of his overcoat free.

'You been up all night, on the bottle?'

'What difference?' Terry said, excited. It was like sticking a knife into your own carbuncle. You put it off as long as possible, but then it felt good to feel the pus ooze out. It hurt and felt good to squeeze the sore lips of the boil and empty out the infection. 'I'm tellin' ya it was me, Father. I'm the one who set Joey Doyle up for the knock-off.'

'Well, I'll be damned,' Father Barry said.

'Now this is strictly between you and I,' Terry said.

'I don't want it that way,' Father Barry said. 'When you're ready Father Vincent can hear your confession. I want to be free to use whatever you tell me.'

'Listen, it's you I feel like tellin' this to. I'm taking a chance you won't rat on me.'

'I'm making no deals, Terry. I won't rat on you, as you put it. But you'll have to ride along on my judgement.'

'Why can't I have it like confession?' Terry persisted. 'What the hell difference does it make whether it's in that phone booth or out here with Palooskie lookin' over my shoulder?'

'Because you can't have it both ways,' Father Barry said. 'Now come on. Let's keep walking and give it to me straight. Fish or cut bait. Spill or button up. Go on, I'm listening.'

'Well, it started as a favour,' Terry began, and then the thumb of truth pressed against the sides of the inflamed lie and the pus oozed out in a relieving flow:

'Favour? Who'm I kiddin'? They call it a favour, but you know their favours—it's do it, or else. So this time the favour turns out to be helpin' them whop Joey. But, Father, I didn't know that. I figgered they was only goin' to lean on 'im a little bit. Honest t' God, Father, I never figgered they was goin' t' go all the way.'

'You thought they'd just work him over, and that didn't bother you,' Father Barry said.

'Yeah, yeah, I thought they'd talk to 'im, try 'n straighten 'im out, maybe push 'im aroun' a little bit, that's all.'

'And what I said on the dock yesterday about silence, that's what brought you to me?'

'Well, sorta. I'll tell ya the truth, Father. It's that girl. The Doyle broad. She's got a way of lookin' at me. I wanna yell out the whole goddamn truth. All the girls I know are like the Golden Warriorettes, crazy kids. But this Katie is, well, I didn't know they made 'em like that. She's so square, it's funny. I walk down the street with her and I feel like—well, like I'm back in trainin' and I just stepped out of the shower. I'd come home with that liniment smell on me and I'd feel clean for a while.'

'What are you going to do about this?' Father Barry cut him off brusquely.

'What d'ya mean, do? What d'ya mean?'

'You think you should know a thing like this and keep it to yourself?'

'I told ya, this was just between you and I,' Terry said quickly.

'In other words you're looking for an easy out,' Father Barry said. 'You tell it to me so I can help you carry the load. But it's still an open cesspool for other people to fall into—and drown in. Like Runty Nolan. Isn't that right?'

'You're a hard man,' Terry said.

'I'd better be,' Father Barry said. 'I'm having a hard day.'

'You should talk,' Terry said. 'A week ago I was doin' lovely. Now I'm in more trouble than a one-armed fiddle player.'

'What are you going to do about it?'

'What? What? About what?'

'The Commission? Your subpoena?'

'How come you know about that?' Terry said defensively.

'You know the waterfront Western Union,' Father Barry said. 'I heard they were looking for you. Well? What are you going to do about it?'

'I dunno. I dunno. It's like carryin' a monkey around on your back.'

Father Barry nodded. 'A question of who rides who.'

They had reached the grilled fencing at the far end of the park. Beyond them at the river's edge a giant pile driver began pounding an ear-shattering rhythm. A new pier was under construction.

'I'm no rat,' Terry said. 'And if I spill, my life ain't worth a home-made nickel.'

Father Barry stopped walking and put it to him hard. 'And how much is your soul worth if you don't? Who are you loyal to? Murderers? Killers? Hijackers? You've got the nerve to put the bite on me for absolution when you're still buddy-buddies with that human meat you think are men?'

'Lissen, what are you askin' me to do, put the finger on me own brother? And Johnny Friendly. I don't care what he done, he was always a hunnerd per cent with me. When I was a snot-nose kid, everybody lookin' to rap me in the head, Johnny Friendly used t' take me to ball games. He done that for a lot of us kids. Just pick us up off the street 'n take us in to the ball games. I seen Gehrig 'n Lazzeri. 'N Hubbell 'n Terry in the Polo Grounds.'

'Ball games!' Father Barry exploded. 'Don't break my heart. I wouldn't care if Johnny Friendly gave you a life's pass to the Polo Grounds. So you got a brother, huh? Well, let me tell you some-thing. You've got some other brothers, and they're getting the short end while your Johnny's getting mustard on his face at the Polo Grounds.'

Father Barry grabbed Terry's arm in a tight grip. 'Listen, I think you've got to tell Katie Doyle. I think you owe it to her. I know it's a hell of a thing to ask you, but I think you ought to tell her.'

Terry pulled his arm away angrily. 'Hell, ya don't ask much, do ya?' Terry worked the fingers of his right hand into his scalp. 'Ya know what you're askin'?'

'Never mind, forget it.' Father Barry said abruptly. 'I'm not asking you to do anything. It's your own conscience that's got to do the asking.'

'Conscience . . .' Terry muttered as if he were trying to translate a foreign word. 'You mean that bill of goods you fellas keep tryin' to sell? Conscience 'n soul 'n all that stuff? That stuff c'n drive you nuts.'

'You're making me late for Mrs. Glennon,' Father Barry said as he walked away from Terry, down the steps, out of the park. 'Good luck,' he said crisply over his shoulder.

'Is that all you got to say to me?' Terry called after him. He hated this smart-aleck priest, but he didn't want him to walk away. He didn't want to be left alone.

'You want to have it both ways, brother,' Father Barry called back over his shoulder. 'Well, you got it.'

He took the small park steps to the street-level sidewalk three at a time at so rapid a pace he almost seemed to be running.

'The round-collar bastard leaves me standin' here with my ass hangin' out,' Terry muttered to himself in a fury of confusion.

The pile driver had been silent for a few moments, but now it swung into action again, pounding, pounding, pounding its steel pilings down through the soft bottom muck to the river floor. Pound! Pound! Pound! Pound! It echoed through all of Port Bohegan.

'Goddamn the goddamn noise,' Terry said, with his hand to his head. A cock pigeon on the frost-yellowed grass was fussing himself up for the benefit of a tacky female cull. He blew out his chest and spread his tail, cooed importantly and cake-walked around her. Terry watched the performance and thought of his own birds. Of Swifty with his powerful frame, his shiny blue-purple neck and his fine, powder-blue head. He wished he was a carefree kid, running from the cops, swimming in the scummy river and watching his birds skim across the sky.

20

BACK ON THE roof tending his birds again. Terry was able to sidestep his troubles for a while. He went into the loft and busied himself cleaning out the nest boxes. One wall of the coop was lined with orange-crates, with each pair of birds occupying one compartment. Terry liked to watch the mates building their nests from the clean straw and he enjoyed the regular way the cocks and hens took turns sitting on the two small white eggs, the males by day, the females by night, in well-regulated shifts. He liked to watch the growth of the grotesque, featherless, Durante-beaked, one-day-old squabs into plump, fluttery, thirty-day-old adolescents ready to leave the nest. Boy, how they hated to get their fannies out of that nest! They were squawkingly scared of the big, open world beyond their nest box and they hung on for dear life when their old man and old lady tried to push them out over the edge. It used to make Terry laugh and feel sorta sad at the same time—all that flapping of wings and squealing commotion. Then the full-grown rejected squabs, big enough to fly, but still too dumb to know they had it in them, would flop heavily to the floor of the loft.

For a few days they'd go through hell, unweaned and unwanted, miserably suspended between their old nest-box dependence and an independence they hadn't latched on to yet. Each time Mr. and Mrs. Pigeon flew down to the scratch-grain feeder the dispossessed kids would rush over to them with their beaks wide open, their wings flapping, clamouring for a hand-out. It was pitiful, the way the old birds pecked them away. Just a couple of days earlier this same mom and pop had been on the nursing shift, regurgitating the soupy, digested grain into these waiting twenty-eight day-old throats.

Hundreds of times he had watched those squabs, confused, more and more frantic, finally driven so nuts they'd turn to other adult birds and cry to cadge a meal, only to be pecked and bullied away. Terry would look in at night to see the disappointed waifs huddled together on the floor, starved, abandoned, demoralized. But they never starved to death. Sure, they were more confused than an Irishman caught in Liverpool on Paddy's Day. Finally the homeless birds, without knowing what they were doing, would pick up a grain of cracked corn. The food filled a hole in the empty crop. The squab went for repeats. Eureka! He had learned the old lesson of the empty belly. You've got to get out and get it yourself.

Strengthened by the food, the little guy would be ready to try the self-serving watering can. Then his wings. Many a time Terry and Billy watched them hurl into the air, up a few feet, flap, flap, and then down they'd go. And try again. A week later the poor little bastard would be air-borne, able to make short, practice hops, a little unsteady yet, but each day learning some new wrinkle about his new-found stunt.

In one of the nests was a fuzz-yellow, ungainly squab nearly ready for its ordeal of joining the flock. It was a fat, oversized fledging because its twin had died after a few days and this one had doubled up on the regurgitated grub. Terry put his finger toward it and it fluttered its undeveloped wings and tried to peck him with its not yet hardened ludicrously large brown beak. It takes a pigeon a couple of months to grow into its beak. At first he looks all nose, like that infant from the old comics, Bunker Hill, Jr. Terry laughed at the futile pecking rage of the big squab. Then he put his hands carefully down over its wings and picked it up. It looked at him with frightened eyes.

'Kid, you got it made for another day or two and then out you go. No more . . .'

Christ, he thought suddenly, it almost seems to fit, the bull voice of Johnny Friendly, roaring, 'No more cushy days in the loft.'

Gently, he put the squab back in the nest of dirty straw, held together with a mortar of pigeon dung.

Young Billy Conley came up the skylight steps, jumped out on the roof and looked around for Terry.

'Hey, Terry, guess who's here.' He hurried over to the coop.

'Rose La Rose? Sorry, I'm too busy,' Terry said through the chicken wire.

'Listen, Terry,' the boy said. 'It's that joker from the Crime Commission. He's comin' up the stairs.'

Terry shook his head, dazed. 'What? Lookin' for me?'

Billy nodded. 'I heard him askin' the super on the first floor. He's got his nerve gum-shoein' around here. I hear you really blistered him in the Longdock.'

'Yeah, yeah . . .' Terry said absently. He came out of the coop wiping his hands on his dark corduroy trousers. Suddenly he grabbed his sweet-looking, foul-mouthed young friend. 'Billy, listen. Suppose you know something, like a job some fellas did on a certain fella. You don't think you should turn 'im in?'

The boy looked at him in amazement. 'You mean holler cop? Are you kiddin'?'

Billy stared at him. His young lips pressed together in a tough neighbourhood sneer. 'You off your rocker?'

Terry felt the hook. The code held for the teen-age gang just as it did for the outfits on the dock. He tapped Billy's dimpled try-to-be-hard jaw affectionately. 'You're a good kid, Billy. A good, tough kid. A couple of Golden Warriors.' He hugged the kid's head roughly. 'We got to stick together, huh, kid?'

'You was our first ace-man,' Billy said. 'You in some kind of a jam?'

'Kid, I got the bases loaded, no outs, and Dusty Rhodes is comin' in to bat,' Terry said.

'He's on his way up,' Billy said, nodding toward the covered stairway leading on to the roof. 'Duck behind the coop and I'll tell 'im you're gone.'

'But I ain't gone!' Terry said loudly. 'I'm here. I'm here. Who'm I kiddin'?'

'It's a good thing you ain't boxin' no more,' Billy said. 'You'd get a sixty-day suspension for talkin' double.'

The tall, well-built investigator in the tweed overcoat stepped out on the roof with his brief case. 'Mr. Malloy?'

'See ya later,' Terry dismissed his young side-kick. Then he walked across the roof-top to where Glover was sitting on a low-walled partition rubbing his feet. 'You lookin' for me?' Terry asked. His voice had a chip on its shoulder.

'Oh, not exactly,' Glover said, rubbing his ankles. 'I was just resting my dogs a minute.' He took off his hat and rubbed the line where his hat-band had been. 'Next investigation we get into, I hope it's buildings with elevators in them. So far this one has been nothing but climbing stairs.'

214

'What d'ya climb 'em for?' Terry said.

Glover smiled. 'I'm what they call a public servant. They tell me the taxpayers have a right to know what's going on down here.'

'Politics,' Terry shrugged it off.

Gene Glover knew enough about his job not to press the point. He had been trained as a Treasury investigator and there were definite techniques for these interviews. He had been studying Terry's record and he had discussed with his colleague, Ray Gillette, the best approach. Terry's mind would be shut. Any waterfront question would put him on guard. Now, let's see . . . They had talked it over together in Glover's kitchen over some beer the night before. Terry used to be a fighter. Ex-fighters like to talk about their lives in the ring. For a lot of them it was the biggest they'd ever be. Headlines. Back-slappers. Money. A sense of achievement. When he was no longer sport-page copy, every fighter who ever hung up his gloves knew the let-down.

So now Glover tried to make his question sound spontaneous, but it was rehearsed:

'Didn't I see you in the Garden three-four years ago with a fellow called Wilson?'

'Wilson? Yeah. I boxed Wilson.'

Terry walked away, back toward his coop. Out of the corner of his eye he had seen Swifty flying into the coop and he wanted to check his beak. He had noticed some dampness around the nostril holes. It could be a slight cold.

Glover followed Terry, moving casually. He knew his business. He stood outside the coop looking in as Terry grabbed Swifty and felt his beak.

Glover hadn't seen the Malloy-Wilson match, but had gone to the trouble of checking on it with a boxing writer he knew.

'I thought you were going to take him that night,' Glover said. 'You won the first two rounds by a mile. But he sure caught up with you. Man, he really dumped you.'

Terry let Swifty fly back to his perch and came closer to the wire netting.

'He dumped me, huh? What would you say if I told you I hadda hold that bum up for half a round?'

'I see. I see. You mean he was hurt?'

'Whatta you think I was doin' with them combinations, pettin' 'im?'

'You mean you had him, but you just couldn't finish him off, huh?' Glover asked.

'Finish him off,' Terry said scornfully. 'Hell, I could feel him goin'. I coulda finished 'im off.'

'The record book shows he finished *you* off,' Glover reminded him. 'Fifth round, wasn't it?'

'Who the hell cares?' Terry said. The truth boiled up in him. 'I was doin' a favour for a couple of fellas . . .'

'Favour!' Glover said. 'I'm glad I didn't bet on that one. So that's the way it was.'

'Yeah, yeah, that's the way it was. Ya know if I had copped that one I'd 've been in line fer the title? Wilson was rated third and I was right behind him and the two bums ahead of us didn't have the connexions.' Terry shook his head a moment, remembering the road work, the rata-ta-tatta of the light bag, the strategy. 'I was real sharp that night.'

'You sure looked it, those first few rounds. I figured you started too fast and that counter-punching of his took it out of you.'

'Hah!' Terry snorted. The Wilson fight was a crimp in his mind he could never work out. 'The sports writers said the same thing, but it was a lousy bet took it out of me.'

'You don't say?' Glover said quietly and stretched. 'Well, guess I better get going. Hit those stairs again. It's been nice talking to you. I watch the fights on TV twice a week. I think you could clean up on those middleweights they got messing around today.'

'Once in a while I get thinkin' I could make it back,' Terry said. 'I'm only twenty-eight. I still got my legs.'

'And you could punch,' Glover said. 'By the way, a friend of mine and I were arguing about the Wilson fight the other night. Was that a hook or a bolo you caught him with in the third round?'

'Bolo,' Terry said contemptuously. 'That's for the birds. Some writer made that up to give Gavilan some colour. A bolo is just a telegraphed uppercut.' He burlesqued one. 'A big nothing.' The stance of shadow boxing and a whiff of the old flattery excited him.

'I was strictly a short puncher,' he said proudly, and came out of the coop. 'Look, you put your left out and I'll show you somethin'.' He manœuvred Glover into an awkward semblance of a boxer's pose.

'I had that bum all figured out, see. He had a good left hand, ya know what I mean? Okay, so I let him slap me with the left for a couple of rounds. Build up his confidence, see? And all the time I'm watchin' how he drops his right. So just when he thinks he's gettin' cute and can tag me whenever he wants me, I step inside the jab—whop, with a right!'—he threw his right hand viciously—'whop with a left, then when his hand comes down I bring up the upper-cut—six inches, but I know how to throw it—WHOP! He falls into my arms. He don' know if he's in the Garden or in Roseland and from there on we're just dancin', dancin' . . . That Wilson couldn't fight too much.'

'I believe you,' Glover said, apparently interested.

'Well, that's a fact! That's a fact,' Terry said excitedly. 'Jesus, how I wanted to put him away. But no dice. All for a lousy bet. Hell, my own bro——'

Terry heard himself and stopped short.

'Your own who?' Glover encouraged him.

'Aah, it's ancient history,' Terry subsided. 'Who'n hell cares about me 'n Wilson?'

'Well, I better get going,' Glover said. 'Sorry to hear they wouldn't let you win it. Better luck next time.'

'Hah, hah,' Terry said bitterly. 'With my luck and a subway token I couldn't get to Times Square.'

'See you soon,' Glover smiled. 'I'd like to hear the whole story some time.' He disappeared into the roof-top stairway.

An hour later Terry was still up there, sitting on an upturned box, watching his birds. He heard someone come up on the roof three houses away. It was Katie. She was wearing a blue scarf around her head to keep her hair from blowing. It was windy on the roof-top, although the sun was filtering through the cold marble sky. When she lingered at Joey's coop. Terry didn't know whether to call over to her or not. He had tried to avoid her on the dock at Runty's im-promptu send-off the day before and he was resigned to the fact that his chance was one to fifty that she would ever speak to him again.

217

Well, he'd settle for that. Bohegan was a fishbowl and sooner than later it would get back to Johnny. Things were tough enough now.

'Don't see her no more,' Johnny had ordered.

'You owe it to Katie to tell her the truth,' Father Barry had insisted.

Terry felt like a one-man tug-of-war with his body on both ends and his head in the middle. 'Kee—*rist*,' he said out loud.

Katie turned from the coop on the other roof and came toward Terry. When she was close enough for him to see her face clearly, he felt panicky. She was so damned fresh looking. When you looked at her you liked her, you trusted her, you wanted to take care of her. Christ! She was the kind of girl a hood like him had no right to be in the same room with. The same world. She wanted too much.

'I was hoping I'd find you up here,' she said.

'Yeah, I—got a sick bird.'

'I was thinking about Joey's birds,' she said. 'We have got to get rid of them. Pop says the butcher will take them, but I . . .' She paused and he was very close to her and again he felt the urge to touch her cheek, put his arms around her, but of course he wouldn't dare. In his whole tenement roof, pool hall and street corner life he had never been unsure of himself with any girl before. 'But I—I thought maybe you could take them in with yours,' she continued. 'At least they'd have a nice life. I know you'd take good care of them. I could trust you for that.'

'Sure, sure. Anything you say,' Terry mumbled. Then he took a small step forward, a big step inwardly. The tarpaper floor of the roof was vibrating from the concussion of the piledriver at the river bank a block away.

'Katie, listen to me,' Terry said. 'I'—he reached back for Father Barry's words—'owe it to ya to tell ya somethin'.'

'You do?'

'It's been jabbin', jabbin' in my mind ever since that night in the church,' he said.

'I'm sorry I lost my temper with you,' she said. 'It's a sin not to forgive people, even when you want them to be better.'

'I wish you wouldn't keep sayin' stuff like that,' he said.

'Why?'

'Because it makes me feel like even more of a louse. It makes me feel like I'm crawlin' in snakes. That's why I gotta tell ya, Katie. You'll hate my guts all your life, but I can't keep it from comin' out no more. It's—it's like—forgive the expression—like puke. Once ya feel it comin' up in your throat ya've got to let it out.'

'Then do,' Katie said. 'Let it come out.'

With a terrible panic he looked at her a moment from across the gulf. Then he plunged in.

'Katie, I—I just told the Father what I did—what I did to Joey.'

She put her face in her hands and shook her head into them. 'No . . .'

'What I did to Joey,' he raised his voice to overcome the insistent pounding of the pile-driver. Unconsciously Katie moved her hands from her face until they were pressing against her ears. Terry went on shouting, the guilt pouring out of him in a relieving purge—*lissen—lissen—my brother Charley—and Johnny—good to me—a favour—the pigeon—got Joey to the roof—Specs and Sonny*—the guilt and filth of it pouring out of him into Katie's innocent, no longer trusting face and her horrified whisper 'No . . . no . . .'

A mighty ship swinging into mid-channel on its way to the Narrows let out a harbour-shattering blast with rows of ear-splitting Zs and Ns in its BZZZZZNNNNN . . . but nothing could stop Terry from spewing it forth. It had to come out to the last shred of gagged-up phlegm. His voice rose hysterically to make itself heard above the giant thumping of the pile-driver and the violent intrusion of the ship's whistle. 'Katie, I'm tellin' the truth. I'm not holdin' nuthin' back. I set Joey for 'em. But, Katie, honest to God, I didn' look to see 'im killed. I didn' know. I DIDN' KNOW . . .' The blast from the ship had suddenly stopped and Terry's voice was so loud it sounded as if it could have been heard all over Bohegan. A moment later the pile-driver paused too, as if to catch its steam-engine breath. It was suddenly still. Terry lowered his voice almost to a whisper now. 'Katie . . . Katie . . . I never thought they'd . . .'

'You never thought *anything*—except how to stuff your mouth or your pockets,' Katie said with a fierceness that lashed Terry with a steel tip because it was so unexpected in her. 'You weren't killing him or not killing him. You were just looking out as usual for number one.'

He put his hand out, tentatively to restrain her, but she turned and ran across the roof, dodging the skylights and ducking through the steel branches of the TV forest that had spread from house to house.

Okay, he did it, he did it, he was thinking. Now what? What's the deal? He had felt a kind of crazy exhilaration to get the thing off his chest to Katie. And now—nothing. He felt tired and just wanted to stretch out and be quiet—like after a hard ten-round fight. The pile-driver began its pounding again. Goddamn it, would it never quit? Was there never gonna be no peace nowhere? He envied Runty Nolan, wherever he was. At least he didn't have to make any more moves. It was this having to decide things one way or another that drove pointed sticks into your head.

'Jesus, Mary 'n Joseph . . .' Terry said, meaning to curse. But his mind was so battered and his spirit so torn that it issued from him softly, more like a prayer.

21

THE GATHERING OF Johnny Friendly's 'pistol local' officials in the weather-beaten office on the wharf was only one of a chain of meetings going on in the longshoremen's union offices all along the Jersey waterfront and around the harbour from Staten Island, the West, South and East Sides of Manhattan and far out into Brooklyn. There had been emergency sessions of the District Council. High-up members of the syndicate like Jerry Benasio's dreaded brother Alky, who had Brooklyn and most of Jersey, and Wally 'Slicker' McGhee, a big dealer from the Lower West Side, had flown up from hideouts in Miami and Hollywood, Florida, to help work out a common strategy for the dock bosses who were being subpoenaed.

In other words, the heat was on. The Crime Commission had an order to call in and examine all the union books. Company records were being subpoenaed too, and the scuttlebutt was that shipping executives were being asked tough questions in private about the practice of keeping 'phantoms' on the payroll to line the pockets of local officers and of systematically paying off the union leaders at Christmas for 'keeping peace on the docks'. There were rumours that stevedore officials, faced with proof in cancelled cheques or confiscated payrolls—or a tell-tale absence of records—were talking in order to shift the blame away from the 'respectable' shipping associations and on to the muscular shoulders of the crime boys who had been running the longshore locals as private mobs.

Sure, there had been investigations before, at least a dozen of them, producing a week of headlines, but usually with no result more serious than the conviction of a hapless loan shark or two, or a loud-mouthed hoodlum the mob was ready to slough off anyway.

But this time the dread tide of waterfront reform seemed to be on the rise. Metropolitan papers had begun to editorialize against a whitewash. An underground of rebel longshoremen seemed ready to erupt. There were even rumours that the Commission had the goods on Willie Givens, who had quietly appointed Sing Sing and Dannemora boys as union organizers, or had handed them charters to start new locals they could run as their own. But Willie himself was a civic leader. Willie was a vice-president of a state labour organization. Willie's florid bulk was a familiar sight on the platform at political rallies in the Garden.

The annual banquet of the Willie Givens Association boasted a guest list of political brass that rivalled anything in the State. And side by side with the mayors, borough presidents, councilmen, senators and judges you would find the Benasios, the McGhees, the pride of the Brooklyn Mafia, the social register of the narcotics trade and the gunmen and shake-down artists who had made the docks their own. At last year's dinner Johnny Friendly had reserved Table 17 for himself, Charley, Big Mac McGown, Police Commissioner Donnelly, Bohegan Mayor Bobby Burke and assorted councilmen, local judges and bodyguards. Now Bobby Burke, who was about to run for re-election and was a crumb-picker from the Keegan table in Jersey City, was panicky. He and Donnelly had a piece of the numbers in Bohegan, as well as something coming in from the docks. All he was looking for was to get out with his take without a Grand Jury or a State investigation.

Johnny Friendly was the strength in the Bohegan sector. Now he was ready to show what he had that had put him up where he was. The thing to do was to close ranks and hang on, hard. 'Tough it out' was Johnny's motto. Admit nothing. Bull it through. The men around him could feel the bull, animal strengtn, not so much in the muscles but in his mind. In his mind he was right, he was justified. The way he ran the docks not only paid off for him, but kept the ships moving in and out. Not only had he mastered the larceny side, but he prided himself on knowing all the technical tricks of loading. He could spot a mistake quicker than old Captain Schlegel. He belonged down here. He had come up out of the hold. He knew everyone's job. This was all his, and his mission in life was to keep it that way.

Sitting with him was Charley and Truck and Gilly and 'J.P.' Morgan and his hiring bosses, Big Mac, Socks Thomas and Flat-top Karger who had just been parolled on a manslaughter rap. Specs and Sonny had beat it to Florida as soon as Father Barry raised his stink on the dock. Johnny would have to stake them until the heat was taken off.

There was no gavel here and no solemn oaths, but everybody knew that a court was in session, with Johnny as judge, jury and prosecutor, Terry Malloy on trial in absentia and his glib brother Charley on the anxious seat for the first time. The groundswell of resentment against Terry for hanging around the Doyle girl had mounted with reports of his having gone back to the church to see Barry. And from a roof-top across the street, where he had been instructed to maintain a lookout, the ubiquitous 'J.P.' had seen plenty.

'I couldn't hear what they was sayin', boss, but Terry and this bum from the Commission was nose to nose for ten fifteen minutes. Terry was doin' a lot of talkin', that's for sure, and this flatfoot looked like he was eatin' it up.'

'Nose to nose,' Johnny Friendly said, looking at Charley.

'Like a pair o' lovers,' 'J.P.' said.

'Some brother,' Johnny said, looking at Charley.

Charley swallowed and said nothing.'

'Well, you usually got something to say,' Johnny said.

Charley took a deep breath and made an effort to trade on his slightly educated gift of gab.

'Nose to nose might not mean too much, Johnny,' Charley tried to sound confident. 'He could have been telling him off too, like he did before. I still don't believe he's going to talk. There won't be any evidence of that until he gives public testimony.'

Johnny pushed a cigar into his mouth and talked around it. His cold, sarcastic voice made second-string tough guys like Truck, Gilly and Big Mac feel relieved that they weren't on the receiving end.

'Thanks for the legal advice, Charley. That's what I always kept you around here for. Now how do we keep this no-good son-of-a-bitch from giving public testimony? Isn't that what you call—ah—the main order of business?'

Big Mac muttered something in back of his hand and Truck's fat-muscled shoulders shook with troubled mirth. Charley glared at them. Meatheads, the lot of them. And every one of them drawing down a couple of union salaries and expenses because Charley had set it up for them.

'Johnny, he's not the brightest, but he's a good kid, you know that.'

'He's a bum,' Big Mac said. 'After the days I gave him in the loft, he's got no gratytude.'

'You shut up,' Charley suddenly raised his voice at Big Mac. 'How about your gratitude to me? I kept you on the job. Schlegel wanted to fire you half a dozen times.'

Johnny put both hands out in front of him, fingers spread wide, to signal silence.

'All right, Mac—Charley—I'm conductin' this—investigation.'

There were a few cautious smiles from the claque. But they were all worried. Charley was a valuable member. He was good at talking to the Central Trades Council and in the wage-scale negotiations and to the press. Now things were heating up all over the harbour and a legitimate-looking fella like Charley the Gent would be handy to have around. One of the best 'sea lawyers' in the harbour.

'Terry's done a few favours for us, Johnny. We mustn't forget

223

that,' Charley tried again. 'It's simply that this girl and maybe the priest too have begun exerting some kind of influence over him that's, well, that's affecting his mental attitude. See what I mean?'

This had been velvet talk for confusing honest members of the District Council or a militant wage-scale delegate. But Johnny had no patience with it now.

'Goddamn it, talk English so's I can understand it,' he shouted.

'I mean the Doyle broad and the priest may be getting their hooks into him so deep he doesn't know which end is up any more,' Charley said, in what was actually his native tongue.

'I ain't interested in all that mental attitude crap,' Johnny said. 'We're into a bi-state investigation. This ain't no two-bit city deal Willie Givens c'n talk or buy his way out of. This one is make or break. Your little brother can hang us. All I want t' know is, is he D 'n D or is he a canary?'

Charley took a long time answering. He was conscious of his sweat pores moistening. There was no use giving Johnny Friendly any bent nails for answers. Whatever Charley said, he would have to deliver on it. No one was safe around Johnny who didn't deliver on his word. In his own way, according to his own rules, he was a fanatic for the truth.

'I—wish—I—knew,' Charley mouthed his answer deliberately.

'So do I, Charley,' Johnny said. 'For your sake.'

Johnny looked at his lieutenant, his eyes drilling cold holes in him. A shudder rippled through the room. Men who passed themselves off as real tough in the embattled bars and alleys of Bohegan were afraid for Charley. They kept very still. They tried to look neither at Johnny nor Charley for fear of making the slightest misplay.

'I was never for tying that kid in close,' Johnny continued. 'We're not playing for marbles. This is business. There's no room for goof-balls in this business. It's time to straighten out that brother of yours.'

'Straighten out how?' Charley asked, in the fewest possible words this time.

'Okay, all you fellas, vamoose,' Johnny said to his local officials and collection boys. He trusted them, but there was no sense in having extra witnesses. This was best between him and Charley, so the rest of them could plead with a straight face they knew nothing about it.

As soon as they were out of there Johnny said, 'Look, it's simple. Drive him out to the place we've been using. Try to straighten him out on the way over. Maybe stake him and ship him out somewhere. But if he won't play, if he tries to stiff ya, you'll have to turn him over to Danny D.'

Danny D. was a black flag on the waterfront, an old Murder, Inc. boy who did jobs on order. He had beaten half a dozen murder raps. There were never any witnesses. All he could be held for himself was as a material witness. He was a cousin of the Benasios and he had broken some strikes for Interstate. There were cops who privately accused Danny D. of two dozen murders. He was a ship jumper convicted only once, years ago, on the Sullivan Law. He sized up as a clean deportation case, but his lawyers kept stalling it off in the courts.

The name Danny D. thickened Charley's tongue. 'Danny D. Johnny, you can't mean that. I mean, all right, maybe the kid's out of line. But Jesus, Johnny, I can handle him. He's just a confused kid.'

'Confused kid,' Johnny shouted. 'Listen, shlagoom, first he crosses me in public and gets away with it. Then the next joker, an' pretty soon I'm just another fella down here.'

'But it's a risky thing, messing with a psycho like Danny D. right now. It's time to lie low.'

'Don't give me that lie-low shit. I lie low now and they pile it on me. I'm a crap shooter, Charley. When I get behind I don't pull in. I double up on the bet. I go with everything I got. I came up that way. And, brother, I'll go down that way—if I gotta go, which I wouldn't take no bets on if I was you.'

'Johnny, I love ya, you know that,' Charley said. 'I know the guts it took to muscle in on this thing and build it up into a beautiful machine. Anything you asked me, I was always there, you know that. But Johnny, this thing you're askin' here, I can't do that. I just can't do that, Johnny.'

'Then don't,' Johnny said.

'But Johnny . . .'

'Forget I asked ya,' Johnny said.

Charley knew what that meant.

'Johnny, it's my kid brother,' Charley tried for the last time.

'If it was *my* kid brother,' Johnny said, 'hell, if it was my own mother, God bless 'er, I'd have to do it if they crossed me. I ain't sayin' I'd like it. I'm just tellin' ya what ya have to do if ya wanna be a real man in this business. The men and the boys get separated awful fast when it gets hot.'

'Jesus Christ Almighty,' Charley said. He could feel the sweat running into his pants where his comfortable thirty-five year old belly folded into the thickening flesh of his thighs.

'Okay, on your horse, deep thinker,' Johnny Friendly ordered.

Charley tried to make his exit casual, but the blood was running out of his face and his silk, white-on-white, twenty-dollar Sulka shirt was sticking to his skin.

Terry was lying on his bed, skimming through a racing pigeon magazine and trying to get his mind off the squeeze he was in. He had the door locked. He wasn't going out any more that evening. Where could he go? Who was there left to see? Only the kid, Billy, and even he was beginning to ride Terry for letting himself get caught in the switches. The mob was off him and the friends of Joey Doyle wanted no part of him. Truck and Gilly had walked out on him. Johnny had lowered the boom on him; the priest had given him a hard time, and finally when he did what this Barry had softened him up to do, the girl had run away from him as if he was a one-man epidemic or something.

He picked up the magazine and tried to read about a special race from Havana, but in a few moments he tossed it on the floor and stretched out on his back, trying to think. Until this thing had happened, he had never had to think. He could just drift along from day to day, picking his spots. He still couldn't quite figure out how he had let himself get jockeyed into this corner. It was like a dry-mouthed whisky morning when your head is coming apart.

There was a knock on the door and he half rose, tensing at the threat of intrusion.

'Yeah?'

'Hey, kid, it's Charley,' the voice came through the door.

Terry jumped up to let him in. Charley looked big and prosperous in his camel's hair coat. He was breathing hard from the walk-up.

'You're out of shape, Charley,' Terry tried to keep his tone light. 'Been living it up too good.'

'Yeah, I'm going to start going to the Y,' Charley said. 'Listen, kid, get your jacket on. We're going to the fights.'

'Jees, I been so . . . I didn't even notice who's on the card,' Terry said.

'What difference?' Charley said. 'A couple of tough niggers like it always is these days. I got a good pair, first row behind the press.'

'I been wantin' to talk to ya,' Terry said.

'Get your jacket on. We'll have time to talk on the way.'

Usually there wasn't a cab for blocks, but tonight they found one on the corner. It was mean, early December weather, with hard rain crystallizing into sleet.

'Jesus, some lousy night,' Terry said.

'The paper said snow,' Charley said.

'The weather's cockeyed. It's this new bomb,' Terry explained.

'Where to?' said the cab driver.

'Turn left on Bedford,' Charley said. 'I'll tell you where to stop,'

'I thought we was goin' to the Garden,' Terry said.

'Sure, but—I want to cover a bet on the way over,' Charley said. 'Anyway it'll give us a little more time to talk.'

Terry tried to relax against the fading leather seat. 'Well, nothing ever stops you from talking, Charley.'

'Yeah, I guess I was born garrulous,' Charley said. 'But—this isn't for the pleasure of hearing my own voice. Terry, I want you and I should have a serious talk.'

'Mmmmm-mmmm,' Terry said, watching carefully.

'Er—the grapevine says you've got—you got a subpoena.'

'Check,' Terry said without expression.

'Of course the boys know you too well to put you down for a cheese-eater,' Charley said, feeling his way cautiously.

'Mmmm-mmmm,' Terry grunted.

'Just the same, they think you shouldn't be on the outside so

227

much,' Charley went on. 'They want you a little more on the inside. They think it's time you had a few little things going for you down there.'

Terry shrugged. 'A steady job. A couple extra potatoes, that's all I want.'

'Sure that's all right when you're a kid,' Charley agreed. 'But you're getting on. You're pushing thirty pretty soon, slugger. It's time you got a little ambition.'

'Well, I always figgered I'd live longer without it,' Terry said.

Charley looked at him and then turned his head away and lowered his eyes. 'Maybe,' he said. Then to cover his feelings, he added quickly, 'Look, kid, you know this new pier they're building . . .'

Terry thought of the pile-driver and the way it kept beating in his head.

'It's going to be a beaut—two million bucks. The Pan-American Line is coming in there and our local's going to have the jobs. There'll be a new slot for a boss loader.'

'So?' Terry said.

'You know the set-up,' Charley said. 'Six cents a hundred pounds on everything that goes into a truck. It don't sound so big, but it snowballs. And the lovely part is, you don't have to lift a finger. I think it's the sweetest touch in the harbour. It's three, four hundred dollars a week just for openers. Guys like Turkey Dooley and Dummy Ennis can do thirty, forty G a year and pay tax on five. That's how I see you, kid. A month in Miami every winter.'

'And I get all that dough for not doin' nothin'?' Terry said.

'Absolutely nothing,' Charley said. 'You do nothing. And you say nothing. You understand, don't you, kid?'

Terry sighed and shook his head, struggling with his unfamiliar problem. 'Yeah, I guess I do. But there's more to this than I thought, Charley. I'm telling you. A lot more.'

Charley was disturbed to see how shaken his brother was. 'Terry, listen to me,' he said sharply. 'I hope you're not trying to tell me you're thinking of testifying against . . .' He pointed a suede-gloved thumb in the direction of his immaculate camel's hair coat. 'Kid, I hope you're not telling me *that*.'

Terry rubbed the back of his hand across his face. 'I don't know,

228

Charley. I mean, I'm tellin' you I don't know, Charley. That's what I been wantin' to talk to you about.'

'Listen, Terry,' Charley said patiently, as if he had to begin at the beginning, 'those piers we control through the local, you know how much they're worth to us . . .'

'I know . . . I know . . .' Terry said.

'All right,' Charley said, steaming himself up as he reminded himself how much trouble this kid was causing him, 'you think Johnny can afford to jeopardize a set-up like that for one lousy, rubber-lipped ex-tanker who's walking on his heels . . .'

'Don't say that!' Terry begged.

'What the hell!' Charley said.

'I could've been better,' Terry said.

'That's not the point,' Charley said.

'I could've been a lot better, Charley,' Terry said.

'The point is, we don't have much time,' Charley reminded him.

'I'm tellin' ya I haven't made up my mind yet,' Terry cried out. 'I wish I could tell ya what it's like, Charley—this goddamn makin' up your mind.'

'Well, make up your mind, kid. I beg you.' Then he added with shame and resignation and desperation in his half-whispered voice, 'Before we get to 2437 Bedford Street.'

The address rang a bell in Terry's mind, a deadly, sombre bell. 'Before we get to *where*, Charley?' he asked in disbelief. 'Before we get to *where?*'

Outside the cold sleet swirled and slowed the progress of the cab. Charley's forehead was hot and moist. All the years of clever words, the smart operator's arsenal of rapid-fire speech had brought him to this—to this bedrock pleading: 'Terry, for the last time. Take the job. Please take the job.'

Terry shook his head.

Charley prided himself on his good manners, on his intelligence and reserve, but now the frustration and the danger exploded something in him and without knowing what he was doing he reached into his shoulder holster and pulled out a short-handled .38. 'You're going to take the job, whether you like it or not. And keep your goddamn mouth shut. No back talk. Just take it!'

When Terry saw the gun in the folds of the overcoat, he was not frightened; the shock of this final gesture seemed to carry him beyond fear into a state of stunned, intuitive compassion he had never known before.

·'Charley . . .' he said sadly, embarrassed for both of them. He reached out and gently turned the barrel to one side.

Charley leaned back against the seat and lowered the gun into his lap. He pushed his hat back to let his forehead breathe. He took an initialed handkerchief out of his breast pocket and mopped his face.

'Please take it,' Charley whispered. 'Take that job.'

Terry had pulled away into his corner of the back seat. He was still shaking his head in shock and disappointment. 'Charley—oh, Charley.' A deep sigh welled out of him that said, 'Wow . . .'

Charley bit his lip and let the gun slip down into his overcoat pocket. In the silence that followed they could hear the sleet driving against the windows and the sound of the wet tyres slurping against the cobblestones. It was an old road, leading inland from the river into the flat, drab backland of Jersey.

When Charley began to talk again, he was groping, almost gasping for words, trying to work his way back toward some relationship with Terry.

'Look, kid. I—look, I . . .' He reached out and tried to squeeze the biceps of Terry's right arm, an old affectionate gesture between them. Terry neither pulled his arm away nor made it easy for Charley to reach him.

'How much you weigh these days, slugger?' Charley suddenly wanted to know.

'Seventy-five, eighty. Who cares?' Terry shrugged off his question in a sullen monotone.

'Gee, when you weighed a hundred sixty-eight pounds you were beautiful.' Charley lapsed into the past. 'You could've been another Billy Conn. Only that skunk we got you for a manager brought you along too fast.'

Terry had been slowly shaking his head. Now the past and all the abuses it had stored up in him seemed to cry out. 'It wasn't him, Charley. It was you!'

Terry came out of his corner, leaning toward Charley, incited by the old humiliation that was like the blood from a cut that won't coagulate. 'You remember that night in the Garden? You came down to the dressing room and said, "Kid, this ain't your night. We're goin' for the price on Wilson." You remember that? This ain't your night. My night! I could've taken Wilson apart that night. So what happens? He gets the title shot, outdoors in the ball park. And what do I get? A one-way ticket to Palookaville. I was never no good after that night. You remember that, Charley. It's like a— peak you reach, and then it's all downhill. It was you, Charley. You my brother. You should've looked out for me a little bit. You should've taken care of me. Just a little bit. Instead of makin' me take them dives for the short-end money.'

Charley wasn't able to look at Terry. 'At least I always had some bets down for you,' he said softly. 'You saw some money.'

'See you don't understand,' Terry raised his voice as if to bridge his failure to communicate.

'I tried to keep you in good with Johnny,' Charley made an effort to explain.

'You don't *understand!*' Terry cried out again, 'I could've had class. I could've been a contender. I could've been somebody. Instead of a bum, which is what I am. Oh, yes, I am. It was you, Charley.'

There was silence again for perhaps ten seconds, while Terry continued to stare at Charley and Charley looked anxiously into Terry's face and saw the days of their youth, saw Terry the dirty-faced urchin and Terry the twelve-year-old gutter fighter and Terry in his flashy towel robe prancing in his corner as he waited for the bell and Terry the twenty-eight-year-old has-been hanging around Friendly's Bar, a bum—which is what he was.

'Okay, okay . . .' Charley was fighting himself for a decision. He glanced out to see how close they were to the isolated two-storey frame house casually identified by the Danny D. crowd as 'the gas-house'. 'I'm gonna tell 'em I—I'll tell 'em I couldn't find you. Ten to one he won't believe me, but . . .' He quickly reached into his pocket and slipped Terry the gun. 'Here, you may need it.' Then he leaned forward and slid open the glass partition between them and the front seat. 'Hey, driver, pull over.' He opened the door while the car was still moving. 'Jump out, quick, and keep going.' He slapped Terry hard on the back. Half a block down was a suburban bus. Terry shouted to hail it and ran toward it down the dark, glistening road.

Charley leaned back against the seat, exhausted. 'Now turn around, driver,' he said wearily, his eyes closed. 'Take me to the Garden.'

The driver made a violent left turn that half threw Charley to the floor, high-balled his car up into Danny D.'s driveway, and sped right on into the garage, where a couple of specialists had been stationed to handle what came in. Charley Malloy opened his mouth to protest, but the men knew their work and he never said another word.

22

WHEN THE BUS dropped Terry off on a side street near the centre of Bohegan he jumped out and kept on running for half a dozen blocks through the hard, slanting rain until he came to the Doyle tenement. He had lost his cap on the way and his hair was wet and tangled. The icy rain dripped down his forehead and along his unshaven cheeks. He raced up the stale, creaky stairs two and three at a time, carried along by an obsession that had seized him and driven away all sense of safety and precaution. It was the image of Katie Doyle's turning her back on him after his confession that tormented him—her cutting angry words, her running away, His mind was a motor propelling him forward. He reached the fourth-story landing, ran to the door and shouted: 'Katie! Katie!'

Katie was in bed, trying to fall asleep. Pop was out with Moose and Jimmy and the door was latched. 'Keep the door locked,' Pop had told her, 'and don't let nobody in. I don't care if it's God Almighty Himself.'

'Katie! Hey, Katie!' Terry shouted through the kitchen door. Katie didn't answer and Terry called her name again while pounding on the door.

Katie ran to the door to make sure it was latched. 'You can't come in. Get away from here!' she shouted angrily.

'Katie, please open the door. I gotta talk to you.'

He kicked at the door and she screamed, 'Stop it! Stop it! Stay away from me.'

She made sure the latch was fastened and hurried back into her narrow bedroom and tried to push her metal bed over against the door. She was terrified by the sound of Terry's body crashing against the flimsy wood of the kitchen door. Then she heard the sound of the latch giving and Terry was rushing in on her. She tried to pull the bedclothes over her. His hair was wild and his arms were flailing. His eyes frightened her.

'Get out of here—out of here!' she shrieked, and when he tried to come close to her, whimpering, 'Katie, lissen . . .' she shook her head and said, 'If Pop finds you in here, he'll kill you. You've got to stay away from me.'

As he came closer she leaped from the bed and hurled herself against him, trying to push him back out of the room. He held her off, gripping her arms hard and shouting into her face, 'You think I stink, don't you? You think I stink for what I done.'

She wrenched herself free and said furiously. 'I don't want to talk about it. I just want you to . . .'

'I know what you want me to do,' he cut in.

'I don't want you to do anything except get out of here and—let your conscience tell you what to do.'

'Shut up about that conscience.' He beat his right fist viciously against the metal bedpost Katie had tried to use as a barrier. 'Why d'ya hafta keep usin' that goddamn word?'

She backed away, still fearful of him, but fearful for him too. 'Why, Terry, I never mentioned that word to you before. Never.'

He stopped, surprised and dazed.

'No?'

She shook her head. She was no longer afraid of him. No longer did he seem a vicious hunter animal running wild in the street. Rain-soaked and wind-swept, he seemed more like some smaller, hunted animal, bewildered by his uncertainties as to where to turn.

'You're beginning to listen to yourself,' she said. 'That's where that word is coming from.'

'Katie,' he said quietly, 'don't get sore now. But I—I guess it's somethin'—somethin' what ya feel when, well, when you're in love with somebody.'

Again he wanted to put his arms around her and hold her close and kiss her and bury his face in the sweet warmth of her neck. But he stood there, staring wildly at her. And strangely for Kate, Terry Malloy was like the dark, evil dream of carnal sin that would come to her in her bed at Marygrove—never the nice boys she met at the outrageously over-supervised school dances, but the fierce, rowdy spectre of naked male passion that would steal into her room and press down upon her until some nights she would actually turn on the light and get up out of bed and plead with Mary to protect her from this stain. There was an overwhelming impulse in her now against every habit and belief to throw herself, barely dressed, shamelessly into his arms.

'Terry, please—not now—let's talk about it—some other time,' she said. 'Now you have to go—please.'

'Okay, okay, forget I said it,' Terry mumbled. 'I got no right . . .' He started to turn away. 'I'm sorry about that door. So much has been happenin'. I guess I can't take it so good.'

'I'll put you in my prayers tonight,' Katie said seriously.

'Boy, c'n I use 'em!' Terry said.

From the courtyard behind the tenement came a muffled cry, 'Hey, Terry. Hey, Terry . . .'

Startled, Terry hurried into the kitchen and peered down the fire-escape. He couldn't see anybody in the darkness, but he heard the voice, louder this time.

'Hey, Terry, your brother's down here. He wants to see you.'

'Charley . . .' Terry said.

'Hey, Terry,' came the cry from four stories below, 'come down and see your brother.'

'Terry, don't go down,' Katie begged.

'He may be in trouble.'

'Lock yourself in your room,' Katie said.

'Charley?' Terry called out the window into the courtyard.

'Come on down—he's waitin' for ya,' the strange voice answered from below.

'I gotta go down,' Terry said, climbing out to the fire-escape.

'Terry, be careful,' Katie called.

'I got *this*,' Terry said, patting the invisible gun.

'Terry, please be careful,' Katie cried out after him as he started down the fire-escape through the sleeting rain.

'We're over here, Terry, over here,' the muffled voice rose through the darkness.

Katie could hear Terry's metallic steps hurrying down the fire-escape. Across the narrow courtyard, strung with clothes-lines, a window opened two stories below. A woman put her head out and looked up toward Katie. It was Mrs. Collins. Katie didn't recognize her for a moment with her hair tight around her head in a hair-net.

'You hear that?' the woman called.

Katie nodded, holding her arms around her shoulders against the bitter cold.

'It's the same way they called my Andy out the night I lost him,' Mrs. Collins said.

Katie ran to closet and pulled out her cloth coat. Then, heedless of Mrs. Collins's cries, she started down the fire-escape, crying down into the winter night. 'Terry! Terry!' When she reached the bottom landing, a shabby, indistinct figure shuffled toward her out of a coal shed. To her amazement he was singing at the top of his hoarse, cracking voice an old popular song meant to carry a gay beat but which was now rendered like a dirge.

'Tippi . . . tippi . . . tin . . . tippi . . . tin . . .'

Katie recognized the neighbourhood derelict Mutt Murphy. He had an almost empty bottle of wine in his hand and he was singing toward the lighted windows.

'Tippi . . . tippi . . .'

A ground-floor window opened and an angry voice shouted out, 'Shet up!'

'Tan . . .'

Another window opened on the rubbish-strewn court and a furious voice shouted, 'Drop dead!' An old shoe, aimed at the staggering figure of Mutt, backed up this suggestion.

Mutt shook his fist at the offending windows. 'Spit on me, curse me 'n stone me,' he shouted hoarsely, 'but I suffer fer yer sins . . .'

The man who had thrown the old shoe shouted back loudly, 'Go suffer somewhere else, ya bum.'

The windows banged shut. Under the fire-escape Katie had been looking around for some sign of Terry or his caller, but the raw night seemed to have swallowed them.

'Terreee . . .' her small panicked voice echoed down the squat row of tenements. Mutt staggered toward her, brandishing the bottle of wine. His slobbering lips horrified her.

'I seen him. I seen him . . .'

'Which way did he go?'

'I seen it happen. With me own eyes I seen it.'

'What? What did you see?'

'I seen 'em put 'im to death! I heard 'im cry out!'

'Who—who did you see? Tell me—tell me!' Katie grew hysterical.

'His executioners. They was stabbin' 'im in his side. An' his soft eyes was lookin' down at 'em.'

His reddened St. Bernard's eyes began to leak great tears down his bleary, unshaven face. 'Oh, I weep fer 'im—I weep fer 'im.'

'Who? You mean Terry?'

In his right hand Mutt raised the bottle aloft in a grand, apostolic gesture.

'Our Lord Jesus when He died to save us . . .'

Katie pushed him away with loathing. 'Oh, get away, you—you *slob!*'

Mutt drained a last swallow from the nearly empty bottle and crashed it against the tenement wall. 'Tippi . . . tippi . . . tan . . . tippi . . . tan . . .' He picked up his persistent lament and wandered back into the coal shed to sleep off his fears and burrow in his visions.

The space between the tenements, built back to back, led into a narrow alley. Katie thought she heard a sound in that direction and hurried toward it, calling Terry's name. As she neared the alleyway, Terry answered her in a strained, hurt voice. 'I'm over here.'

She ran toward him and found him staring at the lifeless figure of Charley Malloy, hanging by his camel's hair coat collar from a cargo hook fixed to the wooden alley wall. The usually spotless golden-tan coat was soiled and blood had stained the lapel. Katie gasped but made no other sound. Terry was trembling with hatred.

'I'll take it out of their skulls,' he said.

'Terry, come back inside.'

'I said I'll take it out of their skulls. I'll take this out of their skulls.'

He had the gun in his hand. He kept staring at Charley. He didn't seem aware of Katie at all. He walked over to the wall and lifted Charley down. He stretched Charley out with his hands folded together at his waist.

'Look at the way the sons of bitches got his coat all dirty,' he said.

'Terry, you're crazy,' Katie said. 'Give me that gun. You sound like you're going crazy.'

Terry pushed the small revolver securely into his pocket. 'Go get the Father,' he ordered. 'Tell him to take care of Charley. Charley was a Catholic. He's got to have it right. I don't want he should have to lay out in this stinkin' alley too long.'

He started down the alley toward the street.

'Where are you going?' Katie called shrilly.

'Never you mind,' Terry said. 'Just do like I say.' He kept on walking, not once looking back to see if Katie was carrying out his orders and hurrying toward the church. She was, however, running sobbingly through the foul-weather night and reaching the church nearly at the same time Terry was entering the Friendly Bar.

A dozen regulars were lined up at the bar looking at the fight on TV.

'Johnny Friendly here?' Terry said abruptly from the entrance.

Jocko, the horse-faced bartender who was a lot smarter than he looked, couldn't see the gun on Terry, but he sensed that he had one. In his ten years' service behind this bar he had become an uncanny judge of these things.

'He's not in now,' he said curtly. Usually he was a good friend of Terry's, with plenty of cuff where the kid was concerned. But now he knew things were wrong. He didn't have to be told. He could smell trouble.

'You sure?' Terry said and slowly walked the length of the bar to the door of the back room. Most of the customers took their eyes off the television screen to watch Terry. When Johnny Friendly was on the warpath, the harbour of Bohegan was alive to it. Some of the regulars even stayed away from the bars. As Terry approached the back door, Jocko reached below the bar and grabbed a wooden ice-crusher he used for a billy. He held it behind his back, waiting to see what the steamed-up kid was going to do.

Terry kicked open the door to the back room so he could have his hands free to fire and use the door as a shield. There was only one occupant, 'J.P.' Morgan, spreading his loan slips out in front of him and conscientiously making notations in his little black book.

'Seen Johnny?' Terry said.

'He's at the fights,' 'J.P.' answered without looking up.

Terry went back to the end of the bar and waved Jocko over. 'A double shot.'

'Take it easy now, Terry,' Jocko said.

'Don't gimme no advice. Gimme the shot.'

Jocko gave a big-shouldered shrug and filled two jiggers.

'Look, kid, why don't you go home before the boss gets here?'

Terry gulped the contents of the little glasses. 'I'm not buyin' advice, I'm buyin' whisky,' Terry said.

'Slow down, boy, down,' Jocko said.

Behind Terry, 'J.P.' was soft-shoeing to the phone booth in the corner to warn Friendly. Terry heard him, whirled around and yelled, 'Stay out of that phone booth!'

'J.P.' did as he was told.

'Kid there's ten bars in every block around here,' Jocko said. 'How's about you go drink somewhere else?'

'I like it here. I like your beautiful face,' Terry said.

Jocko shook his head. He had lived a long time on the waterfront. He had seen Johnny Friendly take over the docks just by walking into this very bar and beating down the tramps who had hold of them back in the late thirties. One of the old mob, Fisheye Hennessey, was chopped right outside on the corner. Half a dozen fellers had seen it with their own eyes, and when it came to a coroner's hearing, not one of them could remember who had done it. From that day on Jocko had been impressed with Johnny Friendly. Of course he didn't bother with these jobs himself any more. But it had been an effective way of establishing confidence in

238

the beginning. Jocko wondered if Terry was taking nose candy or something. What else would spark him into open warfare with a big engine like Friendly?

Father Barry was in the small rectory library, answering letters he had received from various people around the harbour who had read of his hard-hitting sermon on the dock. It gave him hope that he and his little group weren't alone even though they seemed isolated and nearly helpless in Bohegan. An old Italian longshoreman who was under the gun in Jersey City and afraid even to sign his name said he was praying for him. An Irish wife from Manhattan's West Side said she was for throwing those bums out even if Joe and I and the two kids have to live on relief for a while. There were anonymous letters mailed here in Bohegan from dockers who said they kicked back to Big Mac and had to chip in on all the phony welfare collections but were afraid to protest. This is the way it has been for years, one of them wrote, and you're lucky you've got that collar on backwards or they'd never let you get away with that talk you made. In fact, I hope you watch yourself, Father, because they've got too many ways of having accidents.

As Father Barry paused to consider this, with a faint, weary smile, Katie burst in. Her hair was wet and she was out of breath and almost incoherent.

But when he heard that Charley was dead and that Terry had a gun and was talking out of his head with grief, Father Barry jumped up and said he'd go out and find him. If Terry was gunning for Johnny, there were only a few places to look—the union office, the Friendly Bar, the local political club.

'Don't worry, I'll find him,' Father Barry promised. 'Get Father Vincent for Charley. Call your uncle at the station house. Tell him where Charley is. And ask him to see you home.'

'Be careful, Father,' Katie said.

Father Barry shrugged. 'There isn't time to worry.'

It was only when he was trotting down the block with the sleet now turning to wet snow in his face that he wondered if this unexpected mission was a defiance of the Pastor's orders not to leave the church again on waterfront business. But where did approved

Christian charity for the Glennons leave off and a battle for a more Christian life for all of them here in Bohegan begin? Terry Malloy, trying to crawl out of the slime, was part of that battle. Must he love Mrs. Glennon, pious, sick, maternal and long-suffering, more than he loved Terry Malloy, dark-souled, blood-stained and hiding from God and conscience and himself? Oh, it was much easier to console the tearfully grateful Mrs. Glennon. But Terry Malloy was the problem. This seething waterfront was the problem. And Father Barry's mind raged on to the terrifying boundary of disobedience. Pastor or no Pastor, Monsignor or no Monsignor yes, Bishop or no Bishop, this was the problem the Church couldn't afford to duck if it wanted to be a moral force that had the virility of the living Christ.

Ahead of him he saw the red neon smear of the Friendly Bar, inviting men to quick courage or a short cut to well being.

Terry was crouched down against the bar with his hand ready to reach the gun when the door began to open. Everybody was watching as the door squeaked ajar. Everybody was surprised when in walked a priest.

Father Barry spotted Terry quickly and he came right on walking until he was half-way down the bar from him.

'I want to see you, Terry,' Father Barry said.

'You got eyes. I'm right in front of you,' Terry sneered.

'Now don't give me a hard time,' Father Barry said, coming closer.

'Who asked ya here?' Terry said. 'What d'ya want from me?'

'Your gun,' Father Barry said, close enough now to put his hand out for it.

'Hah, hah,' Terry gave a forced laugh.

'Your gun.'

'Go and chase yourself.'

'I said give me that gun. I'm not going out of here without that gun.'

'You go to hell,' Terry said.

'What did you say?' Father Barry's face reddened.

'Go to hell!'

As a youngster, Father Barry had fought in the streets and the punch he threw now seemed to come from him naturally. It was a right-hand driven hard from the shoulder and it caught Terry by surprise and off balance and knocked him down.

'Let me help you up,' Father Barry said.

Terry pushed him away hysterically. 'Get away! Keep your hands off me!'

'You want to be brave?' Father Barry said angrily.

'It's none of yer business,' Terry shouted at him.

Father Barry shouted right back at him. 'You want to be a brave man by firing lead into another man. That's being brave, huh? Well, firing lead into another man's flesh isn't being brave at all. Any bum can pick up a .45 in a pawn shop and be that brave.'

'It's none of your business,' Terry kept saying, almost sobbing. 'Why don't you mind your own business? It's none of your god-damn business.'

'You want to hurt Johnny Friendly?' Father Barry talked right through him. 'You want to hurt him? You want to fix him? Do you? You really want to finish him?'

'Goddamn right,' Terry said.

'For what he did to Charley,' Father Barry poured it on. 'And a lot of men who were better than Charley. Then don't fight 'im like a hoodlum down here in the jungle. Sure, that's just what he wants. He'll hit you in the head and plead self-defence. And beat that rap like he beat all the others. Now listen to me, Terry, the way to fight him is in the hearings with the truth. Hit him with the truth, instead of with that—that cap pistol of yours.'

Slowly Terry had begun to listen. He frowned and screwed up his face as if it were hurting.

'Just a minute. Don't rush me,' he said.

'Get rid of the gun,' Father Barry said. 'Unless you haven't got the guts. Because if you haven't, you'd better hang on to it.'

Terry took the gun out of his pocket and studied it thoughtfully. Father Barry's lips were dry. He ran his hand over them, looked anxiously at the gun and called to Jocko. 'Give me a beer,' Father Barry said, slapping his cigarette money on the bar. Terry was still looking at the gun. 'Make it two,' Father Barry said. He pushed a glass toward Terry. He drank his down thirstily. Terry drank his slowly.

'If you don't want to give me that gun, leave it here,' Father Barry said.

On the wall in the back of the bar was a framed picture, taken in happier days, of Johnny Friendly and Charley Malloy flanking their International president, Willie Givens. It had been taken at Jamaica and caught the three of them arm in arm and wreathed in exaggerated smiles.

'The hell with it,' Terry said aloud, and hurled the gun over the bar into the middle of the glass-encased picture. 'Tell Johnny I was here.'

Father Barry gave an audible sigh of relief when they got outside. 'I'm going to put you up at my place tonight,' he said.

'I ain't afraid where I am,' Terry said.

'Did I say you were?' Father Barry said. 'I thought I'd go over your testimony with you. You can really slam 'em with your stuff on the Doyle and the Nolan jobs. And what they did to Charley. There are going to be three or four other fellas you know over there working on what they're going to say. We want to get the picture as full as possible. That'll hit Johnny where it hurts.'

He took Terry by the arm and started to walk through the sleet toward the rectory.

'Hey, Terry, don't happen to have a cigarette on you, do you?'

23

FROM THE COURT House, where the waterfront hearings were conducted by the Crime Commission, the years and decades and generations of corruptive filth, of criminal sludge, of collusive mire were being dredged up and poured out over the city. The headlines were thick and black. Radio and television commentators conjured the spectre of New York harbour as a contaminated giant. National magazines, awakened at last, threw open their pages to the inhumanity of the shape-up, the waterfront distortion of trade unionism and the shameless complicity of the shipping executive and tainted city officials. The lid was off the waterfront and the sewage was spilling out at last.

As if the warning to stay away from the waterfront unless on pastoral duties had been a preliminary danger signal, now there followed a last minute order from the Bishop to Father Donoghue forbidding Father Barry to take the stand at the hearings. But the curate was too elated at the way things were going to feel discouraged. He knew, through his own underground, that Monsignor O'Hare was bringing into play every strategy he could devise to protect his old friends Willie Givens and Tom McGovern, and he was sure his high-ranking rival was doing everything in his power to prejudice his case with the Bishop. Just the same, he had his Pastor moderately, or perhaps judiciously, on his side, and he felt secure in his conviction that the overwhelming evidence of waterfront racketeering and violence would swing the diocesan headquarters over to his side.

On the opening morning of the hearings he had added to his prayers at Mass a special plea for the successful outcome of this investigation, so that the men of the waterfront could begin to enjoy the human dignity of labour which Christ understood and which God intended for them. O God, knock those Johnny Friendlys out of the box for good, he had prayed, and while You're at it, God, don't forget their respectable protectors. The same ones Xavier used to beef to the king about in the 1550's.

Father Barry did his best to keep up with his hour-to-hour religious and parish duties while sending out for every new Extra, sneaking in radio reports and getting excited telephone calls from Moose and Jimmy and some of the other of his boys who were sitting in on the hearings or waiting to be called. At least, if he wasn't there, he had the satisfaction of knowing that some of the harbour workers who had consulted him were in there taking the oath to lay the facts on the line. Not that he had gone by any rule of thumb conviction that they should testify. Luke, for instance, had come in with the problem of how to feed a family of five if he was to get up there and tell how Negroes got the short end of the short end on the docks.

'My wife is so scared she's been cryin' every night,' Luke had said. Father Barry promised he would talk to the Commission Counsel about that. He didn't think they could ask men with families to take chances without some assurance of physical and economic protection.

A bandy-legged member of the watchmen's union, affiliated with and in fact dominated by the longshoremen bosses, told Father Barry he had been subpoenaed because of the high percentage of pilferage on the pier he was supposed to watch. It happened to be a Johnny Friendly pier. 'My first week on the job I was so green I saw some stealin' of ladies' gloves, whole cases of 'em, and so I reported them to the police. Next day this fella Truck comes up to me, asks if my name is Michael McNally, and when I says "yes" he hauls off and cracks me nose. "From now on, mind your own business," he says to me. "I thought watchin' is a watchman's business," I told him. "You just watch yourself," he says to me. "That's all the goddamn watchin' you have t' do." '

Now McNally's problem was: should he tell that story? It meant the end of his job, and at his time of life there weren't too many jobs a man can do. Father Barry hadn't urged him to testify, as he had Terry, preferring to let his old man make up his mind for himself. The troubled watchman had come back the following day to say that he and his wife had talked it over and decided that he had to testify. 'Our faith is supposed to teach us a right and a wrong,' he had said, and Father Barry, whose parents came from a Kerry where courage counted more than safety, had to smile. He would talk to Father Vincent, whose family owned a chain store and perhaps might have a watchman's opening for McNally. 'I knew you'd get me into this circus of yours,' he could hear Harry Vincent saying, good-humouredly disapproving.

Port Watchman Michael McNally was the first witness called, and when, after describing his violent initiation to the job, he said: 'If I knew at that time what I know now, I never would've bothered to try 'n save those boxes of gloves,' the honesty of his admission was so startling that a laugh of recognition ran through the audience. The truth has a lovely ring, like a ship's brass bell, Father Barry thought to himself as he heard a playback of McNally's testimony over the radio at lunchtime. But to millions of people McNally's testimony would be just so many lines of questions and answers, Q—, A—, Q—, A—. Behind this long line of witnesses were human beings, with fear, doubts, bread-and-butter problems, and for the rebels and turncoats the big Question—Life, and the possible answer—Death.

The watchman was followed by an insurance company detective who gave a chalk-talk with charts on systematic wholesale pilferage. 'It's like fighting an army of locusts,' he admitted before he stepped down.

A florid-faced head of a stevedore company admitted he had given an East River union boss $15,000 to pay for the wedding of the boss's daughter.

'Isn't that an unusually generous wedding gift?' the dignified Commission Chief Counsel asked with a straight face.

'We were personal friends and she happens to be a very nice girl,' the stevedore executive insisted.

'Isn't it a fact that the $15,000 was paid out by the McCabe Stevedore Company and not by you personally?'

The stevedore employer got a little redder in the face and asked if he could consult with his lawyer before he answered.

A raw-boned thug admitted that he had come directly from Sing Sing back to the docks, had gone back on the union payrolls as a delegate at a hundred and fifty dollars a week salary and expenses and had cut himself in for a share of the loading graft. Only he put it more delicately.

A. 'I went back to this here perishable pier and bein' I done the work there before I went away, we talked it over and decided the three of us would be partners.'

Q. 'And you didn't use any pressure to get them to agree to that?'

A. 'You c'n ask them if I done anything.'

Q. 'You became a working partner?'

A. 'If there was anything to do. But as a rule there was nothin' to do.'

Q. 'Isn't it the real honest-to-God truth that you came back from Sing Sing after serving three years for assault with a deadly weapon, that you muscled your way into this loading racket and took half the profits, at least two hundred and fifty dollars a week, while holding down your union job?'

245

The public loader asked to consult his lawyer.

A Negro longshoreman testified that he had to pay a double kick-back, first two dollars to a coloured strawboss who shaped the Negroes in the basement of his own home and ran what he called a kickback club. Three dollars went to the white hiring boss on the pier. The witness had finally given up longshoring, he testified, because 'you got to pay up too many dollars to get those jobs and even then a coloured man don't get no good chance on the waterfront.'

A frightened Italian longshoreman from Brooklyn testified that he had protested paying his three dollars a month dues when there were never any meetings or financial reports.

Q. 'Who did you protest this to?'

A. 'Our business agent and there were two other fellers with him.'

Q. 'And then what happened?'

A. 'I got kicked by someone. I don't know who it was.'

Q. 'You got kicked in the groin?'

A. 'Yes, sir.'

Q. 'And sent to the hospital?'

A. 'Yes, sir. I was out of work nearly five weeks.'

Q. 'And this assault took place right in front of the pier where you work?'

A. 'Yes, sir, where I used to work.'

Mrs. Collins took the stand to tell how her husband, as assistant hiring boss on Pier B in Bohegan, had refused to hire short gangs, which meant that fewer men had to overwork in order to support the hoodlums who did no work. 'Andy was a good man,' she said, and began to cry. 'Every time I hear a key in the latch I get the feelin' it's him comin' home.' She dabbed at her prematurely lined face. 'I've got a boy thirteen, and one thing I promise, he's not going to be no longshoreman—not while that bunch of gorillas are running the thing.'

The criminal record of Alky Benasio was examined and a former Brooklyn assistant district attorney was questioned as to how it happened that a report on a waterfront murder in the 40's associated with Alky had disappeared from the police files. The former official spoke at some length, but was unable to clarify the point.

Alky himself was called to the stand, a medium-sized, unimpressive, self-contained figure whose name was known to have sent murder to at least two dozen victims.

Alky would admit nothing, not even that his brother, Jerry Benasio was now a power on most Italian-manned docks. At one point when the cool-mannered Chief Counsel was asking him a particularly vexing question, he cried out with deeply felt indignation. 'Look, you got the records in front of you. You went to college. You got the Government with you. You got everything on your side. I had to work my way up from the bottom.'

'Where do you think you are now?' the Counsel asked, perhaps baiting him unfairly because Alky Benasio, in the eyes of the law, was a free man and those murders of his were artistic jobs that would never be proved.

Slicker McGhee, up from Florida with a sun-tan, in a tailored flannel suit and a tastefully striped tie, listened politely to a reading of his record of five convictions, his appointment by Willie Givens as an organizer and his association with the country's underworld elite. He looked like a Madison Avenue advertising executive, and the recital of the waterfront murders with which the Commission investigation implicated him seemed incongruous. To any and all questions, including the name and address of his mother, he replied in perfect diction rarely heard on the waterfront, 'I refuse to answer on the grounds that the question will tend to degrade or incriminate me.' He stepped down from the stand with a bland smile, as if forgiving the authorities for this gratuitous waste of time, and a few hours later he was winging back to his life of pleasure in the Florida sun.

A very nervous Mayor Bobby Burke of Bohegan claimed he did not know his Police Commissioner Donnelly had once been a bootlegger employed by Johnny Friendly. And he denied using the docks as an outlet for petty patronage, although a disenchanted precinct worker testified that Burke paid him off by sending him down to Friendly with a note to carry him on the payroll week-ends to get time-and-a-half. Mayor Burke also denied that the late Charley Malloy was known as a City Hall 'fixer' and go-between linking the Mayor's office to Johnny Friendly's operation. But there was something about the Mayor's answers that did not carry conviction.

Often his responses were ludicrously evasive, and when he was asked how he had managed to bank sixty thousand dollars on an annual salary of fifteen thousand, he took refuge in long, fevered consultations with his attorney.

'If that's the Mayor, I hate to think what the rest of Bohegan is like,' a Manhattan reporter at the press table said, grinning.

'You should talk—over there in Manhattan!' a Jersey reporter threw back at him good-naturedly.

A few minutes later the Chief Counsel was offering in evidence documentary proof that all the officers of the local that serviced the luxury-line piers on the midtown West Side were habitual criminals with long prison records. These boys were not only the union leaders for the luxury liners, but had their own stevedore company as well on the piers serving nearly all the high-class tourist trade. In fact, the terminal superintendent for the Empire Lines was asked:

Q. 'Now the police record of the secretary-treasurer of the stevedore's company that does the work for your piers shows he was convicted of grand larceny and that he was a fugitive from the New Jersey State Prison. And the president of this company was charged with carrying a concealed weapon and subsequently jumped bail. Also his familiar nickname on the dock is "Sudden Death". Are you aware of that, sir?'

A. 'No, I didn't know that.'

Q. 'Another loading boss on your piers is Timmy Coniff who has been convicted three times for burglary, robbery and attempted grand larceny and has spent five years in Sing Sing and three years in State Prison. Do you know him?'

A. 'I may have met the gentleman once or twice.'

Q. 'Were there ten tons of steel stolen from Mr. Coniff's pier?'

A. 'Yes, sir.'

Q. 'Wouldn't you call that a remarkable piece of pilferage?'

A. 'Yes, sir.'

Q. 'Now, as an executive of one of our greatest shipping firms, doesn't it strike you that there may be some connexion between pilferage of such proportions and having habitual criminals in position of authority on your docks?'

A. 'You might say so.'

Q. 'Might? You *would* say so, wouldn't you?'

A. 'I wouldn't want to say exactly, sir.'

Half a dozen other shipping executives had heard of pilferage and criminality on their docks but were strangely vague as to the source of it.

One unhappy vice-president of a world-famous line even admitted accepting a twenty-five thousand dollar bribe from an Interstate stevedore official in order to swing his company's business to Interstate.

Witness after witness—some of them lowly 'insoigents' hoping for a change, some reluctant fence-sitters forced to describe overt acts of violence, some defensively respectable, some openly hostile—recited almost casually their tales of bribery, thievery, intimidation and murder. The crimes of extortion and criminal exploitation were being proved not once or twice, but monotonously, day in and day out, through hundreds of hours and thousands of pages of damning testimony.

Father Barry devoured every line of it and was jubilantly ready to bet that the Johnny Friendly type of labour racketeer, as insidious a gangster figure as violent America had ever known, was ready for the skids. What could save him or his underlings or his superiors now that the bottom muck of waterfront viciousness was finally being dredged up to the surface for all to see?

And the show had hardly begun! Not one, but eight waterfront local treasurers in a row all maintained with various degrees of indignation that their financial records had mysteriously disappeared on the eve of the investigation.

'Strange,' said the Chief Counsel, 'that there should be this rash of robberies and that the only property stolen in a dozen different parts of the city should be financial records.'

Big Mac McGown, who served as treasurer of Johnny Friendly's pistol local as well as hiring boss for the Hudson-American Line, was an uncomfortable witness to this mysterious case of the vanishing record books.

He sucked his apple cheeks in, scowled and looked plaintively toward his lawyer, the silky Sam Millender, as the Commission Counsel read off his list of convicted crimes. As preparation for his

249

vital job as dock boss for one of the major American export lines, Mac had robbed a bank and done time for manslaughter. An interesting development was that Johnny Friendly had promised him his hiring-boss slot while he was still 'away', as they called it, in the State can. The inference was painfully clear that the manslaughter rap was a favour for Johnny Friendly and that the choice hiring spot was Johnny's way of discharging an obligation.

Q. 'You mean to tell me that the local which you serve as treasurer takes in six thousand dollars a month in dues alone, not to mention special assessments and frequent cigar-box collections—a minimum seventy-five thousand dollars a year—and keeps no financial records?'

A. 'Sure, we kep' records.'

Q. 'Perhaps, Mr. McGown, you could help our investigators locate them?'

A. 'Well, the trouble is, we was robbed last week, and we can't find no books.'

Q. 'Did you report this—unfortunate robbery to the police?'

A. 'Well, we—we . . .' Big Mac rolled his eyes in agony. He wasn't used to thinking this much on his own. It was a unique experience for him. 'We—wanted t' make sure the books wasn't lost somewheres around the office before we put the police to any trouble.' He turned to look at Sam Millinder for approval.

Millinder was unhappy. He was a knowledgeable, rather sophisticated figure who did not mind counselling Willie Givens for his seventy-five thousand dollar a year retainer, but these muscle heads who couldn't even parrot-back what you had rehearsed with them were more than Sam had bargained for. Somehow Sam Millinder had managed to maintain his position as a respectable cloak for the Longshore International, but now this cloak seemed in danger of being shot through with too many holes. At one point Sam Millinder was unable to restrain his own mirth at one of his client's inane evasions.

Big Mac was asked to explain how he had managed to bank fifty thousand dollars over the past four years on a salary of nine thousand five hundred dollars. Was it, by any chance, as a result of kickbacks from longshoremen over whom Big Mac had absolute economic control?

A. 'No, sir. I been lucky on the horses. I got a barber who gives me pretty good tips.'

Q. 'Has this—good fortune of yours been reflected in your income-tax returns? I see no evidence of it here.'

A frown of puzzlement clouded Big Mac's face.

A. 'Uh, I—I'd like to ask my counsel the answer to that question.'

Sam Millinder signalled for the microphone to make a nice distinction. 'I wish to make it clear to Counsel and the Honourable Commissioners that I am not supplying the answers to any questions you may ask, but am simply here in the rôle of adviser as to the constitutional rights of the members of the union I represent.'

An air of expectancy ran through the crowded court room the day that International president-for-life, Willie Givens, took the stand. Sam Millinder's conduct had verged on discourtesy to some of the more obvious criminal types, but now he hovered around the flabby bulk of Weeping Willie like a fond mother mystified because her little darling has suddenly grown into a monster. And two of Millinder's assistants were close at hand, like lesser tugs trying to nuzzle a disabled leviathan into safe harbour.

Willie's face looked like a great clod of clay which a careless sculptor had thrown together and never bothered to finish. Occasionally the powerful, brawling, hard-drinking longshoreman of forty years ago peered through its prison of fat and easy living. The jowls were formidable and the bulbous, blue-veined nose was held aloft as an ornament to its owner's long nights of congenial fellowship. Yes, Willie Givens was a good fellow, a professionally Irish good fellow who could sing 'I'll Take You Home Again, Kathleen' as huskily as any 12th Avenue or River Street dock walloper.

Weeping Willie had come a long way from the horse cars and the meat wagons of 1912. Once upon a time he had worked side by side with Runty Nolan and Pop Doyle for thirty cents an hour, and he was no smarter than they were or braver or better at his work. But he had something that was still paying off big in America. Call it cupidity or a gift for the main chance, the art of doing nothing in particular and doing it very well, doing it with a flourish, doing it with a knowing rap of the gavel, doing it with a torrent of official-sounding words and a fix in here and a cut back there, doing it with a nod to the Mayor, doing it with a wink from the shippers, doing it with his big red hands making seemingly heartfelt gestures, ready to cry for his forty thousand longshoremen to whom his life was devoted, working day and night for them with no thought except for their welfare, their economic advancement, their social security. Weeping Willie Givens, who had worked his way up from a two-and-a-half dollar a day horse-truck loader to a mover and shaker of the metropolis who could be asked such questions as:

Q. 'Now, Mr. Givens, isn't it a fact that five of the seven organizers you appointed in the past ten years had serious criminal records?'

A. 'Nobody asked me to check back on their records.'

Q. 'But as an International labour leader, you would not wish to appoint known criminals to organize your workmen, would you?'

A. 'I appointed men who had the confidence of their fellow members. I appointed the best men available.'

Q. 'When you appointed Mr. McGhee an organizer at ten thousand a year and expenses, were you aware of the fact that he had served two terms in Sing Sing and had fourteen arrests, including twice for murder?'

A. 'I'm not sure I knew that at the time.'

Q. 'But when it was pointed out to you by members of the local to which you yourself belonged, did you take any action to remove Mr. McGhee?'

A. 'I can't take any action without the recommendation of my Executive Board.'

Q. 'Well, did your Executive Board ever take any action?'

A. 'Yes, sir. They appointed a sub-committee to investigate the conduct of Brother McGhee.'

Q. 'I see. And did this sub-committee come to any conclusion?'

A. 'I'm not sure. I don't think they made their report yet.'

Q. 'Now, Mr. Givens, who was chairman of this sub-committee?'

A. 'Oh, I think it was Mr. Malloy.'

Q. 'Mr. Charles Malloy, better known as Charley the Gent?'

A. 'I knew him as Malloy, Charley Malloy.'

Q. 'Isn't he the same Charles Malloy who was found murdered in an alley in Bohegan recently?'

A. 'I imagine that would be the same man.'

Q. 'Now, Mr. Givens, when you appointed Mr. Malloy to head a committee to look into the fitness of Slicker McGhee as a union organizer, didn't you realize that Mr. Malloy was the business agent for the Bohegan local headed by John Friendly, who is waiting to be called as a witness here and whose police record shows convictions for bootlegging, for grand larceny and for criminal assault? And to whom stevedore and shipping company executives have testified in this court room that they have given him over the past five years bribes exceeding fifty thousand dollars?'

Old Willie Givens asked for a glass of water, more familiar to him as a chaser than as a drink to be enjoyed for its own sake. He had sat with the mayors and the judges and the city machine bosses in the boxes at the ball games, but now his hand had begun to tremble. His putty nose seemed to go a shade bluer. His jowls hung limp as surrender flags along his neck. Pop Doyle and Jimmy Sharkey were in the audience, having arrived at the Court House door two hours early to be sure to get in. Watching Willie's discomfort, they knew that somewhere Runty Nolan must be enjoying himself and maybe drinking his toast, 'Here's mud in the eye of Weeping Willie.'

Well, there was a little justice left in this sin-soaked world, they chuckled to each other as they listened to Willie ramble through one of his characteristically circuitous explanations.

A. 'You see, as regarding John Friendly or anybody else, we have in our organization what is known as local autonomy, and before I could take any action regarding any individual, I could only suggest to the Executive Committee that they appoint a sub-committee to examine all the evidence of anything detrimental to our organization or to the industry as a whole, and inasmuch as I . . .'

Q. 'Yes, yes, now I quite understand that, Mr. Givens, but what I am asking you directly is whether you knew that Mr. McGhee and Mr. Benasio and Mr. Danny Dondero and Mr. John Friendly, all ranking officers in your organization, were known and habitual and dangerous criminals who merely use the longshoremen's union as a screen for their continuing criminal activities? Now after your forty years as an officer of this organization, can't you honestly answer that question "Yes" or "No"?'

253

A. 'There may be a little crime on this waterfront, but I don't see how it's any worse than any other waterfront or any other section of society for that matter, and if anybody's breaking the law down here, then it's not my job to clean it up, but a job for the police and the district attorneys.'

Q. 'And you think they have been doing a good job?'

A. 'I think it's been pretty well taken care of.'

That's about the way it went with Willie Givens. Only there was a whole day of it. If one-third to a half of all the longshore officials had criminal records, he was certainly surprised to hear it. But Willie's jowls hung lowest when he was forced to admit that he had reached a sticky hand into his union's own emergency fund for such items as:

Q. '$1,450 for golf club dues?'

A. 'Well, I . . .'

Q. '$11,575 for two Cadillacs?'

A. 'Mmmm, that . . .'

Q. '$850 for a Caribbean cruise?'

A. 'I—uh . . .'

Q. '$9,500 for premiums on his personal insurance?'

A. 'The Executive . . .'

Q. '$600 for ties and shirts from Sulka's?'

A. 'Now just a . . .'

Q. '$1,000 for the funeral of his wife's uncle?'

A. 'I can ex . . .'

By the time Willie stepped down from the stand at the end of the day, mopping the sweat from between the folds of his face, straightening his dapper, fat man's grey double-breasted suit and doing a feeble imitation of his old good-time-Willie smile, by that time the mighty president-for-life seemed to have come not only to the end of the day, but perhaps to the end of the road, and Pop and Jimmy and Moose only wished that Runty could be with them to enjoy the wake. As the headlines proclaimed next morning, there was mud in Willie Given's eyes, more mud than even Runty could have hoped for.

There had been rumours that Big Tom McGovern, at the top of this pinnacle—or dungheap, as some were beginning to call it—would manage to escape a subpoena, but Mr. Big—as the newspapers preferred to call him—finally had his day in court. Father

Barry got a private chuckle out of this, for he had played a small, sly and possibly effective part in McGovern's questioning. There had been a prevalent rumour that Tom McGovern had enough political power to frighten off the State Commission. One of his old friends, a former magistrate, was sitting on the Commission, Judge Gilhooley, and it was being said along the waterfront that Gilhooley would see to it that Big Tom was never called. Father Barry, with the touch of larceny that peppered his personality, called the Bohegan *Graphic* waterfront reporter to ask if this was true. The reporter said he didn't know, but he would ask the Commissioners. When the Commission Chief Counsel heard that the press was calling, he was persuaded that they would all be leaving themselves open to criticism and perhaps an aroused public opinion if they failed to call the man whose dominance on the docks had become an open secret.

Like Willie Givens, Big Tom McGovern had risen from a thirty cent an hour horse truck job forty years earlier. He and Willie had been young, ambitious roughnecks together, but they were a different breed of men. McGovern was paunchy and meat-faced too, but there was a power in him that was lacking in Windbag Willie. Tom McGovern had longshoreman's hands and eyes that were used to being obeyed. His hair was white, but he still had all of it, worn in a crew-cut that accentuated the size of his neck and the stubborn cut of his fleshy but hard and intelligent face. He owned a seventy-foot yacht and he was known as a good tipper at the Colony, El Morocco and the Stork, but his voice had never lost its hard River Street edge. He had sons who had gone to Harvard and were something of a disappointment to him, but he prided himself on maintaining his original, even his uncouth, vigour. He had become the chairman of boards, the officer of exclusive city clubs, the intimate of many leading figures in the State, a director of charitable institutions and the Mayor's favourite trouble-shooter for labour management problems in the harbour. He even had referred to himself, humorously, as a 'one-man port authority'.

He listened patiently while his various waterfront enterprises were read off: He was the president of the Interstate Stevedore Company, the largest firm in the harbour, operating with a dozen different lines at fourteen piers from Bohegan to Red Hook. He owned half a dozen tug-boat and lighter companies. He owned the oil company that sold the harbour cities all the oil the local administrations consumed. His sand-and-gravel company had nearly all the city contracts. He owned the National Trucking Company, one of the largest in the harbour. He owned a dry-dock, a paint company, a wholesale fruit company.

The list grew laughably long, but Big Tom McGovern did not laugh. He had done this, he whose father had come to this country penniless and who died penniless, a poverty-ridden dock labourer glad to work for two bits an hour. Young Tom had seen the beaten look in his old man's eyes and had sworn it would never shadow his own. So now he sat firm and heavy on the stand while they laughed at the inventory of the 100 million dollar empire he had built with his own two, tough-knuckled hands. This was America, goddamn it, and he'd play his cards the way he picked them off the table.

Q. 'Mr. McGovern, an inspection of the books of your Interstate Stevedore Company shows a withdrawal of over one million dollars in the last four years, without any vouchers covering this amount. How would you explain that?'

A. 'I don't.'

Q. 'You're not even willing to guess.'

A. 'It's not my business to guess.'

Q. 'As one of our leading businessmen, wouldn't you say it was odd procedure to withdraw an amount of such magnitude without any vouchers to cover it?'

A. 'I don't know. We do a lot of entertaining in our business.'

Q. 'But these sums were not applied to entertainment.'

A. 'I wouldn't know.'

Q. 'The hiring bosses and boss loaders on every one of the Interstate Stevedore Company's piers has a criminal record. Could there be any connexion between the pay-offs to these men and the unexplained withdrawal of one million dollars?'

A. 'I wouldn't know.'

Q. 'As president of Interstate, don't you follow the affairs of your company?'

A. 'Not that closely. It's only one of many enterprises in which I'm interested.'

Q. 'But you did take time off personally to request a parole for Mr. McGown and for Mr. Karger, stating to the Parole Board that you had jobs waiting for them when they would be released?'

A. 'I was told they knew their jobs. That's all I was interested in.'

Evidence was then introduced to show that one hundred and fifty convicted criminals were carried on the Interstate payroll.

Q. 'Mr. McGovern, four years ago you were chairman of the Mayor's Port Committee to report on conditions in the harbour. Your general conclusion was that conditions were satisfactory. Is that true?'

A. 'Yes, sir.'

Q. 'Did you investigate the fact that your own loading operation was gangster-ridden?'

A. 'No, sir.'

Tom McGovern had come up a hard road and he gave hard answers, his *Yes, sirs* and *No, sirs* chopping like axe-strokes into the scaffold the Chief Counsel was trying to erect for him.

When it was all over, no one in the court room had any illusions about Big Tom McGovern. He had been chipped away at, and his wife and his ivy-league sons must have paled a little, but he was still Mr. Big. He surveyed the room with a final, ironic, go-to-hell expression and stepped down. Outside his uniformed chauffeur and his Lincoln town car were waiting to rush him home to the penthouse overlooking Central Park, forty years and fifty million dollars away from River Street.

The morning Johnny Friendly was to testify, Terry Malloy came down the aisle with a police guard and was seated in the row in back of him. Terry had been under police protection since the night he had spent with Father Barry in the rectory. He had protested that he didn't want a police guard, but Commissioner Donnelly was taking no chances. He and Mayor Burke were feeling shakier every day, and if anything should happen to Terry now, it would only dig their political graves deeper.

In these strange, unexpected surroundings Terry felt numb and spiritless. He wasn't on fire to testify, but he wasn't afraid to either. He'd like to see Johnny get his for crossing Charley, but he wasn't too sure, now that he had time to think it over, that this hearing would really put the blocks to Johnny Friendly. Father Barry seemed sure enough, and he had to admit that Father Barry was as smart in one way as Johnny Friendly was in another.

Johnny Friendly was a cold, proud, hostile witness, glaring at the row of Commissioners and the counsel staff as if they were all on trial and he was in the prosecutor's seat. That was the way he felt. Here were a bunch of phonies, politicians, cop-lovers, canaries. Big Tom McGovern, Mr. Upstairs, had pointedly ignored him when they had passed each other in the lobby outside the hearing room. But the Big Guy had shown them how to do it, tell 'em nothing, admit nothing, deny everything in a big, loud, Yes, sir-No, sir voice.

Q. 'Mr. Friendly, has your local ever kept a bank account?'

A. 'No, sir.'

Q. 'Why not?'

A. 'That was up to Mr. Malloy, our business agent.'

Q. 'You don't know why Mr. Malloy never deposited the union funds in a bank?'

A. 'I don't know what he done.'

Q. 'As president, weren't you interested?'

A. 'I don't think we had enough money to put in the bank.'

Q. 'Mr. McGown has testified that it was coming in at the rate of at least six thousand dollars a month, hasn't he?'

A. 'I wasn't in this room when he testified.'

Q. 'But surely you know how much your own union takes in?'

A. 'I don't pay much attention to them details.'

Q. 'Well, what do you do as president?'

A. 'Run back and forth, see that the men do their jobs, keep an eye on the shape-up, handle the meetings, and things like that.'

Q. 'Well, you haven't had a membership meeting in over five years, have you?'

A. 'Yeah, I think we had a few.'

Q. 'Isn't it a fact that one of the changes the late Mr. Joseph Doyle was campaigning for was regular meetings where the members would be allowed to express themselves? And isn't it a fact that this is one of the reasons why you had young Mr. Doyle put to death?'

Johnny glanced around until he located Terry in the audience and fixed him with a baleful look. Terry pressed his lips together and stared back at him.

A. 'I don't know nothin' about them killin's.'

Q. 'I have only asked you about one, so far.'

A. 'Well, you can save yourself some time because I don't know about any murders.'

Q. 'Do you realize that you are testifying under oath?'

Hang on, look 'em in the eye and bull it through was Johnny Friendly's witness-chair conduct, and as he was excused from the stand, he was heard to mutter, 'You bunch o' sons a . . .'

The next witness called was Terry Malloy. He and Johnny passed each other in the aisle. Johnny opened his mouth in a sneer and Terry just looked at him coldly. Inside he felt a nervous quiver. How had he gotten here? It seemed only the other day that he and Johnny and Charley were watching a television fight together in back of Friendly's and having a few laughs.

'Mr. Malloy,' the clerk was saying, 'do you swear to tell the truth, the whole truth and nothing but the truth, so help you God?'

'Yeah—right.'

'I do,' the clerk corrected.

'I do,' Terry grunted.

The Counsel led Terry through a series of sullen answers concerning his own activities on the docks and then dropped the sixty-four dollar question.

'Mr. Malloy, is it true that on the night Joey Doyle was found dead that you were the last one to see him before he was pushed or fell off the roof?'

A. 'Brother, he was pushed!'

Q. 'Yes, we'll come to that in a moment, but you were the last one to see him?'

A. 'Yeah—I mean—yes, you're right.'

Q. 'And is it true that you went . . .'

A. 'Wait a minute, wait a minute, I mean I was the last one to see him except for the guys who pushed him off.'

Q. 'And were you acquainted with those gentlemen?'

A. 'You mean that pair o' bums called Sonny and Specs.'

Q. 'Do you refer to Richard C. Flavin?'

A. 'That's Specs.'

Q. 'And Jackson H. Rodell?'

A. 'Yeah, that's Sonny.'

The Chairman of the Commission interrupted. 'Have Flavin and Rodell responded to their subpoenas?'

The Chief Counsel: 'No, sir. They are said to be out of the State at the present time and beyond our jurisdiction.'

The answers came easier as Terry felt the sharp recoil of how they had suckered him into the murder of Joey. How could he have been so stupid as not to realize what they were up to when he already knew Joey was giving them a bad time, and anybody who gives Johnny Friendly a bad time has only two choices: to change his tune or stop whistling altogether.

Q. 'Now, Mr. Malloy, did Mr. Friendly ever say anything to you that would indicate his responsibility for getting rid of Joey Doyle— for wanting to end his life?'

A. 'Are you kiddin'? Hell, yes!'

Q. 'Now, please, Mr. Malloy, in somewhat less exclamatory language, would you be good enough to . . .'

And the truth, the raw, ugly, purging truth poured out of Terry, unrehearsed, unexpurgated, uninhibited, his own sins merging with the velvet-glove racketeering of his brother Charley and the ruthless reign of terror that in the name of Johnny Friendly had made the docks of Bohegan a one-man show—and a slaughter house.

A. 'Yeah, and I could tell you about the time . . .'

The Chief Counsel stepped forward. 'Mr. Malloy, you may stand down now. I want to thank you for your forthright statements. I might say they offer something of a contrast to some others this afternoon.'

Terry stepped down, excited. Talking about Charley and that last cab ride and how he knew it must have been Danny Dondero who took him out as a substitute for himself, these violent impressions fired off inside him like powder flashes, and he was half dazed and trembling with it when he felt rough hands grab him and shake him. It was Johnny Friendly struggling away from a Commission guard to shriek-spit into Terry's unready face:

'You stinkin', rotten cheese-eater. You just dug your own grave.

Go fall in it. You're dead on this waterfront and every waterfront from Boston to New Orleans. You don't drive a truck, you don't push a baggage rack, you don't even live. You're a walking dead man.'

As the Commission gavel pounded and the guards wrestled Johnny Friendly away, he spat into Terry's face. Terry started his right hand, but someone grabbed it and he was pinned from behind and pulled away. There was a swirl of faces and camera flashes and reporters full of questions. It was almost like winning a fight and being rushed back to the dressing room. But Terry knew, jostled and over-excited and confused, he knew that this one was a lot harder, and it wasn't over yet.

24

STILL MUMBLING ABOUT Johnny Friendly, Terry was hustled into a delivery elevator and led out a back entrance by two uniformed cops who had been assigned to guard him. He had hated cops all his life and the sight of them was no more welcome to him now than it was before.

They drove him to his tenement in their police car. He didn't say anything, and they didn't either. They were Donnelly men, looking to the Police Chief for advancement. Now that the Burke-Donnelly-Friendly team was under fire, their jobs on the Waterfront Squad were in jeopardy. A new police chief might even investigate their own weekly handout from the bookies, crap-game bankers and numbers men who operated on the piers under Friendly auspices.

When Terry got out of the car he started to slam the door behind him, but the cops followed him out.

'What's the story?' Terry said, wanting to walk away from them.

'We're detailed to stay with you,' said Patrolman Novick.

'Who wants you? Get lost,' Terry said irritably.

The officers fell into step with him. 'Orders, kid. You're hot. You ought to be glad we're with you.'

'Aaaah,' Terry snarled at them. 'Y' make me feel like a canary.'

They looked at each other and smiled. 'Well . . .'

'No kiddin', you'll drive me nuts hangin' on my tail like this. How c'n I shake you guys?'

'We've got to park outside your door tonight,' Thompson, the other patrolman said. 'Tomorrow, if you still feel the same way, we'll take you down to Headquarters and you can sign a release. At least then if they leave you like a Swiss cheese, our boss'll have something to show the papers to get him off the hook.'

'Ho, ho, very funny,' Terry said.

Terry spent the rest of that day and most of the next morning in his room. Nobody called him or came to see him and it gave him a creepy feeling, as if he was sealed in a tomb, like being buried alive. He played three-handed poker with the cops, and one of them went out and brought in some sandwiches. Then he lay on his bed, sulking and wondering where the hell everybody was. He thought about Katie; he had half hoped she might come and pat him on the back for what he did. Then he thought: for what, for admitting I had a hand in the knock-off of her brother? And could've told Runty what he had coming, but didn't quite work up the guts to? And let Charley throw himself into the pot to give me a chance to jump out of it? Yeah, I'm one heroic sonofabitch. Katie ought to run in and kiss me all over, I'm such a goddamn noble character.

By noon next day he was too restless to imprison himself any longer. So he went down to Headquarters with Novick and Thompson and signed some kind of paper, blowing them off. Some of the detectives down there gave him the horse laugh. 'How's the big reformer?' one of them said. 'Did you say informer?' another asked archly. Terry glared at them and told them where to put it.

Just the same it felt funny-peculiar, walking down the street alone. He felt exposed. The Bohegan *Graphic* carried his picture that day with a subtle caption: *Marked for Mob Vengeance?* It was queer seeing it in print like that. It didn't really feel like him. Somebody with the same name who looked like him. In a way he still felt as if he could saunter in to the Friendly Bar and have a beer and kid around with Johnny. Actually he was being careful to make a wide circle around Friendly's. He wasn't afraid, or anything. It was just that it would be easier not to have to see any of those guys for a while. He had a queasy feeling inside him that he would not have been able to explain to anybody. He knew he had done right. He knew Father Barry had it pegged right when he said the only possible way to get Friendly off their necks was to pack in the facts so the guys who wanted a better shake could have a chance. What the hell, if Johnny and the rest of them were going to do these things, they had to take their chances of guys on the other side getting up and fingering them. It wasn't so much that Terry felt he had done right as that he had done what he had to do when they had pushed him to the edge. Still, there was some hangover of guilt in him, something that was just there, small but uncomfortable, like an infinitesimal pebble inside a sock.

He dropped into a bar he had never patronized, a few blocks in from the waterfront, and had a few beers. He felt people staring at him. He felt alone. A couple of customers walked out. Maybe they were ready to anyway. But Terry imagined that they wanted to get out of gun range in case that crap in the *Graphic* turned out to be true. He decided to drop in on Hildegarde. Fat Hildegarde always liked him. She'd sort of be a test.

Hildegarde said, 'Hullo, mein sweetheart. I buy you a trink,' and seemed to be her usual good-natured slob self. But Terry was more sensitive to mood than he had ever been before and he wondered if Hildegarde wasn't forcing her gaiety in order to show him that everything was as it had been before. To make it worse, a couple of longshoremen friends of Pop Doyle were in the place and they pointedly moved farther down the bar from him, whether through physical fear or ostracism, who could tell? I go down the line for them and the Doyle crowd still treat me like a bum, Terry thought bitterly. And the other side's looking to chop me. Some deal.

On his way home he passed his chums, Chick and Jackie, with whom he used to have breakfast nearly every morning at the Longdock.

'Hi, Chick—Jackie boy,' he called.

They looked right through him and kept on going.

Terry was jolted. Chick and Jackie, who were always laughing at his jokes and telling him what a fighter he was. Then his divided

263

mind tried to reassure him. What made them so great, a couple of mob hangers-on, with not enough guts to go straight and not enough moxie to qualify for a spot with Johnny Friendly? What gave those two shlagooms the right to look away from Terry Malloy?

He passed a couple of real small kids, ten or eleven, playing stick ball, and he stopped to talk to them. He had to talk to somebody. He thought of Billy and the Warriors, and his pigeons up on the roof. That was it. He'd go up and talk to them. Sometimes it seemed to him as if those pigeons could talk. Swifty would throw his neck out and make a noisy cooing sound and Terry would swear he could understand what the guy was trying to say.

He felt a little better when he stepped out on the roof and saw Billy at the far end of it, near his coop.

'Hiya, champ?' He tried to put some of the old ginger into his voice. 'How's the kid?'

Billy didn't answer. Billy just stared at him. There were tears of bitter rage in his eyes.

'A pigeon for a pigeon!' The boy's terrible contempt was hurled across the roof at Terry, and with it an object that struck him and fell at his feet. Then Billy was hurrying down the ladder to the fire-escape. But Terry was conscious only of the dead bird in his hand—Swifty—his lead bird, his favourite, whom he and Billy had waited for at the end of races so many times, shouting and slapping each other when Swifty came winging home high above the buildings, out over the river, Swiftly, the strongest, the fastest, the best goddamn bird in the neighbourhood. Feeling sick, with the bird's limp, wrung neck hanging down from his hand, dreading even having to look, he walked slowly over to his coop.

'Oh, Christ!' he moaned when he saw what had been done. 'Oh, Christ, oh, Christ, oh, Christ . . .'

Every single pigeon of Terry's flock lay dead. Every single bird had been wrung by the neck. They lay in a sickening pile where they had been tossed on the floor of the coop.

Terry sank down in the doorway of his coop and put his face into his hands and cried. When had he cried last, he had no idea. Not since he was seven, that's for sure.

How long had he been sitting there? It could have been half an hour. He looked up and Katie was coming toward him. He didn't bother to greet her.

'I've been wanting to see you,' she said.

'Yeah. Well, you took your time.'

'Pop wouldn't let me come near you. He said it was dangerous.'

'He's probably right,' Terry said.

'I'm going back to Marygrove tomorrow.'

'That's a good idea,' Terry said.

'But I had to tell you that what you did . . .'

'Aah, forget it,' he cut in. 'It's done.'

It was only then that she looked behind him into the coop and saw the pigeons.

'Oh, my God!' she said. 'Oh, no, oh, no . . .'

'Every goddamn one of them,' he said. 'Every one.'

'Oh, Terry, why, why?'

He hesitated and then said in a low voice, 'I guess that's the kids' idea of showin' me what they think of stool pigeons, I guess that's it.'

'But what do they want instead, murders and . . .'

'Forget it,' he said.

'Terry, you've got to get away from here now,' she said. 'Maybe on a ship or out West, a farm . . .'

'Farm!' he said with disgust.

'Well, I don't care, anywhere, as long as it's away from here, from Johnny Friendly, from the whole horrible . . .'

'Look,' he said. 'Save your breath. There's an old sayin' on the waterfront. If they're goin' to get you, they're goin' to get you. They'll follow you out West. They've gotten guys in Sing Sing. I even heard of them catchin' up with a fella in Australia.'

Katie pressed her fist hard against her lip so as not to cry.

'Anyway, don't worry about me,' he said. 'You'll go back to school. Get to be a teacher and try to pound some sense into a lot of snotnose kids. Maybe meet a man teacher, so the two of you c'n starve to death an' live happily ever after . . .'

He tried to laugh at her trying not to cry.

'Now you better beat it,' he said. 'Your old man's right. I know

265

how to duck. But you want to get back to that daisyland of yours lookin' as good as when you come down.'

She almost bent forward to kiss him and then at the last moment she put out her hand.

'I'll pray for you,' she said. 'I won't forget you.'

'That goes for me double,' he said. 'Take it easy now, Katie.'

She turned and walked back across the roof. She had the most graceful way of walking of any person he had ever known. What if he called out to her? What if he said, 'Hey, Katie, come back!' Ten to one she would have. That's what was so strange about it. He never went too far in school, but this he knew. The basic stuff he knew. And, brother, that lovely kid with her head in the clouds, maybe she wasn't quite with it yet, not quite ready for it, but this was the basic stuff. And he never kissed her, never even so much as touched her, except that minute and a half when they found themselves dancing. Boy, that was some minute and a half:

> . . . *I left my love in Avalon*
> *And sailed—away* . . .

He watched the last bit of her long, streaked-brown hair disappearing into the stairwell three roofs beyond. The pile driver on the waterfront was still banging away, busy at the new pier where Terry had been offered the boss loader slot, but Terry was oblivious to the pounding. He stood there thinking about her.

A few days later he was walking along Dock Street, wondering if he could wangle a job as a teamster with an anti-Givens local in the near-by town of Hoboken. A car pulled up to the curb near the corner and Johnny Friendly got out, followed by Truck and Gilly. There had been some newspaper demands for Johnny Friendly's arrest for his part in the various waterfront murders cited at the hearings. But the local district attorney, part of the old City Hall crowd desperately hanging on, had explained that it was impossible to indict Friendly as accessory to a murder when the two principals in the case were out of the country. Specs Flavin and Sonny Rodell were believed to be in Cuba, and even if they were extradited,

Friendly could hardly be indicted unless they were willing to identify him as the instigator of the plot.

Terry's immediate reaction when he saw Johnny Friendly at the end of the block was to turn away and drift over into a cigar-store entrance and keep his head averted until Johnny had disappeared around the corner. But as he tried to hide himself on a public street in broad daylight, he remembered what he had told Katie about the mob's being able to track you down. Hell, they were their own F.B.I. And with this, some of his old cocksure, I'm-with-me feeling poured back into him. He pivoted in Friendly's direction and quickened his steps and even called to him. 'Hey, Johnny. I wanna see ya.'

Johnny Friendly stopped and waited. He was calm. He had been working around the clock to hold everything together and he had a good grip on himself. It was Terry who was overwrought now.

'Hey, Johnny, you want to know the trouble with you?' he slugged it in. 'You take them heaters away from you, you take the tailored suits and the kickbacks and the shakedown cabbage and the pistoleros away from you, and you're nothin'! You're nothin'! Your guts is all in your wallet and your trigger-finger! You know that?'

Truck and Gilly looked at Johnny, but he signalled them with the slightest of nods to ride it out. Johnny had already passed down the execution order. 'He's got to go.' Johnny didn't know where or when the party was going to take place, but he could sit back and let it go through channels.

'I know you think you're the last of the tough guys, but you know what you are? You're a cheap, lousy, dirty, stinkin', mother-lovin' bastard and I'm glad what I done to you. You hear that. I'm glad what I done. I'm glad what I done! And I hope they burn ya till you come out like a piece of black bacon that breaks to pieces when you touch it.'

'Listen, dead man,' Johnny said, speaking quietly, 'I'd lay you out right here for the mother crack. But I can wait. Only I want to remind you one thing. Don't get brave all of a sudden because you figure I'm on my way out. Because I ain't. I'm still in. And I'll be in when you're eatin' worms for breakfast, with the dirt thrown in free with every order.'

He turned and walked away. Truck and Gilly didn't even bother to look at Terry as they hurried to fall back into step with the boss.

Terry watched them turn the corner, on their way to business as usual at the Friendly Bar. He was shaking now, but it was not from fear. It was exhilaration. This, even more than his hour on the stand, had cut him free of Johnny Friendly.

Father Barry went to see Terry a few days later and didn't find him in his room. He returned the following evening and Terry still was not there. He left a note on the door for Terry to phone him, and when no call came through, the priest reported the facts to the police. They did not seem too concerned. They suggested that a loner like Terry might have shipped out or hitch-hiked west. However, if he failed to return to his rooms within a week, they would list him as missing.

Three weeks later the remains of a human being were found in a barrel of lime that had been tossed on one of the multi-acre junk heaps in the Jersey swamps. The coroner's report after the inquest attributed death to twenty-seven stab wounds, apparently inflicted by an ice pick. No next of kin came forward. The lime-mutilated corpse was never identified. But the boys along River Street, pro mob and anti, knew they had seen the last of a pretty tough kid.

25

FATHER BARRY LOOKED around at the monastic room that had been living quarters, office and a place of worship these past two years. He wondered what was being decided at the conference between his Pastor and the Bishop. Father Donoghue had been called up to the Bishop's residence that afternoon, and it was rectory scuttlebutt that Pete Barry was marked for a transfer, perhaps to the small, Jersey harbour town of Leonardo, some seventy-five miles from Bohegan, near Sandy Hook.

Father Barry picked his baseball encyclopedia up off the floor and gathered up some of the waterfront mail that was strewn around.

Mrs. Harris sometimes complained good-naturedly that Pete Barry was the sloppiest tenant the rectory had had in a long time and now the curate was doing his best to set his room in order, as if unconsciously preparing to take his leave of it.

There was a rap on the door and Father Vincent called in, 'Pete, can I do anything for you?' Harry Vincent had disagreed with him bitterly, but now that Pete Barry was on the hot-seat, Father Vincent was rather surprised to find how concerned he was about his headstrong colleague. Even when Pete had called him a 'smoke-pot-swinging metaphysician', Father Vincent had been more amused than angry and even half willing to admit the beam in his eye if only Pete would acknowledge that he had a mote or two in his own.

'No thanks, Harry. I'm just doing a little spring cleaning.' He preferred being with his own thoughts as he prepared himself for the possibility of having to move on from Bohegan and the work he had begun. He checked the time on the silver wrist-watch his mother had given him upon graduation from college. She was living with a married sister in Yonkers. His Sunday afternoon visit was a family ritual. They would both miss that weekly talk if he was to be ordered to Lower Jersey. Mrs. Barry had been ashamed of herself for having to dab her eyes when she heard that her son might be transferred to some strange-sounding place she had never heard of. 'Now what's the name of the place they're after sending you?' she had asked in her spry Kerry brogue. When he had repeated the persistent rumour, 'Leonardo,' she had shaken her head disapprovingly. 'Leonardo? I never heard of it.' Her world was bounded by Kerry on one side and now Yonkers on the other, and she was already convinced that her favourite son was being exiled into the wilderness. Pete had tried to reassure her. Leonardo was a perfectly respectable town of about 2,500 on the South Jersey shore. The Navy had a pier there, but, except in times of emergency, the local longshoremen doubled as clamdiggers and lobstermen on this isolated waterfront.

'Waterfront,' Mrs. Barry had snorted. 'Lord have mercy. You mean they've found you another waterfront!'

'Leonardo isn't another Bohegan.' Pete had tried to smile to allay
269

his mother's fears. But inwardly he had been anxious and tense all week. He was beginning to get a grip on the job to be done in Bohegan. To him the act of raising the Host had become far more than a routine duty; it was a deep and intense identification with the Saviour who walked the streets of Bohegan. Christ not only rose from the altar but came down to the waterfront and on to the docks. Christ in dungarees and a checked wool shirt, with a cargo hook in His belt, had one hell of a job on River Street, and Father Barry had been bracing himself to give Him a hand. Oh, brother, what a bunch of God-forsaken Catholics, Christians, citizens, human beings, human beasts He's up against in *this* diocese! He couldn't help wondering if the Pharisees here in Bohegan wouldn't like to see Him packed off to Leonardo if He started talking out of turn, say, at the foot of River and Pulaski Streets, and assembled there the longshoremen and checkers and truckers and watchmen and stevedores and union officials and shenangos and coopers and the steamship staffs and the boss loaders and the loan sharks and the numbers men and the hired squeezers of .38's, and hit them with the beatitudes, 'Blessed are they who suffer persecution for justice's sake'— hit them hard between the eyes and straight from the shoulder in the lingo of Port Bohegan.

He had tried to hide his anxiety from his mother. She had suffered years ago when her husband got the Siberia treatment for being an honest maverick as a patrolman, and now she was disturbed that this chip off the hard block had ventured beyond the bounds of his duty as a curate and thus had incurred the disapproval of the Bishop. He had done his best to convince her that he was already overdue for a transfer, customary for any curate after two or three years. He didn't tell her, naturally, what he had said to Father Vincent when the Pastor had been called over to the Bishop's residence: 'Well, Harry, looks like I'm being sent down to the bush leagues.'

Father Barry went into the bathroom to wash his dirty celluloid collars. Then he bound his waterfront mail together with a thick rubber band and slid this batch of correspondence inside the cover of his much-thumbed volume of Xavier's letters. He was going to sit down and answer every one of those letters at length, wherever he was. 'The Power House'—as he and his fellow curates referred to the chancellery—had the authority to remove his body to Leonardo—or Timbuctoo—and he was ready to follow obediently if not resignedly. But, by God, they couldn't cut his lines of communication—of identification with the hard-pressed dock wallopers of Bohegan. If they did it to the least of them, they'd still be doing it to him, whether he wound up in Leonardo or God knows where. Isn't that what he wore the vestments for? Isn't that what these uncomfortable celluloid collars made his neck sweat for?

Half an hour later when the Pastor called him down to the office there had been an emotional flash recall of a boyhood panic, the stealing of the money for his kid brother's red fire engine and his childish defiance, 'If the priest gives me too much hell, I'm out of the Church.' But that priest of years ago had let him steal the base and called him safe. Now Father Donoghue was pretty much the same kind of man, a father who did his best to help his sons, even when he wasn't altogether sure he was able to understand them.

Father Donoghue had let the curate express himself, and strongly, as to what he thought of his predicament. Some pastors would have pulled the check lines tighter, but Father Donoghue admired fighters. He had a growing respect for Pete Barry, and he remembered and approved of the Holy Father's often neglected warning. 'The Church is a living body and something would be lacking to her life if expression could not be given to public opinion within it. For such a lack, both pastors and the faithful might be to blame.' Father Donoghue could think of pastors, monsignors, bishops, archbishops, cardinals and even popes who had not always measured up to that wisdom.

'Pete, I had a good, long talk with the Bishop,' Father Donoghue began.

'Leonardo, here I come!' Father Barry broke in irresistibly.

'Pete, there you go again, jumping to conclusions,' Father Donoghue said quietly. 'The Bishop has agreed to hold up the transfer for the time being. I must say he heard me out when I tried to point out the positive things you've been doing. But he does want you to, well, stay out of the limelight, no more interviews and sensational broadsides and that sort of thing, at least not until he's had a chance to get the whole picture a little more clearly in his mind.'

Father Barry felt a sense of relief, even if this were only a temporary reprieve. 'Father, I sure appreciate this. You've been a hundred per cent. That's more than I can say for somebody else around here.'

'I hope your feeling about the Monsignor won't leave you bitter or sour,' the Pastor said. 'We're not infallible. We're men. All kinds of men.'

'Father, you can say that again.'

'I've run up against bad men in the Church,' the Pastor admitted. 'But I always found comfort in the thought that we'll all be judged in time.'

'In the meantime,' Father Barry laughed, 'this ecclesiastical infighting can get pretty rough.'

'Yes, it can,' the Pastor agreed. 'I've always tried to stay out of it myself. But our Church is plagued with it like any other institution. Wherever there are honours, positions of authority and power, you are going to find men jockeying for them, men who are supposed to be above such things, great scientists, surgeons, philosophers scheme in their hospitals and their universities and their great foundations. And I'm afraid they will until the day that Christ comes for all of us.'

'I wonder if I can wait that long.' Father Barry's sense of humour often cut into his most troubled moments.

'That may be one of your shortcomings,' Father Donoghue said gently. 'But I think you made an important contribution in putting our faith into action on a front that can make religion a real force in the lives of our parishioners. You're right, of course. Christ *is* in the shape-up and knows what it feels like to be left out in the cold or to be crucified for speaking up. I was very much interested in your leaflet. And I think we should continue the basement meetings. I understand there's a group of at least a hundred who want to keep them going now. I call that progress. I think you're on the right track about the Encyclicals too. They're not meant to be abstracted away in lofty discussion. They're to be applied on River Street. Yes, on Pier B. But Pete, you did make certain mistakes. Not briefing me so I could brief the Bishop. You let your opponents get the jump on you, and turn against you your—er—your adventure in the bar when you punched the unfortunate longshoreman, and then were seen drinking with him and later working on his testimony after I had warned you to be more prudent. And your own part in the hearings. It is true that you obeyed the order to remain away from the court room, physically. But you did present in writing a detailed plan of rehabilitation for the harbour which received a great deal of publicity. In it you said exactly what you would have said if you had taken the stand. That doesn't mean I wasn't impressed with the plan.'

'I only hope I have a chance to follow through on it,' Father Barry said.

'So do I,' Father Donoghue said. 'I like your ideas for a control commission to screen out the criminal types, and for supervised, honest elections and regular, open meetings for the union locals, a rotation plan for the hiring, to get rid of the shape-up, a credit-union system to run off the loan sharks, and protection for the older workers, seniority, I think you call it, and a welfare fund. You see, Pete, I have read it pretty closely. I thought it was really excellent and I'm convinced our Catholic longshoremen should be encouraged to work along these lines. But Pete, again, the way you went about it was too far and too fast.'

'But Father, I had to move fast. The clock was running out.'

'Pete, if you had only cleared your plan with me I might have been able to buck it up to the Bishop and I think I could have talked it through. Instead he was hit cold with all those headlines about the "waterfront priest". Don't you see what you did by rushing ahead?'

'I guess I did set myself up for a sucker punch,' Father Barry said. 'Well, it was a gamble, and in a way I lost. But, Father, if anything ever does come out of this waterfront mess, at least I'll have the satisfaction of knowing the stuff we believe in is getting across to some of our boys here in the harbour.'

'Son, you're going to have lots of satisfaction. And lots of heartache. You've got a strong sense of justice and a strong conscience. That's good, as long as you don't defy authority. Some of the best men we had in all twenty centuries were in a lot of hot water trying to adjust conscience to authority. Yet we need both, a hunger for justice and acceptance of obedience.'

'It's the acceptance of some of those other things that I find it tough to go along with here,' Father Barry said.

'If it makes you feel any better,' Father Donoghue said, 'I happen to know the Bishop is planning to have a long talk with the Monsignor. He thinks O'Hare has overstepped his bounds the other way in condoning waterfront evils. So don't think too harshly of our Bishop. He may think you're a little too chesty and want to cool you off a little bit. But he's very much interested in the idea that we may be allowing our waterfront communicants to stray from the Church because we're not taking a firm enough moral position in defence of their God-given rights. Believe me, Pete, you've stirred up some embers here that we're going to keep burning. I want you to fan those embers, if at the same time you learn how to control the fire all round you—and in you.'

Rising, the Pastor put his arms out to Father Barry and embraced him. 'I see it's time for me to work on my sermon for High Mass on Sunday. God be with you, Pete.'

'God bless you, Father.'

Back in his room, Father Barry fingered the rosary given to him by the girl he used to go steady with in high school, and about whom he wondered now and then. She reminded him just a little bit of Katie Doyle. Katie had been in to see him before she left for Marygrove. She had changed; she was older; there was less of the onward-Christian-soldier, I-want-it-to-be-just-as-it-is-in-the-Missal. She had embarrassed him by apologizing for expecting him to solve everything overnight. Now she had had a taste of the complexities, a bitter taste. Now she knew that the sins of avarice and theft and murder in Bohegan were not to be shucked off like a snake's skin, but had infected the body, deeply.

'Katie, I hope you never lower the fine flame of your indignation,' he had told her. 'Even when you learn as you have learned that it's going to burn you a little bit too.'

They had looked at each other a moment, and he had known that both of them were thinking of Terry and the way evil often intertwined itself with good, and the way life had of rubbing some of the quality of one on to the other.

It still hurt him to realize that Runty Nolan and Terry Malloy actually had been torn from this world and hurled into the next. Day after day he had tortured himself with the question of their sacrifice. Had human life been given in vain, and had he been worthy to ask this terrible price of them before weighing more carefully the value of their offerings? I took their lives in my hands, he prayed. I stumbled upon these two most unlikely of martyrs, an old, tough-flint of a bar-fly and a fringe hoodlum. I took these two, and, right or wrong, I made them dare as St. Ignatius dared when he chose the Coliseum, saying: 'I am God's wheat: I am ground by the teeth of the wild beasts that I may end as the pure bread of Christ.'

From his desk Father Barry picked up the preliminary report just issued by the Crime Commission and flipped a page: 'Criminals whose records belie any suggestion that they can be reformed have monopolized controlling positions in the longshoremen's union; under their régime narcotics traffic, loan-sharking, short-ganging, pay-roll phantoms, shake-down and extortion in all forms—and the brutal ultimate of murder—now flourish and continue unchecked.'

Continue unchecked. In Father Barry's mind those words ticked on: *Continue unchecked.* Tom McGovern was untouched. Everybody knew his word still thundered on the docks. Oh, yes, he had been passed over for the Order of Saint Gregory, and Father Barry took some slight satisfaction from that, but he was still a Catholic paying his own men less than the going rate and hiring gunmen to keep them in line. Still a Catholic . . .

Had the mountain strained to bring forth a mouse? And was the mouse poor Weeping Willie Givens? Yes, it's true, Willie was under indictment for misappropriation of union funds. He had resigned, tearfully, avowing his concern for his beloved longshoremen to the end. Willie had been retired on half his salary, and the new president was Matt Bailey. He was fifteen years younger than Willie and not quite as paunchy. For years he had been president of the checkers' union that worked jowl by jowl with Willie. And, of course, for Tom McGovern. That reform was the laugh of the waterfront, especially since the new Fat Cat was known as Smiling Matt Bailey. Father Barry could almost hear Runty laughing, 'So now we got a smiler for a cry-baby an' it's the same difference.'

In Bohegan, it was true, the hearings had shaken up City Hall, and Mayor Burke had just announced that he would not stand for re-election. That meant the end of Donnelly too. There was talk of a new reform ticket. Interstate had been fined five thousand dollars for commercial bribery and had lost its licence to operate on the docks. But it had quickly rebounded as the National Stevedore Company. An Interstate vice-president had resigned and a pier superintendent had been given a six months' sentence, suspended.

But to Father Barry the most mystifying fact of all was that Johnny Friendly had been tried merely for perjury and given a year in the State Prison. He'd be back in seven or eight months, Moose and Pop had told the priest. Meanwhile everybody in Bohegan was in on the secret that he'd go right on running his docks from inside the pen.

The national labour federation had expelled the longshoremen's union as 'hopelessly gang-ridden', but the Johnny Friendlys and the Jerry Benasios, with the tacit support of Tom McGovern and the shipping association, hung on to those docks. Longshoremen like Moose and Pop and Jimmy and Luke, in nearly every part of the harbour, were trying to buck them. But they were still on the outside looking in.

Just the same, Father Barry's handful had grown to a hundred. And for each one who showed up at the meetings there could easily be ten more ready to follow, when they thought they had a chance. I call that progress, the Pastor had said. Maybe so. Maybe progress was to be measured not in hundred-yard dashes, as Pete had tried to do, but in mere centimetres, painfully crawling forward.

Restlessly, Father Barry went down into the church to meditate, to examine his own conscience, since he was finding so much fault with others', and to ask for guidance. The small church was empty, but in the flickering, shadowed light of the altar, and the shrine candles it seemed very large, and Pete Barry, on his knees in front of his favourite Saint Xavier, seemed very small. If there was any figure in the whole great gallery who would understand and intercede, it was the hollow-cheeked Basque who administered to the souls of the 7,000 Paravas pearl divers with a loving heart while venting his rage on the baptized Portuguese who swindled them out

276

of the harvest of pearls for which they had risked their lives and health in the depths of the oyster beds.

That's the kind of saint Pete Barry wished and prayed he had the courage to be, the spiritual courage to be, a man who didn't merely intone 'and the last shall be first', but lived it, dangerously, every day.

He knelt for an hour, and his mind wandered, but the intensity of his feeling remained concentrated. He prayed for his friends, and he prayed for his enemies, and he prayed for the dead, and he prayed for surcease from the stalking evil of Bohegan. And finally he prayed for forgiveness for hating Tom McGovern and Willie Givens and Johnny Friendly. At the same time he was sure his Xavier would like to see Johnny Friendly get more than eight or nine easy months. And greedy merchant princes and worldly princes of the Church could—and did—make even a saint lose his temper. O Xavier, worn out with too much living and loving at an age when lesser men are coming into their prime, make me see so that I may make others see that our Church is not for the O'Hares and McGoverns taking the easy way, but a Church that suffers as Christ suffers when they crucify Him on a tenement roof or in the hold or on the stringpiece or in the stinking Jersey marshes.

It was midnight. Father Barry listened to the familiar tone of the chimes. He wondered if he was going to be able to function within the Pastor's benevolent but somewhat limiting restraints. For a moment he felt a twinge of self-pity. Then he caught hold of himself. Hang on, Pete. What have you got to beef about? What was the name of that old Cardinal who said, 'If you say nothing and do nothing, you will escape criticism'?

Hell, he hadn't been accused of heresy as Saint Basil was before Pope Damascus. He wasn't condemned as a heretic and then deposed as Saint Cyril was by a council of forty bishops. He wasn't accused of witchcraft like Saint Athanasius. Or burned like Saint Joan. And he hadn't been charged with vile immorality like Saint John Chrysostom. No, and he hadn't been reviled and rejected by the Holy See like Saint Joseph Calasanctius who died in disgrace in Rome at the age of ninety-two. And he wasn't thrown into a windowless prison, persecuted by Pope Clement and deprived of the consolation of saying Mass, like the great Father Ricci, Xavier's noble successor. Somehow those bearers of the cross survived all that, or their memories did, and waited for the Church to catch up with them. And the Church had been richer for their daring.

Solaced, he made the sign of the Cross, rose and genuflected. Then he walked out of the church and crossed the street into Pulaski Park. Now the early winter sleet had given way to snow and there was a white hush over the park. It seemed for a moment as if all the turmoil of Bohegan had finally come to rest. The snow was falling softly, a pure white cloak under which the ugliness of Bohegan might hide—for a little while.

Peering through the grille work at the far end of the park, Father Barry looked out across the majestic waterway of the Hudson to the most powerful harbour city in the history of the world. From the darkened faces of the buildings on the opposite shore, ten thousand yellow eyes twinkled and stared back at him. Having eyes, they see not, he thought to himself. Hang on, Pete, inch along.

Down river a ship sounded its whistle in a melancholy, echoing farewell as it eased down the Narrows. Slowly, Father Barry turned away from the old North River—Johnny Friendly's silent partner still—and walked back to answer some of those letters in the rectory.

New Hope, Pennsylvania, July, 1954
Princeton, New Jersey, April, 1955